THE FIGHTING

THE LATE DR. JIGORO KANO
Founder of the Kodokan

THE FIGHTING SPIRIT
OF JAPAN

The Esoteric Study of the Martial Arts
and Way of Life in Japan

E. J. Harrison
(3rd Dan)

THE OVERLOOK PRESS
Woodstock, New York

First published in the United States in 1982 by
The Overlook Press
Lewis Hollow Road
Woodstock, New York 12498

Copyright © E. J. Harrison 1955. First published in
England by W. Foulsham & Co. Ltd.

Library of Congress Cataloging in Publication Data

Harrison, E. J. (Ernest John), 1873-
The fighting spirit of Japan.

1. Hand-to-hand fighting, Oriental. 2. Martial
arts—Japan. 3. Japan—Civilization. I. Title.
GV1112.H36   1982   796.8′15   81-83227
ISBN 0-87951-142-7   AACR2
ISBN 0-87951-154-0 (paper)

Third Printing, 2000

Printed in the USA

CONTENTS

ILLUSTRATIONS

AUTHOR'S ACKNOWLEDGMENTS

For practical help and encouragement in the compilation of these pages my thanks are due first to my friend Mr. Y. Umewaza, whom I have mentioned more particularly elsewhere, then to the famous judo instructors Dr. Jigoro Kano, Mr. Yokoyama and Mr. Kunishige, who have contributed valuable data. My great friend Mr. D. T. Weed, also a fellow student of judo, was of great assistance in furnishing hints and material bearing on phases of that art.

For the inspiration that led to the addition of the chapter on Japanese physiognomy I am deeply indebted to Mr. R. J. H. Mitwer of Tokyo, and to the Japanese expert himself, Mr. Seki, who went out of his way to furnish me with a valuable exposition of a fascinating subject.

AUTHOR'S FOREWORD

In response to a steadily growing demand which has more or less kept pace with the increasing popularity of judo as reflected in the phenomenal post-war expansion of the art throughout the world, my publishers have had the enterprise to issue my book *The Fighting Spirit of Japan*, written in early pre-war years and perhaps more topical today in the light of past and present happenings in the world. The retention of the original title must not be construed as condonation of Japan's lamentable record during the last war but simply as an indispensable recognition of the fact that the Martial Arts are closely connected with the esoteric mind of the Japanese.

For despite the crimes of the Japanese militarists in the last war it cannot be denied that the Japanese soldier always has been a first class fighting man and that the well authenticated feats of arms of individual members of the *samurai* or *shizoku* class and of old-time exponents of jujutsu have rarely if ever been equalled in other parts of the world. Moreover in our own less spacious and colourful epoch by no means exempt from "moving accidents by flood and field", the best Westerners are still no match for the best Japanese judoka for reasons connected not only with congenital characteristics but also with subsequent physical and mental training, to which reference is made later on in these pages.

I have discarded a few chapters on subjects not strictly apposite to its overall purpose and therefore redundant to it. On the other hand I have interpolated a certain amount of fresh material designed to bring the story up to date, *e.g.* the passages descriptive of karate and aikido more especially. I have retained the chapters on the Zen school of Buddhism, the practice of Za-Zen, the cult of cold steel, Nō dancing, the Japanese theatre and the art of Ninsō, or physiognomy because they seem to me to illuminate distinctive, so to say, "spiritual" components of the Japanese national mentality.

I also ask the reader to bear in mind that the book was written before the turbulent years which have passed, and at the same time to appreciate that the explanation of Japan's behaviour may perhaps be found in her ancient arts.

19 Mornington Avenue,

   London, W. 14

CHAPTER I

INTRODUCTORY

THE following pages, whatever their merits, represent the fruits of nearly twenty years' residence in Japan, where for the greater part of the time I was engaged in newspaper work for English papers published at Yokohama and Tokyo and later as resident correspondent for English and American home papers.

I made my way to Yokohama from San Francisco in the steerage of the P.M. ss. *China* during the early summer of 1897, having been engaged at the latter port to join the staff of the *Japan Daily Herald* as sub-editor. At the risk of somewhat dimming the dignity that should hedge that office, but in the interests of truth, I am bound to say that the aforesaid staff consisted at that time of one other foreigner besides myself, in the solid person of the late Mr. J. H. Brooke, then over seventy years of age but in his day and generation a power to be reckoned with by the Japanese Government as a stalwart opponent of Treaty Revision and a staunch defender of what he conceived to be the interests of all resident foreigners. Subsequently, after the death of Mr. Brooke, I became connected with the *Japan Times*, the *Japan Advertiser*, and during the Russo-Japanese war, with the London *Daily Mail* as its base correspondent in Tokyo. In the course of my residence in Japan I undertook various professional trips beyond the boundaries of the country returning to England via Siberia immediately after the war and again travelling more recently in Korea, South and North Manchuria, other parts of North China and East Siberia to study the situation. This book, however, is not intended to describe in detail my personal experiences as a journalist in Japan; that task would require more space than I have at my disposal and leave little or no room for other purposes more germane to the plan I have mapped out. The talented and witty author of *Letters of a Self-made Merchant to his Son* speaks somewhere of an old reprobate who took normal sustenance now and then just to be sociable, but lived chiefly on tobacco. Somewhat

13

analogously of myself I might say that although I was obliged to
work as a journalist in order to earn my daily bread, yet during
the first few years of my stay in the country I lived more particularly for the study of the language and the practice of the celebrated art of judo, more commonly known abroad in those days as
jujutsu. As a boy in Lancashire I had always been fond of wrestling.
Then for a year or more, while working as city editor of a local
paper at Nanaimo, British Columbia, I studied catch-as-catch-can
systematically under one Jack Stewart, a favourite pupil of Dan
McLeod, otherwise known as the "Californian Wonder", although
he was actually a native of Nova Scotia, and gained his first
scientific experience of mat work at Nanaimo, which small coal-
mining town could perhaps produce among its collier population a
proportionately larger number of skilful wrestlers than any other
spot on the continent. With such strenuous antecedents, therefore,
what more natural than that immediately after my arrival in
Japan I should cast around for some similar method of getting
rid of my surplus energy? I gained my first introduction to
jujutsu about that juncture in the course of a nocturnal adventure
which brought me into contact with the Yokohama police, when
I was rather chagrined to discover that my catch-as-catch-can
repertoire of tricks was of scant avail against even a third-rate
exponent of what is now properly known as judo. Not relishing this
feeling of inferiority in comparison with a man considerably smaller
than myself, although I am no Goliath, I speedily set about
repairing these deficiencies. With the help of the *Japan Herald's*
Japanese translator I found out a local dojo or school of jujutsu
referred to elsewhere in these pages. Its proprietor was a small
Japanese named Hagiwara Ryoshinsai, a disciple of the Tenjin
Shinyo-ryu and a wonderful little man in his way. Although in
stand-up wrestling, known technically as Tachiwaza, he would
have been no match for the black-belt brigade of the famous
Kodokan of Tokyo, yet in what followers of the art have designated "ground work" he possessed remarkable skill and a neck of
such indiarubber-like elasticity and strength as to defy my utmost
efforts to strangle him even when he deliberately exposed himself
to my attack and chokelock. In this small school of not more than
fifteen mats[1] I gained a good deal of rough-and-tumble ex-

[1] The Japanese floor mat called *tatami* is usually about 6 ft. long, 3 ft. wide, and

perience, my opponents being drafted chiefly from the bourgeois element with an occasional coolie thrown in. At the outset I sustained numerous nasty falls, a cracked collar-bone at one stage of the proceedings putting me out of action for several months and almost incapacitating me for professional work, to the no small disgust of my venerable employer Mr. Brooke, who had never in his life been under the spell of athletics and therefore regarded my distraction as more than a mild form of lunacy.

By dint of perseverance coupled with "beef" I began to gain proficiency, and was eventually given the grade of *shodan* at this small dojo. With very rare exceptions I was the only foreigner who ever attended. One disadvantage was that practice took place only at night after dinner, and another was that the interior was always visible from the outside, nothing more substantial than a low hoarding separating the wrestling mats from the roadway. Naturally the sight and sound of incessant struggle invariably attracted a large crowd of spectators, and when I chanced to be holding the floor the rush and scramble for seats in the stalls were fiercer than ever. My own attitude towards this unsought-for publicity was direct and simple. During the initial stages of my novitiate, while I continued to be an "easy mark" for every juvenile "disciple" with blood in his eye and a mad desire to feel what it was like to hurl a foreign devil through the heated air, quite frankly on hearing the noisy laugh and ill-bred chaff of the *hoi polloi* onlookers I asked myself what the deuce I chanced to be doing on board that galley. Later, however, when I began to "put it over" the majority I thoroughly enjoyed this notoriety, and tried to look blandly unconscious every time the downfall of a victim elicited a groan of patriotic disgust from the disgruntled spectators.

I should add that my jujutsu activities were by no means confined to the Tenjin Shinyo-ryu dojo. Reports of my very modest prowess in the "soft art" having reached the ears of the Yokohama police I was invited to practise with them at the central Kagacho police station which exercised jurisdiction over the foreign settlement. This interval happened to coincide with my connexion with a foreign paper which left me more or less free to devote my

2 in. thick, consisting of *toko* (made of rice straw bound together), tightly covered with a straw mat called the *omote*, with the edges neatly bordered with cloth. Mats used in judo exercise are about the same size but much more strongly made. A detailed description will be found in the chapter on the subject.

mornings after breakfast to *keiko* (practice) on the mats of the police dojo. There too I usually got the better of the rank and file without much difficulty but did not fare quite so well when trying conclusions with visiting police *yudansha* (black belt holders) from Tokyo some of whom had no doubt graduated from the Kodokan. Moreover the chief instructor of the Kagacho police station dojo, although not a disciple of the Kodokan but the product of another ryugi or school of jujutsu the name of which I cannot recall, was none the less a decidedly formidable customer and especially adept in Newaza, otherwise "ground work". I am not at all likely to forget this stalwart seeing that it is to him that I owe my first introduction to the Kansetsuwaza known as the Ashigarami, or Leg Entanglement, and that too on no less important an occasion than a specially organized demonstration of jujutsu at the Kagacho police station before the late Prince Henry of Prussia who was then visiting the port with the German Far Eastern squadron of which he was the admiral. I had been paired with the Japanese instructor and greatly to my youthful chagrin it was not long before I was forced to submit to this particular lock of which I had until then been ignorant.

With the outbreak of the Russo-Japanese war in 1904 I moved to the capital and there joined the Kodokan whose 250 mats were in striking contrast to the humble fifteen of the Yokohama wrestling haunt. Here too I soon found that I was a mere tyro in the art and had to unlearn a good many bad habits engendered by the fault of relying too much upon brute strength instead of upon skill.

In connexion with the study and practice of judo my attention was drawn to the part which a certain kind of occultism plays in the armoury of really efficient masters. The relegation of the seat of courage to the lower abdomen (*shitahara* or more elegantly *saika tanden* in Japanese), and the contention that the concentration of strength in that portion of the body is, as it were, the alpha and omega of fighting capacity, at once impressed me profoundly as plausible and original theories worthy of investigation. By actual experiment I found that these claims were more than idle and empty theorizing and that the habit of deep abdominal breathing, if pursued as directed by the Japanese teachers of martial arts, and side by side with the practical study of the latter, would generally lead to a marked development of defensive and offensive power.

That more gush and drivel have been written about Japan than about any other country in the world is a fact too notorious to require special proof and I should be loath to add my "sum of more to that which has too much". Nevertheless, even when due allowance has been made for exaggeration I think it will be generally admitted that the Japanese race as a whole possesses the fighting knack. Of course the country has its full quota of weaklings, and the average Japanese man in the street is by no means an impressive object. Still, if I were asked to sum up the physical characteristics of the Japanese in as few words as possible, I should undoubtedly say that these people are usually stronger than they look, whereas with us the opposite is very often the case—i.e. we frequently look stronger than we are. I have dealt with this aspect of the question in subsequent chapters, but it may be said here that some of the most powerful Japanese of my acquaintance make very indifferent tailors' dummies. I have in mind as I write the judo instructor at Keio University, Mr. Iizuka, who, when clad in Western garments and seen from behind might very easily be taken for a schoolboy but who, when stripped, displays the thews and sinews of a miniature Hercules. Again, admitting that the average Japanese is hardly a match for the average Englishman or American in a fight with Nature's weapons, Europe and America have had ample proof that on these terms the Japanese specialist is nearly always certain to be the victor. Investigation will show that there are purely technical reasons for this outcome, but one object of a portion of this book is to demonstrate that the offensive and defensive ability of the Japanese specialist is not based solely upon technical reasons. I will even go so far as to declare my opinion that, given equal technical skill on either side, until we have learned thoroughly the lesson of abdominal power the Japanese will nearly always defeat his Western opponent in a fight to a finish with or without weapons, firearms of course excluded. In the following pages I have tried to explain in as simple language as possible the secret of this marked superiority. I am prepared to incur in some quarters the reproach of mendacity on the score of what I have written; but if my modest efforts gain an occasional convert I shall not complain, for a little leaven will sometimes leaven the lump, while if those whose opinion really counts will take the trouble to trace my statements back to their original sources they will speedily be satisfied of my *bona fides*.

It should be pointed out that the book is in no sense a technical exposition of these Japanese arts but rather an imperfect first attempt to arrive at their rationale, both esoteric and exoteric; nor is it intended to be that and nothing more. On the contrary, I have ventured to deal with several other distinctively Japanese subjects which, during my residence in Japan occupied part of the leisure that could be spared from purely professional duties. I do not say that these subjects have never before been handled by a foreign author, but I do say that I have handled them here either quite independently or with recourse to Japanese originals. While the chapters devoted to the esoteric and exoteric aspects of judo form a more or less connected narrative, other chapters may be read as distinct and separate studies, and the rest are offered simply as lighter samples of actual personal experiences of Japanese town and country life.

CHAPTER II

PHYSICAL CULTURE IN GENERAL

THE alleged physical deterioration of the Japanese people has for years exercised the minds of public-spirited Japanese. During the feudal era the samurai class were of necessity devoted to the strenuous life, while the common people, save under stress of circumstances, were frankly sedentary in their habits, if we except worthies like the renowned Chobei of Bandzuin, himself of samurai origin, and his fellow wardsmen, the famous Otokodate of the old Yedo. The young samurai was subject to the severest discipline and underwent careful training in all manly exercises. These even included initiation at an early age into the grim ritual imperatively observed by a daimyo or samurai condemned to commit *seppuku* (more vulgarly *harakiri*) or disembowelment. For a detailed account of how this truly blood-curdling method of suicide used to be carried out in those spacious days of derring-do I cannot do better than refer the reader to that delightful classic, Lord Redesdale's *Tales of Old Japan*. Even today, although *seppuku* has no legal sanction, cases are not unknown where members of the *shizoku*, or former military class, and the present-day gentry have voluntarily chosen the method of "happy despatch", as disembowelment is sometimes rather euphemistically termed, as a means of departing this life. In my day the most dramatic and impressive example of *seppuku* was furnished by the celebrated General Nogi, the victor of Port Arthur, in the Russo-Japanese war, who on the very stroke of midnight on the day of the death of his Imperial master, the Emperor Mutsuhito, killed himself in this manner while at the same time his wife cut her throat before the family altar or *kamidana* of the deeply revered national Shinto cult of ancestor worship.

In the present more enlightened era the samurai have lost their former calling and fill other walks in life besides those that are essentially military, naval or official. They may even be found in menial positions, sometimes serving as house "boys" or even pulling

19

jinrikisha in the streets of the capital! I once knew the scion of a Hatamoto family (retainers of the Shogun) who earned his livelihood as a clerk in a foreign firm and devoted his leisure to wine, women and song.

A good many years ago the *Yorozu Choho*, a popular Tokyo newspaper, published the following remarks on physical culture in Japan:

"The patriots of this country will learn with regret that the Japanese people as a whole is growing physically weaker and weaker as years roll on. It is true that physical education has always been encouraged to a certain extent among our younger generation and as a result many of our young men take kindly to Western sports such as baseball and boating. It is also true that animal diet, which was almost unknown in feudal Japan, has been adopted by a large section of our people since this country began intercourse with Europe and America. In the face of these facts it would seem that the bodily health of the Japanese might have improved. Yet the fact is that instead of improving it is slowly but surely declining. And there can be no doubt about this because no less authorities than Lieutenant-Colonel Yokoi and Lieutenant-Colonal Hirano, who have long been engaged in conscript examination, assert that the results of these examinations show a most lamentable tendency towards deterioration in the health of the Japanese. In recent addresses to a small gathering of Tokyo journalists these two officers gave some interesting facts in the above context. From them we learn that the percentage of recruits who are physically strong enough to come under the first and second classes is steadily diminishing year after year. We also learn that, compared with Europeans, the average Japanese male and female are smaller in stature by 3.3 and 3.7 *sun* respectively, and lighter in weight by 2 and 2.6 *kan* respectively. (The Japanese *sun* is a little more than an English inch and the *kan* a fraction under 8 lb.) The Japanese soldier is, on an average, 5 *shaku* 2.4 *sun* in height, while the English soldier is 5 *shaku* 5.5 *sun*, the Russian 5 *shaku* 6.2 *sun*, the German about the same, and the French 5 *shaku* 6 *sun*; so that the stature of the soldiers of these four Powers is, on an average, 5 *shaku* 6.13 *sun* and is greater than that of our soldiers by 3.73 *sun*. (The Japanese *shaku* may be roughly calculated as almost equivalent to the English foot.) These figures clearly show that our men are inferior in physical development to the European troops. This is not reassuring, but what must trouble the minds of Japanese patriots most seriously is a statement made by our authorities that of all classes of society the students of our public and private schools above the grade of middle school are physically the worst. The students of the Imperial University are, on an average, 5 *shaku* 2.8 *sun* in height and about 112 lb. in weight. Walking in Hongo or its vicinity one may often meet a slightly built, pale-faced, listless, spectacled young man clad in a brass-buttoned uniform, carrying a bundle of notebooks and hurrying along with unsteady steps. He is a good representative of the university student of which class the future backbone of the nation is to be composed. Will this nation when it comes to be guided by these sickly men continue with any degree of success the great race for self-preservation against the robust and unflinching peoples of Europe and America?"

Such laments as the foregoing are less frequent today than before the Russo-Japanese war which afforded very striking evidence that superior weight and stature do not necessarily imply greater fighting capacity or staying power. For the rest, my own personal experience and observation are far from bearing out the conclusions of the military men above quoted. I have myself frequently had occasion to observe that many Japanese, to the inexperienced eye small and apparently of no particular strength, were in reality "built from the ground up", as the saying is, and so agile as to more than compensate for the extra "beef" of the bulkier European. It is unfortunately true that men of this kind are not in a majority. But what about our own country? Is a perfectly sound physique the rule instead of the exception in our bigger cities? After having had dinned into my ears for years before I came to the country the smallness of everything Japanese, I was somewhat astonished on visiting for the first time Yokosuka, the seat of the Government dockyard situated at the entrance to Tokyo Bay, to see hundreds of soldiers and sailors well over 5 ft. 7 in. in height and powerfully built withal. In the days before

the First World War, when Russian bluejackets could not infrequently be seen at Yokohama, dapper "boys" in restaurants of
an inferior type have often been known to expel without difficulty
Muscovite opponents apparently huge enough to eat them. In
short the Japanese with additional height and avoirdupois would
not necessarily be a gainer; he would probably have to sacrifice
no insignificant part of his present agility and alertness. It should,
however, be recorded that irrespective of the gigantic professional
wrestlers known as *sumotori* about whom I shall have something
to say later on in these pages, there are today among the thousands
of both practising and retired *yudansha* of the Kodokan many
men who in any country would be regarded as "outsizes" with
weights in many cases of as much as seventeen or eighteen stone
and heights of six feet or over.

It is well known that the Japanese have imported several
Western forms of sport and athletic exercises, but with the exception perhaps of baseball it cannot fairly be said that they excel in
any. Baseball, however, is a game which appeals strongly to their
constitutional preferences and it is one for which their quickness
of hand and eye and their bodily agility admirably qualify them.
There is scarcely a school in the Empire without its "nine", and
during my residence in Japan the leading teams of the higher
schools and universities (notably Keio and Waseda) were as a rule
more than a match for the foreign players of the old treaty ports,
and could give even American collegiate players a run for their
money. Young Japan also takes kindly to lawn-tennis and one
may frequently see the game being played vigorously on open
plots of ground in the capital and elsewhere, sometimes with very
primitive equipment. A foreign instructor at the Keiogijiku
College, Tokyo, many years ago inaugurated Rugby football
among the students and matches were in my time regularly
organized between the local foreign fifteens and the Japanese,
though in these the latter were far less successful than on the
diamond. Cricket too has so far failed to attract the Japanese.
Cycling, however, is immensely popular, and though no Japanese
champion has yet approached the records of the West, the country
has nevertheless produced riders who have beaten foreigners on
local tracks. I was myself a keen cyclist as well as an ardent judoka
in those early days and as a member of a Yokohama cycling club

enjoyed many a collective country run occasionally as guests of a distinctly aristocratic Japanese club of the metropolis. Rowing in foreign style has been taken up enthusiastically, the universities, schools and even many banks and companies having their crews. The periodical regattas on the Sumida River, Tokyo, are red-letter events in the social life of the capital and attract enormous crowds, more especially the spring regatta which is held during the cherry-blossom season. But in my day Japanese crews had not yet adopted the sliding seat and were therefore outclassed by the foreign crews of Yokohama and Kobe.

The Japanese are fond of swimming and among the younger generation of students and the coast population may be found some splendid long-distance swimmers. Schools of natation teach the art in a systematic manner, and although the best racing times in Japan are not quite equal to the best Western figures, a Japanese expert can perform some truly wonderful feats—such, for example, as diving into deep water and maintaining a position with the water no higher than the loins, when he will fire a musket or a bow and arrow, write on a slate, paint a picture on a fan with a brush or move freely in every direction as though walking on solid ground. The expert, while rarely emulating the graceful high swallow dive of the European or American, can plunge head downwards from a great height and strike the surface of the water with his chest without sinking or wetting the face and head. In some mysterious way he contrives to obviate the painful consequences which the impact would inevitably entail upon the foreigner who should essay this feat in the absence of the necessary esoteric knowledge. It is said that the old-time samurai frequently made use of this trick when crossing a river or stream with their armour and weapons on their heads.

The above statements may be accepted as true, but it is to be regretted that the vernacular newspapers in Japan sometimes publish the most startling stories of the marvellous feats performed by indigenous Captain Webbs. For instance, they once described how several bold students had swum from Tokyo to Yokohama, a distance of nearly twenty miles, in less than ten hours. This would mean that they kept up an average speed of thirty minutes per mile or half a mile in fifteen minutes! The best racing speed in Tokyo by the best Japanese swimmer in my day was over nine minutes for the quarter mile; and it took a good foreign swimmer at Yokohama more than eighteen minutes to cover the half-mile in a race. What adds to the improbability of the story is that these ten hours included stoppages for a smoke, "chow" and a call in at a certain swimming-ground at Kanagawa! The feat may indeed be called natation extraordinary. On the other hand, as illustrative of the antiquity of swimming in Japan, it may interest foreign readers to be told that the famous crawl stroke of the Occident, which is there of comparatively recent origin, has been known and practised in Japan for hundreds of years, in addition to not a few other methods of progression in the water which would doubtless come as a revelation to Europe and America.

It is the practice for students of the universities and schools to repair to the seaside during the summer months and there train systematically, regular courses of instruction being given to those who wish for them. Fancy swimming is a popular feature of the periodical competitions which are held and, as intimated above, some of the feats which Japanese experts can accomplish are of a surprising character. Very strict discipline is maintained both on these occasions and at the permanent swimming-schools which exist in various parts of the country. The pupils are carefully classified as in judo and fencing and all other forms of physical prowess. Caps of different colours are worn as distinguishing badges. and pupils below a certain grade are not allowed to swim beyond a specified boundary for fear of accidents. Several international competitions which have been held between Japanese and foreign representatives at Yokohama and Tokyo have for the most part resulted in victory for the Japanese, though by a narrow margin; but in almost every instance the foreigners have carried off the long-distance event less because their powers of endurance are superior to those of the Japanese than because on these occasions the Japanese long-distance champions were unable to compete. Nor must the point be over-looked that whereas the Japanese representatives have been virtually the pick of the nation, the foreigners have had to select their men from among a very small community, the younger members of which, engaged as most of them are in some business occupation, have nothing like the same amount of leisure for training as their Japanese rivals. Considering the circumstances, their achievements against the Japanese are something to be proud of, though it is to be regretted that Japanese papers, in reporting such contests, should usually write as though the elite of Japan had beaten the elite of Europe and America.

Archery is a very common pastime in Japan, nearly every town and village having one or more ranges at which, for a very small pecuniary consideration, all and sundry may try their skill. During my first years in Yokohama I spent many an enjoyable evening at a favourite *daikyuba*, or archery range, in the popular resort known among foreigners as Theatre Street and among the Japanese as Isezakicho. The keeper of the range was a member of the *shizoku* class and a man of splendid physique. He had a fine collection of bows, some of considerable age, the actual weapons of the ante-Meiji clansmen. Some of these bows were so strong that I could scarcely bend them at all, not to speak of using them with any hope of making a bull's-eye, albeit the proprietor could handle them with comparative ease.

Without attempting to enter into a technical description of how the bow is used in Japan, I am safe in saying that there is a right way and a wrong way of holding it, fitting the arrow, drawing and releasing it. And in this context I can still remember the real distress experienced by the burly proprietor on those occasions, not infrequent, when some of my foreign companions and I fitted the arrow on the wrong side of the bow and held the bow in the incorrect position. One of these companions, a fellow-journalist on a local foreign paper, now, alas, no more, was an incorrigible offender in this respect. What added to the enormity of his offences was that in spite of these—so to speak—arch heresies, he always got nearer to the bull's-eye than the Japanese habitués who never drew a bow without having conscientiously indulged in a number of preliminary flourishes such as baring their good right arms by throwing back their ample sleeves over their shoulders, raising the bow with a spasmodic gesture, and so forth. It was really heartrending to note the persistency with which they missed after all this elaborate ceremonial; but I think I am right in saying that they themselves would far rather have missed, and the proprietor would far rather have had them miss in proper form than score by such irregular practices as those indulged in by my friend who, with a cigar between his teeth, the bow held horizontally instead of perpendicularly, and the arrow on the wrong side, would wing his shafts into the very centre of the target with a monotonous frequency which afforded him unalloyed satisfaction and the unhappy and orthodox proprietor ineffable disgust. Archery ranges are generally provided at higher-grade schools and competitive meetings are frequently held. The standard bow is made of inlaid layers of bamboo and is 8 ft. long, while the shaft measures 3 ft., and is tipped with hawk's or eagle's feathers.

Horsemanship is not a form of exercise with which the Japanese betray any promise of witching a wondering world at an early date. As I am a very amateur rider myself I cannot pretend to write as an expert, but even a novice can tell when he is looking at a centaur or at a meal-bag perilously balanced on the top of the saddle. Most Japanese equestrians belong to the latter category. Kipling has said things about the Japanese cavalry with which most foreigners are in agreement; but it must in justice be added that here, as in all other branches of the military service, desperate efforts were in my day being made to effect improvement, although the Japanese by heredity seem to be unfitted to excel as a horse-master. And in any case it must be added that the wholesale military mechanization which has taken place in virtually all armies of the world since the publication of the original edition of this book has largely eliminated the practical need of cavalry in the conduct of actual warfare, although for ceremonial purposes it still survives. Constitutionally your average Japanese would appear to have little love for animals and, as more than one correspondent at the front had occasion to remark during the war with Russia, the trooper as a rule regards his mount more as an enemy to be bullied than as a friend and companion to be treated with affectionate consideration. The Japanese authorities of those days were themselves fully aware of these shortcomings, and in the Horse Administration Bureau established in 1906 under the direct control of the Cabinet and with a Privy Councillor and an ex-Minister of State as its chief, an organ was created whose chief duty it was to better the breed of horses. Whereas prior to the war with Russia horse-racing had been virtually confined to the meets organized by the Nippon Race Club, an institution founded by foreigners but with Japanese members, thanks to the efforts of the above mentioned bureau, which often took the form of substantial subsidies and prizes, numerous purely Japanese clubs sprang up all over the country, and in the season hardly a day passed without its race meeting. The Japanese law forbids gambling, but the pari mutuel had all along been tacitly permitted at the meetings of the Nippon Race Club, and for some time after the Russo-Japanese war similar latitude was extended to the Japanese organizations. Then suddenly the judicial authorities woke up and resolved that both the letter and the spirit of the law must be enforced, and in 1908 the pari mutuel was prohibited. The consequences were disastrous. Most of the newly created clubs whose shares had been boomed up to fabulous figures were reduced to bankruptcy and many went out of business. The popularity of horse-racing had hitherto been almost wholly due to the gambling element, for the Japanese are notorious speculators, and once this incentive and attraction were withdrawn the attendance at the race meetings fell to a vanishing quantity. In this case the interests of the military and civil authorities proved to be antagonistic. The former would fain have had the latter wink at a glaring infringement of the law for the sake of improving the breed of horses through private initiative which was stimulated into action by the prospect of munificent returns, for the most part from the pari mutuel. When this inducement was withdrawn the gilt was off the gingerbread and although race meetings continued they prove to be comparatively spiritless affairs. Nevertheless the Horse Administration Bureau continued to offer prizes and subsidies. Its policy was to keep for the service 1,500 stallions of foreign breed and to distribute them among the principal stud farms where they were to be paired with mares of native breed. The improvement programme was to extend over twenty-eight years and was estimated to require an outlay of Yen 30,000,000 or at the then rate of exchange £3,000,000. The Japanese native stock is traced back to the Mongolian breed with an admixture of Persian blood which seems to have been introduced as early as three centuries ago. The leading stud farms are to be found in the northern districts of the main island and in the Hokkaido where comparatively extensive plains exist. The finest native breed is the Nambu from the Aomori and Iwate prefectures. Other well-known stocks are Hokkaido, Sendai, Miharu and Kagoshima. Thanks to the stimulus afforded by the Horse

Investigation Commission, the Government had begun to import foreign horses in fairly large quantities. Since 1906 it had bought extensively, the breeds comprising Arabs, Anglo-Arabs, Australians, hackneys, trotters, Clydesdales, thoroughbreds, etc. In 1906 the Horse Administration Bureau purchased forty-eight horses, in 1907 forty, and in 1908 some forty mares and forty-four stallions; and it is to be presumed that this practice will be steadily pursued in the future.

It is to the credit of the Japanese cavalry arm that notwithstanding the many natural disadvantages under which the Japanese trooper has had to labour, a good deal has been accomplished since the Russo-Japanese war. It cannot be denied that the average Japanese cavalryman has an execrable seat, but for all that he is no weakling and does not easily tire, as has been proved by several decidedly stiff endurance tests. As an instance of what can be done in this direction I may mention the performance of the Eleventh Regiment then stationed in Manchuria. The test took the form of a long-distance ride from Dairen to Kungchuling, a distance of 500 miles, which was covered in five days, four hours and forty-five minutes, exclusive of the time taken for rest *en route*. According to Japanese authorities, the only previous cavalry feat at all comparable with this was the ride of Austrian troopers between Vienna and Berlin; but in the latter case not only was the distance less but the climatic conditions rendered the test infinitely milder than that to which the Japanese horsemen were subjected. Fifteen men were chosen and divided into three detachments of five men each, commanded by lieutenants. The detachments set out on three consecutive days, from Fushima Park, Dairen, carrying with them an ample supply of ammunition for fear of attack by mounted bandits. As it happened this precaution was justified, for one of the detachments was ambushed by desperadoes near the Shaho River, but after a brisk exchange of fire succeeded in putting the enemy to flight. The same detachment on the second day strayed into swampy ground near Kaiping and spent four hours in covering two miles. On the third day the second detachment overtook the first, and together they indulged in a rest of seven hours, for they had slept on an average only one hour a day during the first three days and were on the point of breakdown. On the fourth day the two detachments crossed the Hun

JAPANESE ARCHER MOUNTED
Feudal period

THE LATE SHUICHI NAGAOKA
10th Dan. Professor of judo at the Butokukai, Kyoto

River and rode into Mukden amid loud cries of "Banzai!" from their compatriots. The best time has been given above. The poorest was six days, one hour, and thirty-five minutes.

Under the modern regime physical culture begins early. From his boyhood every able-bodied Japanese is subjected to a training which smacks of militarism, though the framers of the physical curriculum believe in teaching the young idea to do more than shoot. The system is essentially eclectic. Dr. J. M. Davis, in his work entitled *The Christian Movement in Japan,* has furnished an admirable account of what Japan has been doing in her schools, and from this source I extract a few of the more interesting data. Pupils begin military drill without arms from their fourth year. In the secondary schools, where the drill is compulsory through the entire course of five years, individual and section drill is added in the second year. And before the Second World War during the remaining three years the students were given these drills with arms and in the high schools military training with arms was continued. But from all accounts this system was forbidden by General MacArthur and under the impact of the popular reaction against militarism which attended Japan's defeat has not yet been resumed. As regards gymnastics, Roberts's dumb-bell drill, Ling's ten groups of progressive movements, Barnjurn's barbell drill, certain series of fancy steps and marches of the Springfield Y.M.C.A. are taught. An excellent custom too is that of long-distance walking excursions in which an entire school or class is expected to take part. These trips last a week or ten days. The boys are divided into companies each of which is led by a teacher, and these companies are divided into squads of ten or twelve boys with their chiefs who are required to report three times a day to the company captain on the condition of their groups. Higher-school boys think nothing of doing their twenty-five or thirty miles a day in this manner. Every boy is expected to carry his own extra clothing and whatever else may be deemed necessary in the way of provision for the trip.

The fairer sex is not being neglected in the matter of physical culture. No longer are young maidens taught that it is the proper thing for them to walk with a sort of chronic stoop supposed to evince a becoming sense of deference and that it is indelicate to permit the feet to stray beyond the lower edge of the kimono.

Indeed the very costume of the Japanese school girl has been modified to fit her for her new physical responsibilities. The usual kimono which opens down the front and is confined at the waist with a cumbersome sash called the *obi* is certainly but ill-adapted to strenuous exercise. To protect the wearer's modesty at such moments the educational authorities have devised a light skirt, usually maroon-coloured, which covers the lower part of the kimono and is confined at the waist, the clumsy *obi* being dispensed with. Very frequently too the young ladies wear European-style shoes instead of the native sandals or clogs. In the girls' schools great attention is now paid to confer grace and ease of movement. Fancy marching and dancing steps, calisthenics, the Swedish stall-bars, the vaulting-horse, and basket-ball have all been naturalized and are helping to revolutionize the physique of the futute mothers of the Japanese race. A field-day at one of the leading girls' colleges when to the accompaniment of music the pupils give an exhibition of their skill is one of the prettiest spectacles imaginable.

The most important centre of physical culture in my day but since then prohibited under the allied military occupation was undoubtedly the Martial Arts Association (Budokukai), organized in 1895 in Kyoto. It was a flourishing concern with a membership of nearly 2,000,000, its patron being Prince Fushimi and its president Baron Oura. It had branches throughout the country at which judo, fencing, archery and boating were practised and taught. It possessed magnificent headquarters in Kyoto, a former temple having been reconstructed to suit its requirements. I can even now recall in this context that on the occasion of my first visit I thought that my jinrikisha-man must have made a mistake and had brought me to a place of spiritual instead of physical exercise.

CHAPTER III

HISTORY AND RATIONALE OF JUDO

TURNING from hybrid and imported forms of exercise I shall now try to describe those which have a truer national flavour and which are therefore of superior interest. Many earlier fallacies concerning the Japanese are being gradually dispelled by the limelight of publicity, but even today there are some who doubtless associate the idea of Japanese wrestling almost exclusively with those mountains of fat and muscle who, under the style of *sumotori*, form a class apart and hold periodical contests in various parts of the Empire. But this brand of wrestling would not in itself entitle Japan to peculiar distinction. It possesses forty-eight different throws, many of which are the common property of wrestlers throughout the world but whose repertoire includes a proportion of methods designed not only to throw the opponent but also to push him outside the ring in which event the successful pusher is adjudged the victor. Without in any way posing as a competent *sumo* "fan" I am nevertheless inclined to think that some of these really drastic techniques would repay serious study by our Western mat-men. But in these pages it is to another and more elaborate form of the art of offence and self-defence that I now desire to draw the reader's attention. I speak of judo, earlier confused with jujutsu, incorrectly jiujitsu, which may be said to have become naturalized in the West for many years. Perhaps a pioneer of the Japanese art or a sort of version of it in Europe was the late Barton Wright who studied for some time in Japan, afterwards proceeding to London where he opened an academy and taught what he knew under the name of Bartitsu. He claimed that he had grafted on to the parent stem various shoots of his own invention or culled from other schools in different parts of the world. Without doubt Mr. Barton Wright was a colourful personality in his day and generation and could give a very good and effective account of himself on the mat against all and sundry lacking knowledge of either jujutsu or judo. This splendid veteran passed away only a few years ago on the threshold of his tenth decade. Since those early days however the bibliography of both jujutsu and judo, keeping pace with their rapid world expansion, has grown by leaps and bounds. In the home country of judo, Japan, since the opening of the Kodokan more than seventy years ago at least seventy-six works have been published in Japanese. The founder, Dr. Jigoro Kano himself wrote only one propaganda brochure. Several of these works have been translated into English, notably a pioneer manual by the late Sakujiro Yokoyama and an excellent work by Professor Arima of the Kodokan. I myself have produced an "interpretation" of the Katamewaza section of a book by Tsunetani Oda 9th Dan, and a free translation of a more comprehensive volume by Hikoichi Aida 8th Dan. Of the older jujutsu not more than three books are on record because the then jujutsu masters were wont jealously to guard the secrets of their art. Nowadays the number of textbooks on judo outside Japan in many languages, but more especially in English and French, can be reckoned by the score, and at the present tempo of production we may soon be justified in saying of judo authorship, as the late Basil Hall Chamberlain once said of books about Japan generally, that it is a distinction *not* to have written a book about judo! Personally, while very far from claiming anything like an expert status in the art, I did during my heyday on the mat devote a good deal of time to the study of its history and rationale and thus deem myself to some extent qualified to express an opinion.

It must frequently have puzzled and bewildered a big and brawny bluejacket to find himself easily mastered by a little Japanese policeman half his size. Let me hasten to add that it is *not* every Japanese policeman who is skilled in judo, though at home the conviction has apparently gained a firm foothold that the most anaemic and attenuated native of Dai Nippon has but to touch the most herculean Westerner with his index finger in order to bring his victim to the ground a shuddering heap of helpless, shattered humanity. On the contrary, the average efficiency of the Japanese police in this regard is not very great, and as a general rule, man for man, the Japanese policeman had in my day fared but second best at the hands of American and British Jack Tars in those not infrequent "scraps" between the "liberty men" and the *junsa* (policeman) which in those days helped to create diversion in the unsavoury purlieus of the Yokohama "bloodtown" and the equally salubrious quarters of Nagasaki and Kobe. Elsewhere in these pages I shall have occasion to describe a class of Japanese judoka (exponent of judo) whose skill and strength combined, I make bold to say, could not be equalled, much less excelled, in any other part of the world.

The word jujutsu, to use the older nomenclature, is written with two ideographs, the first *ju*, meaning "to obey, submit to, weak, soft, pliable"; and the second *jutsu*, meaning "art" or "science". The use of the first character is intended to imply that jujutsu relies for its triumphs not upon brute strength but upon skill and finesse, the ability to win by appearing to yield. Thus in jujutsu the opponent undermost may have the other at his mercy, though to the novice he may appear to be defeated. Jujutsu is the art which every samurai under the feudal regime was compelled to learn, and it was often a point of honour among the higher-minded ones, if attacked by a vulgar opponent, whether with or without a weapon, to try first to overcome him by means of jujutsu before drawing their own swords. Authentic stalwarts such as the redoubtable Chobei of Bandzuin, the Father of the Otokodate of Yedo, and the equally formidable Funakoshi Juyemon whose astounding exploits against tremendous odds are so dramatically described by Lord Redesdale in his *Tales of Old Japan*, were clearly adepts in jujutsu. The word *otokodate* means a man of chivalrous spirit or one who takes up the cause of the weak against the oppressor. A synonym is *kyokaku*.

Nowadays, however, jujutsu is no longer a monopoly of the military class, and the various dojo or schools in the larger cities render it possible for any respectable person to practise it. The fees charged in my day were astonishingly small, the principal school in Japan, then as now, the above-mentioned Kodokan founded by the late Dr. Jigoro Kano, collecting but fifty sen a month, or say a shilling at the then current rate of exchange, from every pupil, while those who held the grade of shodan or first grade and upwards paid nothing since they attended in the capacity of teachers, as they do today. It is another characteristic of this cult that its members may not make a public display of their art for money. Thus for the most part all competitions were in those days virtually private functions, admission being by invitation, and jujutsu gossip did not then figure in the sporting columns of the native press like boxing and wrestling in America and England, though ample space was allotted to reports of the *sumo* matches during the season. Similarly kenjutsu or kendo (fencing) is held in equally high esteem. However, the passage of time has brought about a good many changes in the domain of publicity, so that today the periodical judo championship tournaments are to all intents and purposes public displays and are widely reported in the native press. But in my day the etiquette observed in relation to both judo and kendo was appreciably stricter, and I remember how on the occasion of a smoking concert at the old Gaiety Theatre on the Yokohama Bluff, two Japanese fencing instructors of my acquaintance who had agreed to give a display refused to do so on ascertaining that money was being taken at the doors and that the concert was not being given for a charitable purpose.

The origin of jujutsu, like so many other things Japanese, is traced back to the mythological age, the gods Kajima and Kadori having, it is said, availed themselves of the art for the purpose of chastising the lawless inhabitants of the eastern provinces. But from then until the time of the Hojo regime (say from the twelfth to the fourteenth century) no special school (*ryugi*) had developed. Later, however, the various methods employed by physically inferior persons in defeating physically superior antagonists were carefully elaborated until eventually many distinct *ryugi*, sects or schools, came into existence. The suggestion that Chin Gen-pin or Chuen Yuan-pin of the Ming dynasty of China introduced the art into Japan is not generally credited, and in any event it seems certain that it owes its present perfection almost entirely to Japanese exertions. Jujutsu is but one of the names by which almost one and the same thing has been connoted: kempo, yawara, kugusuku, kumiuchi, and now judo are all slightly different applications of identical principles. Irrespective of the eclectic and predominant modern system of judo evolved by Dr. Jigoro Kano above referred to, the best known schools of my day not all of which exist today were the Kiraku-ryu, Takenouchi-ryu, Yoshin-ryu, Shinnoshindo-ryu, Tenjin Shinyo-ryu, Sekiguchio-ryu, Shibukawa-ryu, Asayama Ichiden-ryu, Kyushin-ryu, Kito-ryu, Ryoishinto-ryu, Arataryu, Shimmei Sakkatsu-ryu, etc. I was first introduced to the Tenjin Shinyo-ryu which is an amalgamation of the Yoshin-ryu and the Shinnoshindo-ryu. The founder of the Yoshin-ryu was one Akiyama Shirobei Yoshitoki, a physician of Nagasaki. He had been to China to study, and there learned under one Haku-tei or Pao-chuan three *te* or tricks of jujutsu. The principal features of the art as practised in China were kicking and thrusting. Yoshitoki fully mastered these three *te*, together with twenty-eight different *kassei-ho* or means of resuscitation. Returning to Japan he taught the art to his pupils, but discouraged by the paucity of tricks at their master's disposal the majority abandoned their studies before they had acquired proficiency. Yoshitoki then sought to improve his art, and it is recorded that he retired to the Temmangu Temple at Tsukushi for a hundred days and there finally succeeded in increasing the number of his *te* to 103.

The title of his school arose in this way. He chanced one day in winter to notice that the branches of a willow-tree in front of the temple did not retain the snow even after a heavy fall and that, thanks to the suppleness of its branches, which gave way under the falling snow and thus threw it off as fast as it accumulated, the tree escaped the fate of seemingly sturdier growths whose branches were everywhere ruthlessly crushed and broken under the burden. This circumstance so impressed the onlooker that he gave to his sect the name Yoshin-ryu, i.e. "Willow-heart-school".

The founder of the Shinnoshindo-ryu was Yamamoto Tamizayemon, his school being a modified form of the Yoshin-ryu, and the names of many of the tricks the same in both. They were classified into *shodan* (preliminary rank), *chudan* (middle rank) and *jodan* (upper rank). The founder of the Tenjin Shinyo-ryu was Yanagi Sekizai Minamoto-no-Masatari who was born at Matsuzaka in Seishin. He was attached to the feudal lord of Kishiu, his original name being Okayama Hochiroji. He acquired an early taste for warlike arts and on attaining his fifteenth year proceeded to Kyoto where he studied jujutsu for six or seven years under Hitotsuyanagi Oribe, who was a retainer of Lord Hitotsuyanagi and a well-known master of the art. After the death of his teacher he joined one Homma Joyemon, an exponent of the Shinnoshindo-ryu, whose teachings he thoroughly mastered in six years. This done he travelled through the country and tried

conclusions with different champions and was successful in every
encounter. He stayed two or three years at Kusatsu in Joshiu
where he gained many "disciples" (montei). On one notable
occasion, assisted by Nishimura, one of his pupils, he encountered
more than a hundred lawless ruffians whom he put to flight after
soundly drubbing them. The sceptical West may smile in a
superior sort of way and dub this story apocryphal, but incidents
scarcely less remarkable have come under my own personal
observation during my residence in Japan, and I am therefore
quite prepared to accept it as substantially correct. Yanagi elaborated atemi, or the art of inducing a state of apparent death
by kicking and striking certain vital spots in the body, and kappo,
or the art of resuscitation. In the long run he established his school
of the Tenjin Shinyo-ryu and fixed the number of te or tricks at
124. He again toured the country improving his art and finally
went to Yedo (Tokyo) where, after the characteristic and bewilder-
ing Japanese fashion, he changed his name to Kuriyama Matayemon and became a retainer of the Tokugawa Government. Later he
again changed his name to Iso Matayemon Yanagi Sekizai
Minamoto-no-Masatari. His fame continued to spread and the
number of his pupils increased to 5,000.

"In order fully to master any martial art," says a native
writer on jujutsu, "it is essential to learn under a competent
teacher. The pupil must not be proud or overbearing. He should
constantly practise his art and scrupulously obey his teacher's
instructions. Three vices must be strictly guarded against, viz.
the excessive love of wine, money and sexual immorality. If
the pupil should become addicted to sexual immorality or
unfaithful owing to his love of money, or if he should grow
proud and arrogant owing to drink, he may ruin his life; or
even if he should become experienced in his art he will not
deserve any credit! These evils, therefore, should be studiously
avoided."

Our author continues:

"The jujutsu pupil learns his art without any weapon
on his person. After gaining experience, when he then puts

on arms his mind will be capable of controlling his body. On the other hand, should an inexperienced person put on armour, his bodily movements will be fettered. Thus the mind must be well trained to begin with. The pupil's mind should be sovereign of the body, and his hands and feet his servants. Training his mind and limbs alike, he should then buckle on his arms. The art of jujutsu is an important ally on the field of battle.

"Even in practice one should try to imagine one's opponent an actual enemy. A correct posture should be carefully maintained and the rules of *genshin* (the power to anticipate an attack) and of *zanshin* (how to act after throwing one's opponent) must also be observed. A truculent attitude should not be assumed. When one is attacked with a wooden sword one's fear or caution is not great; on the other hand, substitute a steel sword for the wooden one and caution will be exercised. Let the pupil then try to imagine that his opponent is armed with a real sword.

"The employment of violent physical strength in jujutsu is not desirable but is sometimes admissible. However, the pupil who has not completely mastered his art must avoid the reckless use of force which tends to hamper the free movements of the body and limbs and therefore to prevent him from learning the mystery of the art. He should endeavour to practise lightly and softly and should avoid stiff and heavy movements.

"In an encounter you should watch your opponent's arms, the weapons he handles, and his eyes. At the same time, remembering that a clever adversary will frequently seek to deceive you, the eyes are not to be absolutely relied on. When the enemy remains motionless you may find it impossible to attack. In that case you must keep strictly on the defensive. Above all, avoid entertaining feelings of hatred towards your opponent. Do not keep your limbs at tension, but be cool and wary and prepared for any emergency. If you are over eager to defeat your opponent you may overlook an opportunity. To take advantage of a change in your antagonist's position is called *aiki-no-sen*; the sudden resort to a trick is known as *fui-no-sen*. The act of throwing or otherwise disabling an opponent should be performed as if you were casting a stone to the ground. The body should not be made too hard nor should the shoulders be raised too high. If this advice be followed the lower part of the body will become firm. The *kiai* (literally 'spirit-meeting', i.e. a sort of shout[1]) should emanate from the stomach by which means the lower part of the abdomen is strengthened. In seizing or throwing your adversary care should be taken to protect your own body. In seizing with the left hand do not lose sight of your right hand and leg, and in throwing with the right hand take care similarly of your left side. The human body being formed of angles, try to assault them. In resisting an attack yield, as it were, to the enemy's will, but in the same manner as a gourd afloat on the water, even if pushed downwards, instantly rises again to the surface.

"When opposed to one physically stronger than yourself do not be afraid and, on the other hand, never despise one weaker than yourself. Do not recklessly resist your opponent's physical strength; imitate the action of a boat adrift upon the surface of the ocean. If your strength is inferior to that of your adversary it is useless for you to oppose strength to strength. Try instead to avail yourself of your art and to attack him during an unwary moment in an unguarded spot, deceiving him with fictitious movements. By so doing the weaker but more skilled man will defeat a more powerful opponent.

"In the action of mind and body a negative (*in*) and a positive (*yo*) principle operate. The active state of the mind or body is termed *yo* and the passive is termed *in*. As the proper control of the mind has an important bearing upon the practice of jujutsu, considerable attention has been devoted to it. The mind should be kept energetic and the attention concentrated upon the fundamental principles of the art. The mind will keep watch and ward over every part of the body, whether stationary or in motion.

"The technical terms *shi*, *ki* and *chikara* may be broadly defined as idea, spirit and power. A man's intention to pick up something is *shi*; his compliance with the prompting of *shi* is *ki*; and the actual handling of the object is due to *chikara* which obeys the impulse of *ki*. Where there is *chikara* there is also *ki*, and vice versa; one is really the complement of the

[1]A separate chapter on Kiai will be found elsewhere.

other. But in practising jujutsu it should be remembered that if precedence be given to power (*chikara*) the result is bound to be highly disadvantageous. Power or physical strength should be relegated to a secondary position and efforts should be made to gain experience in the control and employment of spirit or mind, for when that is accomplished the right application of strength will become spontaneous.

"By the term *ki wo mitsuru* is meant the assumption of a correct position, with the mind on the alert. The god Senju-Kannon has a thousand arms and only one head, but still he is accredited with the ability to use all his hands simultaneously. To obviate the danger of an uneven distribution of strength the mind must permeate the entire body from the head to the extremities.

"The word *kurai* means a quiescent state of mind, as if one were afloat in a small boat on the ocean. A boat obeys the impulses of the waves and currents and will not attempt to resist them. Similarly in jujutsu, when powerful pressure is brought to bear do not resist it, but appear to conform to the will of your adversary. Nevertheless, at the moment when he relaxes his efforts promptly avail yourself of a favourable chance.

"Imperturbability of mind in an emergency is called *fudoshin*. An unmoved demeanour on seeing sharp drawn swords or at any other unexpected happening is highly valued, and this attitude of mind should be sedulously cultivated. In an encounter with a powerful opponent the mind should be kept placid and all the tricks of the art should be tried. In ancient times the student had more frequent opportunities than today of witnessing and taking part in warlike actions in order to acquire this mental imperturbability. Some enthusiasts would even go so far as to retreat to mountainous regions or other desolate places in search of mental concentration. Nowadays too many jujutsu pupils merely train their bodies and pay but slight attention to the cultivation of their minds, but this is a mistake; the importance of mental training should never be lost sight of.

"Sometimes when one prepares to attack, the opposite party will not move but will maintain a composed posture as if he had fallen asleep. This conduct is called *muga-mushin* it is highly valued and ought to be carefully studied, though the learner should never scruple to take advantage of a chance favourable to himself and detrimental to his opponent."

Thus far my Japanese author whose remarks will have been sufficient to give the foreign reader a fair idea of the theory and application of jujutsu. Not all that is here written should be accepted in a painfully literal manner; some allowance must be made for Oriental hyperbole, and it is not every theory that is capable of flawless fulfilment in practice. No modern teacher of judo despises strength. Other things equal it is almost certain to turn the scale in favour of its possessor. The vital consideration is that a knowledge of judo enables the student to distinguish between the right and wrong use of strength. I began to realize the philosophy of the distinction early in my novitiate when a Japanese considerably smaller and lighter than myself threw me over his head with what is known as the *seoinage* or shoulder throw and splintered my collar-bone. It is nevertheless a difficult lesson to learn, especially for a muscular pupil who is constantly tempted to try to bear down his opponent by sheer "beef". It is because the adult Sandow type of pupil can rarely avoid instinctive recourse to mere physical strength that the most satisfactory results in judo are usually achieved in the case of the "disciple" who is caught young, say at the age of eleven or twelve, and who is thus enabled to develop skill and strength simultaneously. Such a subject, if to begin with he possesses some natural aptitude, is rarely guilty of the offence of "unreasonably" (*muri-ni*, as the Japanese say) applying his strength. It is not that the powerful adult may not become a very formidable exponent of judo in a practical sense, but simply that his victories in the matted arena are likely to be due less to what the Japanese call *waza* (the neat and finished performance of a trick, technique) than to *wanryoku* or brute strength, albeit the effectiveness of the latter will unquestionably be intensified by knowledge of the principles and practice of the art. But for a true and convincing demonstration of the essential properties and virtue of judo one should not look to such a demonstrator but rather to a comparatively small and by no means heavy expert who, when the accomplishes a given throw, will seem to do so without serious effort.

CHAPTER IV

JUDO IN ACTION

No more remarkable object lesson in the futility of mere physique when pitted against "science" could be desired than that afforded by a visit to a first-class judo school. The highest of all such dojo is Kodokan of Tokyo to which I have already referred as the head-quarters of Dr. Jigoro Kano's eclectic system which has gained the widest recognition and the largest number of followers throughout Japan and the West. The Kodokan of my day, since superseded by a far larger structure described in greater detail elsewhere in these pages, was a very handsome Japanese-style building with an imposing central entrance surmounted by a carved wooden arch or canopy. The entire building was of the same material and was erected at a cost of about £1,000 sterling or 10,000 yen at the then current rate of exchange—a ridiculously small sum judged by present-day standards but whose purchasing power in the Meiji era was immeasurably greater. It was situated in the metropolitan ward known as Koishikawa not far from the arsenal, a forty minutes' tramcar journey from Shimbashi. Although apparently somewhat remote from the centre of the capital it was nevertheless located in a populous student district, while for the rest, a true judo student thinks nothing of spending two or three hours per day in merely travelling to and from the dojo. The interior of the Kodokan is a sort of sahara of straw-coloured mats, a specially strong kind of *tatami* made to resist as long as possible the incessant shocks from falling bodies to which they are necessarily subjected. The bare statement that there were some 250 of these *tatami* on the floor space of the Kodokan will not in itself convey a great deal to the average foreign reader; but when it is added that the approximate dimensions of one Japanese mat of this type are 6 ft. long by 3 ft. wide a better idea of the generous area of the place will be forthcoming. A mat of the above description is composed of a *toko* or bottom, usually made of straw, sewed in eight or nine lines; and of a covering made of rush matting (*ryukyu*) which is tightly sewn to the bottom in ten or fifteen lines, the thread used for the purpose appearing on the surface as little as possible. In the case of a perfect dojo such as the Kodokan these mats lie upon a flooring which in turn rests upon numerous steel springs which cause the entire floor to give perceptibly in response to the smallest pressure from above. The surface of the mat, though seemingly hard and smooth, is none the less of remarkable elasticity, and although a clumsy fall may result in a broken bone it is astonishing with what force one may be thrown and still rise to renew the encounter absolutely intact. At the same time this result presupposes on the part of the victim some knowledge of how to fall, and no judo pupil is allowed to take part in actual practice on the mat until he has mastered what are called the Breakfalls for which the overall Japanese term is Ukemi. The walls of this, as of all jodo, were of wood and as far as possible sharp angles were avoided, corner-posts being concealed within the walls. Immediately behind the main entrance, which was reserved for Dr. Kano and other members of the teaching staff, Black Belt wearers or *yudansha*, was a spacious alcove-shaped platform from which Dr. Kano was in the habit of addressing his disciples from time to time. His portrait hung in a corner, and the rule of the school imperatively required that every member of the dojo should, both on entering and leaving the hall, make an obeisance before this portrait by going down on his hands and knees in Japanese fashion and tapping the mats with his forehead. None the less, "tell it not in Gath", yet in the interests of Truth at this distant date I feel bound to reveal that there were times when this rule was more honoured in the breach than the observance, e.g. on some occasions when all the so-called *mudansha* or judoka below the Black Belt grade had already gone and the hour waxing late the few remaining Black Belts were in a hurry to "perambulate their calcareous strata", in other words, walk their chalks, and so instead of making the customary obeisance (*rei wo suru*, in Japanese) would irreverently exclaim, "Please excuse me, *sensei* (teacher), for being rude!" (*Kore wa shitsurei itashimashita!*) or words to that effect and thereupon beat it for home or some other appointment. On either side of this central dais were two smaller platforms, one of which was intended for the use of occasional visitors, foreigners or

Japanese, who might wish to watch a display of judo; and the other dedicated to members of the grade entitled to wear the black belt from *shodan* (first grade) upwards. As a rule a group of experts, with the then director of the dojo, the famous Sakujiro Yokoyama, now alas no more, as the central figure, might daily be seen on this latter elevation, smoking the eternal cigarette and perennially discussing "stunts". The common herd had to foregather for social intercourse at the other end of the dojo, though for wrestling purposes the matted floor space was free to all. When taxed to its full capacity the then Kodokan would permit a hundred or more couples to practise at a time. The present-day Kodokan of 500 mats can of course accommodate a far larger number. The typical judo costume is made of strong cotton cloth, sleeved and lined. To quote Professor Arima, the author of a standard work on the subject, "it must cover the legs an inch or two below the knees and be so made that its *eri* (which in Japanese clothes forms the collar and extension) can fit both sides of the body. The sleeves should be an inch or two longer than the elbow and loose enough to admit of the fist in addition to the arms. The garment must be thickly stitched crosswise with white thread, but below the waist it may be stitched obliquely or lengthwise and crosswise. The belt should also consist of cotton cloth, folded five or six times, stitched with white thread in four or six lines, and be long enough to encircle the body twice, leaving sufficient length to fasten in front. The trousers must be loose and need not be lined. They should end about midway between the knee and ankle but may be half that length. They are to be fastened around the waist by means of cords attached to their upper part."

In some of the smaller dojo of my day many pupils might be seen wearing nether garments scarcely more voluminous than the bathing trunks used by men, but I do not advise the tender-skinned Occidental to follow the example of these young stalwarts whose epidermis seemed impervious to abrasion. I speak feelingly on this subject seeing that I began by wearing this attenuated kind of costume and endured agonies before my knees became inured to the flaying process every time they struck the mats. I well remember that during one winter season they were cut and torn so repeatedly that suppuration set in, and I had to undergo special medical treatment before I could renew my exertions.

Later on, however, when I joined the Kodokan, the problem was solved by the adoption of the more sensible style of trousers affected at that school.

The idea underlying the use of some sort of costume in the practice of judo may call for explanation for the benefit of Western boxers and wrestlers who in practice often wear nothing over the upper part of the body. The theory of judo, however, is largely based upon the justifiable assumption that in nine cases out of ten your opponent in a quarrel in real life would be clad in ordinary garments, and with equal justice a large number of the tricks in the repertoire of the art depend for their successful fulfilment upon a grip of the upper garment, although it would be a grave error to suppose that the judoka (exponent of judo) is necessarily at a loss when his antagonist is nude from the waist up. The field of action would to a certain extent be reduced in the latter instance, but on the other hand there is an esoteric branch of the art whose application would actually be facilitated by this very circumstance. As a rule, however, the judo expert is loath to have recourse to the often lethal tricks comprised in the latter category, save in the last extremity, and prefers if possible to put his opponent out of action by means of a throw or bonelock which, if the victim is wise enough to know when he has had enough, rarely leaves him much the worse for wear. The esoteric side of judo will be dealt with more in detail later on.

The only outward distinction of rank at the Kano school lies in the colour of the belt. The lowest classification is the *"kyu"* meaning "class". Below the grade of *sankyu*, which may be freely rendered as third-class, the student wears a simple white belt; from *sankyu* up to *ikkyu*, or first-class, the colour changes to brown. Then from *shodan*, first grade, up to *godan*, or fifth-grade, a black belt is worn. The word *dan* in Japanese has the meaning of grade, degree or step, and *shodan* is the lowest rank in the section above that of *kyu* already mentioned. From *shodan* upwards the classification runs numerically, i.e. "second-grade" (*nidan*), "third-grade" (*sandan*), "fourth-grade" (*yodan*), "fifth-grade" (*godan*), "sixth-grade" (*rokudan*), "seventh-grade" (*shichidan*), "eighth-grade" (*hachidan*), "ninth-grade" (*kudan*), and highest of all, "tenth-grade" (*judan*). From sixth-grade up to eighth-grade a red and white belt is worn, and from ninth to tenth-grade an

KYUZO MIFUNE
When Fifth Dan

THE BUTOKUKAI KYOTO

all red belt. But in practice the wearing of these parti-coloured belts is optional and dan-holders are free to wear the all-black belt.

Judoka below the *dan* classification are called *mudansha* or *non-dan*, and dan-holders are called *yudansha*. I should add that in my day the highest grade ever awarded was the seventh and holders of that grade could then be counted on the fingers of one hand. Understandably the number of judoka tended to increase in inverse proportion to that of the dan-holders. Dr. Kano himself, as the founder of the school, may be said to have stood above even the *dan* distinction. After him the most celebrated and, in practice, the most formidable of all judo experts of my day was undoubtedly Sakujiro Yokoyama, already mentioned. He held the seventh-grade, or *shichidan*. The nickname of "demon" (*oni*) which he bore in his heyday is in itself a reflection of the awe in which he was held by his judo and jujutsu contemporaries. Fairly tall for a Japanese but of medium height for a foreigner, Yokoyama, then a man on the shady side of forty, was seen at a glance to be of unusual muscular development, his neck especially rising from between his broad shoulders like a solid pillar of sinewy flesh. Any attempt by even the strongest untrained man to throttle such an opponent would have been vain indeed.

I had occasion to note during my first visit to the Kodokan that several of the *yudansha* were hardly more than five feet high— though many were, of course, far taller—but in spite of their inferior stature it was a comparatively simple matter for them to topple over their opponents, however big, with an apparent absence of effort which added to the impressiveness of the demonstration. Dr. Kano himself was then a middle-aged man perhaps 5 ft. 4 in. in height, but with a thickness of neck and a depth of chest which denoted great strength. Very notably his calves were of abnormal thickness. Very strict discipline was observed among the students and during my visit no one ventured to address him without a bow, and the head of the school on his part gave his instructions with military curtness. In those days Dr. Kano still did a certain amount of practice and would have been an ugly customer to tackle in a serious encounter. His name was one to conjure with throughout Japan.

Catch-as-catch-can wrestling, which I had studied in British Columbia before proceeding to California and from there to Japan, is the nearest approach to judo that we have in Europe and America and several of the pure throws are similar in both schools, though in view of the fact that the catch-as-catch-can wrestler is naked save for a pair of jock-straps and pumps, he is by no means so good a subject for holds and grips as a man who is clothed. Again, the object in catch-as-catch-can is to force your opponent's two shoulders down upon the mat. In judo, though a clean throw of course counts, you are at liberty to try to defeat your opponent by falling voluntarily upon your back or in any other manner, whereas in catch-as-catch-can the man who, voluntarily or otherwise, allows his two shoulders to touch the mat together is defeated. In judo, on the contrary, it may often happen that the man on top is in such pain as to be forced to surrender.

The question is continually being asked by foreigners which is the more effective—judo or boxing? I may say at once that in my opinion the problem can never be satisfactorily solved under the conditions of a friendly contest in which the boxer must wear gloves and the judoka may not avail himself of the more deadly tricks in his repertoire. I may recall in this context that very many years ago, not long after I had taken up the study of judo in one of the *ryugi* outside the Kodokan, the then well-known middleweight Jack Slavin, former champion of Australia, came to Japan and gave several exhibitions at one of which some of my Japanese wrestling friends and I contributed a display of judo. The presence of the Australian was regarded as a fitting opportunity for an international contest, and arrangements had actually been completed for a meeting between Slavin and a famous Japanese champion named Iizuka, professor of judo at the Keio University, Tokyo, when Slavin suddenly sailed for the Klondyke in response to an invitation from his brother Frank, a prominent heavyweight of those days. Jack Slavin, in a letter to his agent, explained that, as his funds were at zero and an opening had presented itself, he would not have been justified in letting it slip. Personally I believe the excuse was genuine enough, but his sudden departure at such a juncture naturally created a most unfortunate impression in Japanese circles and confirmed the very real belief that Slavin would have been defeated. Since confession is said to be good for the soul I do not mind acknowledging that I too shared that belief

and still share it, for Slavin's prospective opponent Iizuka, albeit
not more than 5 ft. 3 or 4 in. in height, was a miniature Hercules
in physique and possessed of astonishing skill and agility. I am
glad to say that at the moment, Iizuka, now well in his eighth
decade, is still alive and well in Tokyo. But even had the contest
come off it would have been hampered by the conditions already
adverted to and would have satisfied only the winning side. The
only logical way of deciding the point would be to put the boxer
and the judoka into an open field and there let them fight to a
finish with nothing barred. But unfortunately for the final settlement of this much-vexed question, though fortunately for the
limitation of international bills of mortality, neither the laws of
the civilized East nor those of the West permit what the Japanese
call a *shinken* (literally "real sword", otherwise a genuine fight
to a finish).

Before taking final leave of this much-vexed subject and
braving at this eleventh hour the risk of being accused of an
indiscretion, I am going to reveal the fact that somewhat irregu-
larly and while holding the modest post of editor of *The Japan
Advertiser* at Yokohama, I acted as an intermediary in
arranging contests between an English bluejacket boxer and a
Japanese judoka in one case and between an American bluejacket
boxer and a Japanese judoka in the other. These contests were
separately staged at a Japanese theatre in the Yokohama native
quarter and in both instances attracted crowded houses. In the
first case the British bluejacket was reputed to be the best boxer
among the crew of the cruiser in which he served, and the American bluejacket was the acknowledged boxing champion of the
American warship in which he served. The Japanese opponent
of the British bluejacket was an exceptionally big and powerful
Japanese who, though nominally only a first *kyu* (*ikkyu*), was
well known to be as good as any contemporary 4th Dan extant,
but he had been expelled from the Kodokan for unseemly
behaviour beyond its borders and had therefore never been promoted to the ranks of the *yudansha*. Be that as it may, he was a
cheerful and likeable ruffian and by his subsequent performance
fully justified my choice by throwing the unfortunate bluejacket all over the place. But in the second instance the tables
were turned, and the Japanese *ikkyu* who tried conclusions with

the American naval pugilist, a superb physical specimen of the "killer" type, was so badly battered that before the end of the second round he had to retire to escape a knock-out. But in neither case could the result be deemed decisive seeing that in the first case the British bluejacket, despite his reputation, was clearly only a crude amateur and in the second, the Japanese judo representative was not even a *yudansha*. Then came an unexpected sequel to all these alarums and excursions when to the consternation of all concerned, with myself in the van, from the heights of the Kodokan Olympus descended the thunderbolt of Dr. Kano's wrath in the shape of a warning that thereafter any member of the Kodokan found guilty of participating directly or indirectly in further degrading practices of this kind calculated to sully the fair fame of judo would be summarily expelled without benefit of clergy. After that I waited not upon the order of my going but went or retired at once from the scene of action, and so as far as I am concerned the issue is still open and bids fair to remain so unless and until contest rules are relaxed and amended along the lines already foreshadowed.

I once asked Dr. Kano how one of the big wrestlers, or *sumotori*, would fare at the hands of an expert judoka?

"Well," he replied, "no doubt the *sumotori* might be able, under the silly rules of his style of wrestling, to push the judoka out of the ring, but in a real fight an expert judoka ought to be able to kill the *sumotori*." Apropos of which there is a Japanese yarn which, *se non è vero è ben trovato*, tells how once upon a time a judoka and a big *sumotori* fell into a dispute on this very subject, until finally it was agreed to try conclusions in order to make certain. At the very commencement of the struggle the big man picked the judoka up and holding him high above his head asked triumphantly, "Now where are you?" Apparently not a whit perturbed by this turn of events the judoka answered, "Oh, this is just where judo comes in. The moment you attempt to throw me down I'll kick you to death!" Terrified out of his wits by this awful threat the fat man, still holding the judoka in the same position, rushed out into the street shouting loudly for help! The sequel is not recorded.

The term judo is not in itself new, but until its adoption by Dr. Kano to designate his system it was by no means so much in vogue as the term jujutsu. Etymologically a single ideograph differentiates jujutsu from judo. As already explained jujutsu means the soft art or art of softness; *do* means a road or way. In other words, Dr. Kano insisted upon the ethical as well as the purely physical aspect of this system, and, in theory at least, a good moral character is as essential to the promotion of the student of judo as practical efficiency. Dr. Kano perfected his system more than seventy years ago after training under the teachers of the older jujutsu *ryugi* and thoroughly assimilating the best they had to offer. In the days following the abolition of feudalism a reaction had set in against the martial arts, and when the prominent German physician Dr. Baelz urged upon the faculty of the Imperial University the necessity of improving the sadly deteriorated physique of the students of the day he encountered strenuous opposition. One result of this tendency of the times was that the jujutsu dojo were almost deserted and the starving teachers were only too eager to impart their knowledge to so enthusiastic a disciple as Dr. Kano then was. Thus in the end Dr. Kano was enabled to establish his own school which has retained all that is really valuable from the repertoire of the older *ryugi* whilst rejecting what the lawyers would call surplusage, adding largely to the list of *waza* or tricks and classifying the latter in a logical and scientific manner. From modest beginnings the famous Kodokan has grown up into an imposing practice hall with a membership which today runs into hundreds of thousands and is continually growing, while among Dr. Kano's *montei* or disciples even in my day were included many of the most prominent military and naval men of Japan, not excepting even princes of the Imperial blood. The young Prince Tokugawa, son of the last of the Shoguns and then head of the house, was a clever exponent of the art personally known to me, with the rank of *nidan* or second grade. Judo is the system officially recognized, compulsory in my day in all naval and military schools, practised at all Government universities and schools and at nearly all the bigger private educational establishments.

The fee charged for tuition at the old Kodokan was astonishingly small—only thirty sen a month or less than eightpence, in addition to an entrance fee which was not usually less than a yen but which could be increased by those disposed to do so. When the student reached the grade of *shodan*, the lowest teaching grade, the charge was remitted in return for the help which he was expected to render to lower-grade students. The method of classification was quite simple. Responsibility devolved upon a select number of teachers who carefully watched the form displayed by the pupils in daily practice and in the periodical contests called *shobu* or *shiai*, and decided all details relative to individual promotion. The applicant who obtained permission to enter the institution was required to present it with a pair of folding fans and the sum of one yen. And today as then until the student attains the *dan* grade he is forbidden to make use of certain locks called *gyaku* which, unless skilfully applied, may result in serious injury to muscles and joints. When the student reaches the *dan* grade he is gradually initiated into the esoteric branches of the art which include *atemi*, already referred to as the art of striking and kicking vital spots, and *kappo*, or methods of resuscitating one who has been rendered unconscious by strangulation or other cause. The non-esoteric branches of judo are called *randori* in which the pupil freely applies his knowledge in open practice (*keiko*) with others, and *kata*, or forms, in which the principal tricks are demonstrated in a prearranged order by two performers. In the *kata* the prearranged winner in every method is called Tori (literally "taker") and the loser Uke (literally "receiver").

In order to inure the pupil to the two extremes of heat and cold and to cultivate the virtue of perseverance, all dojo including the Kodokan hold special summer and winter exercises. For the former the hottest month of the year, August, and the hottest time of the day, from 1 p.m., are chosen; and for the latter commencing in January, the pupils start wrestling at four o'clock in the morning and keep it up until seven or eight. The summer practice is termed *shochugeiko* and the winter practice *kangeiko*. There is likewise the "number exercise" on the last day of the winter practice when as a special test of endurance, the pupils practise from 4 a.m. till 2 p.m. and not infrequently go through as many as a hundred bouts within that interval.

In the periodical competitions the best two out of three falls or other recognized proof of superiority decide the victory, although the umpire, if the contest is unduly prolonged, may announce what is called *ippon shobu* which means that one fall shall decide the issue. Literally *ippon shobu* may perhaps be rendered as "one-point contest". Expert students with exceptional wind often defeat half a dozen or more opponents one after the other and wrestle continuously for an hour or more at a time. More recent modifications of contest rules authorize the umpire, at his discretion, if no point has been scored by either party within the time limit, to award the victory to the contestant who has displayed the more aggressive spirit and initiative.

The two great competitions of the year, held in the spring and autumn respectively, are styled *Kohaku Shobu* (or Shiai), meaning Red and White Contest, in which the competitors are divided into two teams (red and white), each team having its leader and being arranged according to the degree of skill possessed by the members. Thus the contest will begin with the least proficient and youngest opponents of the lower grades, and each bout is decided by the first fall or point scored instead of the best two out of three for the periodical grading competitions. Ultimately the two best men on either side meet and fight it out. Or it will sometimes happen that one side is so far ahead of the other, owing to a succession of victories won by individual competitors, that towards the end the lower-grade men on the winning side must wrestle with higher-grade men on the losing side. At such moments, not unnaturally, intense excitement prevails, and the adherents of the rival colours freely encourage their champions with cries of *"aka"* (red, *"shiro"* (white) respectively, and frequent use of the expression *"Shikkari! Shikkari!*—i.e. "Firmly! Firmly!"—something like our "buck up" or "stick to him", perhaps. At the close of the competition the members of the winning team with their leader (*taisho*) at their head, enter the roped enclosure and in my day from the hands of Dr. Kano himself would receive the championship flag as concrete evidence of their victory. At one time the *Kohaku Shobu* began with the very lowest grades, mere children, and finished with *sandan* or *yodan* experts; but nowadays, owing to the constantly growing number of entries, the contest begins only with the *ikkyu* classes. It is quite a common thing for 400 couples to participate in these historic meetings. The names of the competitors were in my day written in large characters on a wide strip of paper which stretched right across the far end of the hall so that they might easily be perused from a distance. Written of course in Japanese each name must be read vertically from top to bottom, and the entire list from left to right, though the customary Japanese order in books and newspapers is from right to left. Thus, whereas a corresponding list of names in English would take the form of two or more perpendicular rows, the names of each row being written horizontally, in Japanese the separate rows, for red and white contestants, are horizontal, one colour above the other, while the names of members of both teams form perpendicular lines. Nominally each name in the upper row is supposed to appear immediately opposite the name of a prospective antagonist in the lower row, but as a matter of fact, this original order can rarely be preserved; and it was curious in my day to trace the fluctuating fortunes of war on either side by means of the red lines which an assistant, seated high enough to have an unobstructed view of the contests, described with a brush after each bout. Two or more red lines radiating from a name in the upper row and ending at two or more names in the lower one would indicate that the owner of the name in the upper row had beaten the owners of the names in the lower row, or vice versa. It was therefore quite easy for even a foreigner with but an elementary knowledge of the language to ascertain at a glance at the red lines which side was ahead for the time being and by exactly how many men. The *Kohaku Shobu* is furthermore the occasion for numerous promotions which were in my day also announced by Dr. Kano himself in a stereotyped formula from which he rarely if ever deviated. Even after the pruning process above referred to, a *Kohaku Shobu* commencing at eight in the morning rarely finished much before the same hour in the evening, and prior to the pruning process 11 p.m. has seen the young gladiators hard at it in the glare of incandescent lamps and nowadays of the electric light. Ordinary *shobu*, otherwise *shiai*, differ somewhat from the *Kohaku* in that there is no red and white classification and two out of three falls are required for a win unless the umpire, as already explained, announces *"ippon shobu"*, owing to the equal character of the struggle. Also it may be that two or even three couples with their three umpires are bouting simultaneously while, unlike the *Kohaku Shobu*, the onlookers maintain a religious silence. For those who are susceptible to verbal encouragement the ordinary *shobu*, held on an average every six weeks in the case of students below the *dan* grades, is therefore a far more serious and trying affair than the *Kohaku* and a greater test of physical endurance. Speaking from long personal experience I can say that the *shobu* is a genuine mental as well as physical ordeal—for the participant. In the case of the more advanced students who come on at a later hour, there is all the horror of anticipation to be contended against. As one enters the building the only sounds to greet the ear are the "dull sickening thuds" which proclaim successive falls, the deep breathing and panting of the contestants, and the staccato tones of the umpires as they declare victory and defeat. From the umpires' decisions there is no appeal. In the comparatively rare cases where one of the competitors is a foreigner, he finds it difficult to resist the conviction that most of the onlookers who squat on the bleak-looking mats in serried ranks are anxious to see him defeated, not because they entertain towards him any personal animus but simply out of deference to the racial sentiment which is nowhere more assertive than in Japan, and which, while no doubt it makes for national solidarity, undeniably carries with it strong prejudice against the alien and the not unnatural desire for his discomfiture whenever and wherever he runs up against a true son of Dai Nippon. I must hasten to add that in my day at the Kodokan, whether or not this feeling existed, it was never allowed to reveal itself. No outward demonstration signalized victory or defeat on either side except on the occasion of the *Kohaku Shobu* already mentioned. But then as now, so far as the umpire himself is concerned, speaking generally, strict justice may be confidently expected at his hands, irrespective of race, colour or creed.

The pleasure of a *shobu* is not at all enhanced by the sort of weather Tokyo enjoys in winter. Let it be said that in the old Kodokan, as in all other dojo of my day, there was no artificial heating of any kind whatever, and in order to anticipate suggestions from inventive foreigners I must hasten to add that no footgear other than socks or stockings and no overcoats might be worn inside the building. Here, then, in such stark circumstances the expression Anglo-Saxon colloquialism "cold feet" had a very real and dreadful application. For reasons already explained, it was impossible for the heads of the dojo to specify the exact moment when a given competitor must take to the mats against his opponent or for them to determine beforehand who that opponent would be. Imagine therefore the state of being, physical and psychological, of the nervous person while waiting, constrained by the awful fascination of the game to watch as one after the other the contestants preceding him were either defeated or emerged victorious from the strenuous fray. The spectacle of a human being hitting the mats with a bang which literally shook the spring-supported floor and seemed to shake the entire building was hardly conducive to a happy, tranquil state of mind. The feet of the nervous onlooker were by this time so frigid as to be almost destitute of sensation, and what between excitement and the temperature his teeth would be chattering like the proverbial castanets and it would be with extreme difficulty that he could articulate at all. These symptoms of "blue funk", I am sorry to say, were in my day rather more frequently exhibited by the foreigner than by the Japanese. After all the Japanese judoka has usually been caught very young, say at eleven, twelve or thirteen, and is thus to the manner born. Furthermore he is among friends and can as a rule depend upon the moral support of a large proportion of the spectators, while his opponent is usually a Japanese. The average foreigner is necessarily in a different position and is handicapped accordingly. As a matter of fact, however, during the whole of my experience of the game I can recall only five foreigners who had in my day taken part in *shobu*, and of this number two only at all regularly. Since the Second World War, the position in this respect has naturally changed almost out of all recognition and it is safe to say that of the many hundreds of Allied service men among the forces of occupation who had practised judo at the new Kodokan a considerable proportion must have taken part in contests.

Apropos the psychology of the *shobu* the testimony of my old friend Weed, now, alas, no more, is of great value, for he was a well-known athlete among resident foreigners in Japan where he was born of an American father and a Japanese mother, and had won distinction and numerous trophies in football, rowing, baseball, swimming, running and to a lesser extent cricket. When, therefore, a man of this calibre testifies that the judo competition is the most trying of all, and one that imposes the severest demands upon the nervous and physical forces, I think the reader ought to be convinced that in my own appraisement of the *shobu* I have not been guilty of any exaggeration.

What, it may be asked, is the human product of judo? Elsewhere in these pages I shall have occasion to quote the views of authorities like the late Dr. Jigoro Kano, the late Noboyuki Kunishige, and the late Sakujiro Yokoyama; but speaking briefly here from my own experience and observation I do not hesitate to declare that in my day at any rate the teachers and students of the art in Japan constituted a body of men of which any nation and any epoch might well be proud. In saying this I do not lose sight of the fact that there are inevitably black sheep in every fold and that in this respect judo can hardly hope to remain immune from the incidence of what seems to be the operation of a natural law. Also in too many cases, speaking rhetorically, the ichor-like fluid which flows in the veins of the pioneer idealists of any movement as often as not is transformed into commonplace gore in the veins of their venal descendants exposed to the corrupting influence of wordly success.

The foreigner in the old treaty ports who rarely left the beaten track and knew nothing of any other kind of Japanese than the narrow-chested pasty-faced, anaemic *banto* whose principal recreations were tobacco, *sake* and dissipation generally, was wont to smile almost sceptically when told of the existence of a very different type of native—of a young man bubbling over with health and vitality, not tall, perhaps, but extraordinarily broad-shouldered, deep-chested and thick-necked, with beautifully developed thighs and calves, back and stomach muscles. This kind of man appears to walk somewhat from the hips with a suggestion of swagger, probably unconscious and the outcome of justifiable self-confidence. He was then and is now as a rule a student at one of the higher schools of Tokyo and Kyoto; and if, as sometimes happens, devotion to judo tends to detract a little from his devotion to book-learning he is none the worse on that account, and the race as a whole is decidedly better since it cannot be denied that at about the time when the late Dr. Kano succeeded in popularizing his system the greatest physical and nervous deterioration had set in as the outcome of excessive zeal in the pursuit of Occidental knowledge. It is scarcely too much to say that the revival of the old samurai art in an improved form has been the salvation of the rising generation, although it must be confessed there are still too many young men and boys who appear to be committed irrevocably to the sedentary life. Dr. Kano may thus with reason be regarded as a public benefactor, and that his motives were purely disinterested—in a pecuniary sense at least—is patent to all who are familiar with the facts. Owing to the almost nominal charge for tuition it is doubtful whether the old Kodokan did much more than support itself, and in many indirect ways it is almost certain that Dr. Kano was out of pocket for the board and lodging of the numerous *shosei* (a sort of student-dependant) who gathered round him. But to return to our muttons. The type of student whom I am endeavouring to describe is as a rule quiet and well-behaved, but it is not always possible to avoid trouble without sacrifice of self-respect. When, however, trouble does occur, it is usually confined to the opponent of the judo expert. Indeed it might almost be inferred that although hardly likely to have read *Hamlet* yet in such an emergency he is exemplifying the sage precept given to Laertes by his father Polonius which reads: "Beware of entrance to a quarrel, but being in bear't that the opposed may beware of thee." Herewith a few cases in point :

Two Kodokan teachers were assaulted by seventeen coolies in a meat-shop—a sort of popular restaurant. Although some of the coolies were armed with knives the gang were dispersed in a twinkling, three of them with broken arms and all with bruised and battered faces. As fast as one of the experts artistically "downed" his man the other would pick the victim up like an empty sack and dump him into the street. The only evidence of the conflict on the side of the two experts took the form of skinned knuckles where the latter had come into contact with the coolies' teeth. On another occasion a celebrated expert fell foul of a coolie in the upper room of a restaurant and promptly threw him downstairs. The coolie returned to the fray with fourteen comrades, but the expert calmly sat at the head of the stairs and as fast as the coolies came up single file, owing to the narrowness of the passage, he simply choked them in detail and hurled them down again. In the excitement of the moment he was rather rougher than was strictly necessary and so broke one man's neck. The rest fled in terror carrying off their dead and wounded. The judo expert was arrested, but as he was easily able to prove that he had been one man against fifteen he was, of course, acquitted, Nevertheless the Kodokan temporarily suspended him for his conduct which was deemed unduly violent.

In another case the hero, whom I knew personally, was then a youth below shodan grade and was attacked in a lonely part of Tokyo by a footpad armed with a sword. He succeeded in capturing the footpad and handing him over to the police, but received a wound in the foot which laid him up for a month. Dr. Kano himself had more than one adventure. During a voyage to Europe he once engaged in a wrestling contest with a huge Russian, and greatly to the surprise of the spectators, who had anticipated his speedy defeat, threw his opponent with ease by means of a *koshinage* or loin throw, and what is still more remarkable saved the Russian's head from a nasty knock on the deck by placing his hand underneath it as the man fell. Commander Hirose, who perished during one of the famous blockading expeditions before Port Arthur during the Russo-Japanese war, was in his youth attached to the Japanese Legation at St. Petersburg as a student and was once challenged by a certain Russian naval officer of herculean proportions to a friendly trial of strength. Needless to say, Hirose, by means of his art, threw his man with ease. The Tsar, being informed of the episode, invited Hirose to the Imperial Palace where a contest was arranged with a famous athlete, and again Hirose emerged victorious. A well-known fourth-grade expert (*yodan*) named Uchida who travelled extensively in Korea, Manchuria and Siberia, had more than one occasion to utilize his knowledge of judo for purposes of self-protection and was never found wanting. In 1895 while travelling by steamer to Vladivostok, he came into conflict with a big Russian who, thinking to make use of his superior height and reach, seized Uchida by the collar and waist. Uchida, however, quickly applied a *koshinage*, which aptly lends itself to application against a taller opponent, and threw his man. The latter rose again and tried to kick Uchida, but was speedily swept off his feet and brought to the deck with a crash which knocked all the fight out of him. He fled from the arena and thereafter refrained from further interference with this formidable Japanese.

After long association with disciples of the cult, as it may almost be termed, one grows to recognize them anywhere by a sort of instinct. Perhaps their bearing becomes affected by the constant exercise of certain muscles in a certain way. The teacher of judo, who has been accustomed to practise almost daily until middle age, cannot safely retire at a moment's notice and henceforth lead a life of ease. His system has grown to need the stimulus of exercise and the sudden suspension of that exercise is calculated to impair his general health. The teacher who begins to tire of his strenuous calling and to pine for the condition of *inkyo* (retirement) finds it necessary to leave off by gradually reducing the daily number of bouts until in the end he feels it safe to abandon practice altogether.

CHAPTER V

STRANGULATION EXTRAORDINARY

UNDER the general heading of *kubigatame*, or necklocks, the Kano School of Judo has a very extensive repertoire of effective methods of choking an obstreperous adversary into submission, and unless surrender comes in the nick of time the victim will infallibly lose consciousness. Although the recital in the absence of a photographic commentary must be little better than a Chinese alphabet for the majority, as the Russian saw has it, I may mention the *namijiujijme* (literally "normal cross", the Japanese equivalent for the word "cross" being "sign of ten"), *gyakujujijime* (reverse cross), *katajujijime* (half-cross), *hadakajime* (naked stranglehold), *okurierijime* (sliding collar lock) and *sodeguruma* (sleeve-wheel). Many more could be cited but as this is not a textbook the foregoing will suffice.

It must be well within the recollection of any ordinary reader of the newspapers and of fiction that the would-be descriptive, picturesque writer not infrequently indulges in heroics when it comes to dealing with the sensations of an individual undergoing strangulation, while the question whether or not our common form of capital punishment is the most humane one possible in the circumstances also occasionally furnishes food for lengthy polemics. It so happens that I am in a position to write intelligently on the subject of strangulation for the simple reason that I personally have been choked into insensibility, and have scores of friends and acquaintances who have undergone a similar experience. I will say, and they will say that being choked by a competent hand is *per se* a bagatelle not worth making a fuss over. Indeed, beyond the preliminary sensations, as in the case of being chloroformed—another of my personal experiences—the sensation is rather pleasant than otherwise and if the victim is intelligently revived by means of *katsu*—a method of resuscitation afforded by the overall system termed *Kappo*—he feels as fit as ever five minutes afterwards. So lightly do the Japanese practitioners of judo and jujutsu regard strangling that apart from those accidental cases which are bound to occur quite frequently during judo contests, it is the time-honoured custom to choke deliberately all newly appointed *shodan*, or students of the art who hold the lowest teaching grade, the outward symbol of which is the black *obi* or belt. The idea at the bottom of this seemingly cold-blooded procedure is both to steel the victim's nerves and round off his experience, as it were, and to afford the newly promoted members an opportunity of putting into practice certain forms of *kappo* which are demonstrated by an expert teacher before the strangulation takes place.

My particular friend of those early days, D. T. Weed, already mentioned, first underwent the above experience and afterwards furnished me with an account thereof which, I think, makes interesting reading.

Weed first practised the art at the dojo of Keio University, Tokyo, the instructor of which was the famous Iizuka, then holder of the sixth-grade (*rokudan*) but years later promoted to the highest grade of *judan* (tenth-grade). Of stature somewhat below the average even for a Japanese, he was built on the lines of a miniature Hercules, and although in those days some thirty-seven or thirty-eight years of age, was still more than a match for the strongest and most expert of his pupils ten and fifteen years younger. Shortly after his promotion together with some ten others Weed attended the customary lecture and strangulation ceremony —if it may be so called—at the private residence of Mr. Fukuzawa, the son of the revered founder of Keio University, Yukichi Fukuzawa. Mr. Iizuka delivered the lecture which dealt generally with the ethical aspects of judo and this was followed by a demonstration of specific methods of *kappa*, the art of resuscitation, and finally by the choking of all eleven *shodan* and their speedy restoration to consciousness by the application of the appropriate *katsu* the details of which every initiate was under the most solemn pledge never to reveal to outsiders. It should perhaps be added that since those days the veil of mystery wherein *kappo* was then shrouded has been largely lifted and anybody interested can now buy for himself in several European languages quite reliable printed descriptions of these methods. The proceedings were so arranged that every new *shodan* alternately choked a

THE LATE SAKUJIRO YOKOYAMA
When Director of the Kodokan

THREE FAMOUS FENCING MASTERS

colleague, was choked by another, and revived a third by the application of the special *katsu* which had shortly before been illustrated either by Mr. Iizuka or some other high-class *yudansha* present. The room in which the ceremony was performed was of course in Japanese style and matted, and the *shodan* participating in these experiments wore the usual *keikogi* or practice garments, also called *judogi*, as most suitable for such an occasion.

Weed was asked by Mr. Iizuka whether he had ever been deliberately choked outside an actual judo contest. On receiving a negative reply Mr. Iizuka cheerfully rejoined, "Well, in that case you had better go through with it; otherwise you cannot regard yourself as a full-fledged judoka."

Affecting an air of easy nonchalance, which, he cheerfully confessed, was very far from being a faithful reflection of his true state of mind, Weed lay down on his back, and the famous expert, having secured a good hold in the *katajujijime* style, in which the loose collar of the upper garment is tightly constricted against the depression below the Adam's apple by the dual motion of pressing against it with the right hand and pulling the left lapel of the jacket downwards with the left hand, deftly dispatched Weed into the land of nod in forty seconds by actual watch count. Weed informed me however that he lost consciousness after the timekeeper had counted eleven, this being the last sound he heard, but his legs and arms continued to move convulsively for twenty-nine seconds more, so that the full count of forty seconds must be accepted as the interval required in which to "put him to sleep". As a matter of fact, with the exception of one student who took forty-five seconds to go off, Weed displayed the greatest resisting power of anybody present. It should be added that under these conditions the victim does not try to resist but rather to co-operate with the operator in consummating this congenial task. To that end he is required to empty his lungs as far as possible and to relax the muscles of the throat which are at other times brought into play when the subject has no overmastering desire to take a nap merely to oblige another. As already stated generally, so in Weed's case the first sensations were the usual ones of suffocation, the symptoms of which are a singing in the ears and a black void before the eyes. Complete oblivion speedily ensued. While in this state all perception of time and space is lost. Weed's earliest realization of his own identity took the form of a dim, confused attempt to balance a series of conflicting figures which presented themselves to his mind, but to no purpose. Next he heard the dull murmur of voices, and then suddenly regained complete consciousness with a start, and opened his eyes to find himself sitting on the mats surrounded by a circle of grinning comrades.

The older or more advanced *yudansha*, who had on previous occasions undergone this ordeal, did not scruple to indulge in uncomfortable jests at the expense of their juniors whose turn had yet to come on this memorable evening. These juniors, looking decidedly green about the gills, vainly sought to conceal their nervousness and anxiety beneath an assumption of coolness and indifference which succeeded in deceiving nobody, and laughed artificially in response to the grimly jocular comments of their seniors. *"Sayonara!"* ("Good-bye!"), *"Mata chikai uchi ni!"* ("See you again shortly!"), "Have you any last words or messages for your friends?" etc. were among the commonest forms of wit employed as one by one the members of the gallant eleven passed temporarily into the *Ewigkeit*. It is a notable fact that these experiments have no bad effect that can be traced, and seeing that even the Kano School of Judo has been in existence for more than seventy years the data under this head are by this time sufficiently voluminous to enable those responsible to estimate the danger, if any, of adherence to this practice. Weed showed no other sign of wear and tear the next day than a pair of slightly bloodshot eyes, but these symptoms rapidly disappeared and the experience remained thereafter in his memory as something which he was glad to have endured but had no overwhelming wish to undergo again!

In my own case the effect was unrehearsed. It was during the Russo-Japanese war and I had gone to the Kodokan in Koishikawa for my customary afternoon practice, at the end of which I was wont to while away an extra hour or so "yarning" with the rest and occasionally participating in trials of skill and strength not always strictly confined to judo. On one of these occasions a certain genius bethought him of an effective method of testing the resisting power of the human neck. The scheme was for one man to pass a sash round the neck of another from behind, the loop being carefully adjusted so as to press exactly upon the slight depression an inch or so beneath the Adam's apple—i.e. the most sensitive part of the throat and the one which, in conjunction with the jugular vein and the carotid arteries, yields most speedily to attentions of this description. The loop having been thus adjusted, the first man seized the two free ends of the sash, turned his back upon the other man, and passing the two ends of the sash over his shoulders raised the second man from the floor by bending forward at the necessary angle in such a manner that virtually the entire weight of the second man hung from his neck and exerted corresponding pressure upon the impromptu noose by which he was being carried pickaback. The object of the second man was, of course, to resist gradual strangulation by hardening the muscles of his throat. The carrier would then move forward at a rapid pace, but the moment the second man gave notice by clapping his hands that he had reached the limit of endurance, the carrier would drop him. The winner of this novel competition was the man who could hold out while his mount carried him over the largest area of mats.

I was an amused and interested spectator of these proceedings until a dozen or so fellows had with varying fortune coqueted with strangulation, but so far not one had failed to give the signal in time. Then suddenly certain members of the group turned to me and invited me to have a try. I may say without undue vanity that I then possessed a neck and throat of more than average strength and thickness, especially for my height which is only about 5 ft. 6 in. After years devoted off and on to catch-as-catch-can before I went to Japan, and jujutsu and judo almost from the day of my arrival in the country, I had developed special muscles to such purpose that it was no easy task for an ordinary man to choke me even when I made no use of my hands to ward off the attack but relied solely upon those muscles in doing so. I therefore consented with something like alacrity to have a go for the record and was soon under way. I can at this moment recall quite clearly how I took count of the mats as my bearer stepped over them and how the thought passed through my mind that I must be ready to give the signal as soon as I had improved on the distance of my most successful predecessor, if I could possibly hold out so long. The old familiar symptoms were soon declaring themselves. My temples were throbbing, my ears singing and things began to dance before my eyes. I saw that I had gone one better than the previous winner, and I was just thinking to myself, "Now, now I'll clap my hands!" and my arms were raised in the very act when I knew no more. As the Japanese vernacular has it, I fell (*ochiita*). The transition from consciousness to unconsciousness appeared in this case to be exceptionally abrupt. My first awakening thought was one of locality. I felt puzzled to know where I was—whether in England, America, Japan, or where? "Where the blazes am I?" was the problem which never ceased to worry me. Following this stage I became aware that I was sitting on the floor, but where, I could not yet be sure. Then, with a suddenness rivalling that with which I had succumbed to strangulation, I regained my full senses and opened my eyes. But immediately before I did this I had heard the dull confused murmur of human voices which entered into Weed's experience, though I had been unable to distinguish words or to associate the sound with individuals whom I knew. On opening my eyes I found myself surrounded by a small crowd of laughing fellows, but I did not know until some time afterwards that I had been brought round by the application of *kappo* and that the *yudansha* who had performed the operation was one named Karino, holder of the third-grade at that time and a recognized expert in "groundwork". My first words before rising to my feet were "What a pleasant sensation!" ("*Domo ii kokoromochi da!*") whereat everybody roared more loudly than ever. Thus the incident terminated and I felt absolutely no ill effects from the ordeal.

Ever since that time I have been less ready to sympathize with the actual physical sensations of the victims of capital punishment or of hanging generally, since, on the score of physical pain alone, a toothache or a severe kick on the shins is infinitely worse. Still, if it is all the same to the reader, like Weed, I am not hankering after additional experience of a like nature.

CHAPTER VI

A CHAMPION'S REMINISCENCES

I HAVE already spoken briefly about the famous superintendent of the old Kodokan, the late Sakujiro Yokoyama, as perhaps the greatest practical exponent of judo Japan had in my day produced. Mr. Yokoyama and I had been on amicable terms for something like a dozen years, although occasional absences on professional duty in my case had interfered with continuous intercourse. Like so many other adherents of this important art Mr. Yokoyama in private life was the very personification of good nature, although in his time, in pursuance of his calling, he had been compelled to give a good deal of pain to his fellow-creatures. Certainly this latter observation is more true of the past than of the present. Modern Japanese law does not permit human beings deliberately to inflict injuries upon each other, even when all the parties concerned are perfectly willing to run the risk. In Mr. Yokoyama's younger days, while the liberty of the subject was more restricted in other respects, yet in jujutsu and fencing encounters far more latitude was granted to the participants than during the Meiji era during which I was living in Japan.

When I asked Mr. Yokoyama to tell me something about his strenuous youth he readily complied. On the day appointed he took dinner with me at my residence in Kojimachi, Tokyo, and then over the post-prandial whisky and cigarettes promptly fell into reminiscent mood to which he gave verbal expression.

"In the old feudal days," he began, "jujutsu was divided into many schools. I commenced my study of the art from boyhood under a master of the Tenjin Yoshin-ryu. In those days contests were extremely rough and not infrequently cost the participants their lives. Thus, whenever I sallied forth to take part in one of these affairs I invariably bade farewell to my parents, since I had no assurance that I should ever return alive. Competitions were of such a drastic nature that few tricks were barred and we did not hesitate to have recourse to the most dangerous methods in order to overcome an opponent. I have had experiences of this kind without number. Since then the more dangerous tricks have been eliminated from these encounters to avoid serious consequences, and this circumstance, I think, accounts for the growing popularity of the art.

"When I was about twenty-three years old I had a contest with Mr. Samura Masahara, of the Takeuchi School. The scene was the dojo of the Metropolitan Police Bureau and I was fortunate enough to gain the victory. Some time afterwards I had a contest in the same dojo with Mr. Nakamura Haruze, of the Ryo Shinto School. Mr. Nakamura was then in the prime of manhood and enjoyed the reputation of being the strongest representative of jujutsu in the country. Our bout lasted fifty-five minutes—the longest time recorded in matches of this kind—and had not then been decided in favour of either of us. Fearing lest a continuation of the struggle should result in fatal injury to one or both of us—for we were prepared to go the limit—Mr. Mishima Tsuyo, then Chief of the Metropolitan Police, stepped forward and ordered the suspension of the match. The above-mentioned masters are the most formidable I have ever met in my life. For the most part the matches in which I have wrestled have terminated in my favour after two or three minutes. About that time a list of jujutsu masters was published in which Mr. Nakamura appeared as the champion of the East and I as champion of the West.

"From 1890 the taste for jujutsu began to decline and the various *ryugi* (schools) lost their pupils, but with the foundation of the Kodokan the tide again turned and no pains are spared nowadays to produce competent teachers. The art is taught at all the high schools and to military and naval officers. The pupils of the Kodokan number about 13,000, of whom the proportion of *yudansha* who are allowed to wear black belts as a sign of efficiency is about 1,200. The seventh-grade (*shichidan*) is now the highest conferred at the Kodokan and has so far been obtained by only two men, viz. Mr. Yamashita and myself. The sixth-grade (*rokudan*) is held by three men, Mr. Isogai, Mr. Nagaoka and Mr. Iizuka. There are six persons holding the fifth-grade (*godan*) and about thirty the fourth (*yodan*). It may be interesting to note that Commander Hirose, who lost his life in the attempt to block the entrance to Port Arthur during the Russo-Japanese war, held the fourth-grade and was posthumously raised to the sixth-grade by Dr. Kano. The third-grade (*sandan*) comprises about 120 names; the second (*nidan*) about 300, and the lowest of the *yudan-sha* grades known as *shodan* are correspondingly numerous. There are some well-known masters outside the Kodokan School of whom Mr. Imai of Okayama who in point of skill is equal to our fifth-grade, Mr. Tanabe, also of Okayama, and Mr. Yamamoto of Chiba, both of whom may be classed as fourth-grade, deserve special notice. The *yudansha* of the Kodokan are scattered all over the provinces where they are striving to popularize the art. Some of them have gone abroad and are winning a high reputation in foreign lands.

"When I was a young fellow," continued Mr. Yokoyama, "Tokyo was not at all what it is today. Old residents can still recall that there was a licensed quarter at Nedzu, immediately behind the Imperial University. At the back of this quarter there was a road running along the Shimobazu pond, at the foot of Ueno Park, and this road was bordered with bamboo-bushes and was a decidedly lonely spot at night. The licensed quarter was then infested with gamblers and other rascals who were ever on the look-out for a pretext to quarrel with peaceable wayfarers in order to extort money by means of intimidation. The jujutsu dojo where I practised was situated not far from Nedzu, and the pupils found these gamblers and other rough elements excellent raw material on which to test their skill. We were in the habit of repairing to the road I have described, usually choosing a dark night and there taking up our station in the bamboo-bushes. When a party of gamblers came along one of our number would emerge from his hiding-place and intercept their passage. A row was sure to ensue. We had no intention of inflicting serious bodily harm; all we wanted to do was to give them a bit of a surprise and a certain amount of physical pain by way of well-deserved chastisement for their sins. Accordingly we agreed among ourselves not to strike at any vital spot, but to confine our attentions to dislocating temporarily the lower jaws of the bellicose gamblers. We have a simple method of accomplishing this by sharply striking the point with the open palm. Whenever words resulted in blows we would promptly settle the encounter by administering the necessary fillip which rarely failed to place our antagonists *hors de combat*. It used to afford us jujutsu pupils immense amusement to watch our victims as, with their lower jaws out of joint, they would vainly try to cry out, the only audible outcome being a sort of muffled groan as with both hands supporting their damaged jaws they made off at full speed. Sometimes a pupil failed to finish his opponent with one stroke and had to repeat the process, in which case he was regarded as not yet fully proficient in his art. Bone-setting is taught by jujutsu masters as an essential part of the art, and so it happened that the injured gamblers would go to the dojo in the morning to have their jaws reset. Often enough as many as half a dozen victims would require the services of our teacher in a single day after a fracas of the kind I have described, and we would thus have the pleasure of examining at close quarters the effect of our skill, which added to the zest of these nocturnal adventures. We were all high-spirited and mischievous young bloods in those days, and I make no excuse for our delight in these malicious tricks. Times have changed and today practices of this kind, however laudable their motive, must be discouraged. I tell you the story as a voluntary confession of my boyhood.

"Apart from this deliberate seeking of opportunities to make use of judo, I have more than once had occasion to apply the art for offensive and defensive purposes, but I do not care to enter into details since these encounters are mostly connected with the election troubles which occurred during the early days of the constitutional administration, when the political campaign was frequently characterized by displays of brute force between the supporters of the rival candidates. Instead of dwelling upon these unpleasant incidents I will recall a few cases of a less serious nature in which I have had recourse to my art. I remember during the early part of January 1909 I went to a certain restaurant accompanied by Mr. Mifune, a fifth-grade teacher of the Kodokan. (Mr. Kyuzo Mifune is now a veteran turned seventy, a 10th Dan and Chief Instructor of the new Kodokan: Author's Note.) We noticed in one corner of the room a group of thirteen young fellows drinking *sake*, while in an adjoining apartment there were an elderly couple and some other visitors taking food. The members of the first-named group were seen to be putting their heads together at frequent intervals and to be busily whispering, at the same time casting glances in our direction. I did not take any notice of what was going on, nor did I suspect that they had any designs upon us. Mr. Mifune and I went on chatting over our drinks. Presently one of the rascals approached us, calmly picked up my overcoat and hat, and tried to make off with them under our very noses. Of course I remonstrated, when the thief, evidently bent on picking a quarrel, insisted that the coat and hat were his property. A warm altercation arose in the midst of which he assumed a threatening attitude and was speedily joined by half a dozen of his comrades from the other side of the room. There being no alternative Mr. Mifune took a hand in the game. He avoided unnecessary roughness but in less than a minute he had them all down with a succession of swift blows. Then the rest of the gang set upon me but I knocked them down one after the other and the affair was over in less than three minutes. As our victims regained consciousness they lost no time in making themselves scarce. But we detained one of them and forced him to confess. He admitted that their object had been to extort money from us by intimidation. They had been misled by our good clothes and had imagined that we would be easy prey. We let the fellow go instead of handing him over to the police, as we considered that he had received punishment enough at our hands. After the rascals had gone the old couple who had been interested spectators of the occurrence told us that they had just witnessed for the first time in their lives a practical display of jujutsu and were amazed at the wonderful feats which experts were able to perform against such odds.

"It was during the same month that I was called upon to render a friend of mine a trifling service. He had undertaken to finance a theatrical performance and, fortune having smiled upon him, he had netted a few thousand yen profit. One day about the middle of the month he was entertaining a friend at dinner when about half a dozen sōshi (a type of swashbuckler or bravo often reinforced from the ranks of ex-students who have gone under) called on him and demanded an interview. As they were perfect strangers to him naturally my friend refused to meet them, more particularly seeing that he had a guest. But the sōshi would not be denied and forced their way into the room where my friend and his guest were seated enjoying themselves. My friend asked them what they wanted, and they calmly stated that they wished to borrow some money. On his refusal to consider so preposterous a request and a peremptory order that they should leave the house the ruffians produced swords and daggers which they had concealed among their clothing and curtly informed my friend, who sat spellbound, that they would wait until they received a more satisfactory answer, and meanwhile proceeded to help themselves to whatever they fancied among the delicacies on the table, including copious libations of *sake*. Thus my friend and his guest were virtually prisoners. Fortunately a man-servant was able to slip out by a back door and to tell me of what had happened and I lost no time in hastening to the rescue. On arriving at the house I found the *sōshi* threatening my friend with drawn swords in their attempt to extort money. I recognized the leader of the gang, and advised him to decamp with his comrades if he cared to keep a whole skin. He too knew me, and at once changed his tone, apologizing profusely for having given my friend so much trouble. The other *sōshi*, who did not know me, appeared inclined to have recourse to violence, but their leader assured them that if they raised a hand against me they would never cease to regret it and he told them who I was. They then laid down their weapons which I collected and laid aside. I again advised them to quit the house and instructed them to call on me the next day when I would advance them some money to meet their immediate needs. The *sōshi* were escorted from the premises and my friend thanked me profusely for the little service I had been able to render him. Of course the *sōshi* did not call on me the following day, as I had anticipated; but later on one of their number joined the Kodokan, turned over a new leaf, and is now a very promising pupil."

Mr. Yokoyama then recounted a very interesting incident of which he was an eye witness, and in which the principals were a sturdy young jinrikisha-man and an old man.

"It was some seven years ago," said Mr. Yokoyama, "that I chanced to be taking a stroll along Dangozaka to see the chrysanthemum display, and on the way an old man, seemingly about seventy years of age, accompanied by a boy of eleven or so, both riding in a 'rikisha', passed me. Reaching the foot of the hill they alighted, and the old man tendered the puller his fare. The coolie, however, was dissatisfied and demanded more. The old man resented the puller's impudent manner and tried to proceed without taking any further notice of the request. The coolie followed and repeated his demand with the addition of a threat. I watched them from a short distance and was on the alert to interfere should the 'rikishaman attempt to carry out his threat. The old man told the boy to go on ahead, and then faced the coolie and ordered him to discontinue his importunities, whereupon the coolie seized the old man by the throat. I quickened my pace thinking the moment had arrived when my help would be required, but before I could reach the spot I saw the old man quickly grip the hands laid on him, and without any apparent effort bring his assailant to the ground on his back, where he lay pinned helplessly shrieking with pain and praying for forgiveness. A crowd speedily gathered and vastly enjoyed the bully's unexpected discomfiture. Finally the old man let him go. It was a fine sight to see him limping off with the shafts of his vehicle tied to his belt, both hands having been crippled for the time being by the powerful and skilful hold of the veteran who in this encounter had shown really wonderful knowledge of the art of jujutsu which he must have acquired in his younger days.

"I can carry my memory back to the days when all *samurai* wore the two swords and used them as well when necessity arose. When quite a boy I accidentally witnessed an exciting duel to the death between a *rōnin* (an unattached *samurai*) and three *samurai*. The struggle took place in the Kojimachi ward in the neighbourhood of Kudan where the Shokonsha now stands. Before proceeding with my narrative I ought to explain for the benefit of my foreign listeners (there were two of us present besides another Japanese gentleman) the usage of the old feudal days in order that the incident I am about to describe may be better understood. The sword of the *samurai*, as you know, was a possession valued higher than life itself, and if you touched a *samurai's* sword you touched his dignity. It was deemed an act of unpardonable rudeness in those days for one *samurai* to allow the tip of his scabbard to come into contact with the scabbard of another *samurai* as the men passed each other in the street; such an act was styled *saya-ate* (*saya*=scabbard, *ate*=to strike against), and in the absence of a prompt apology from the offender a fight almost always ensued. The *samurai* carried two swords, the long and the short, which were thrust into the *obi*, or sash, on the left-hand side in such a manner that the sheath of the longer weapon stuck out behind the owner's back. This being the case it frequently happened, especially in a crowd, that two scabbards would touch each other without deliberate intent on either side, although *samurai* who were not looking for trouble of this kind always took the precaution to hold the swords with the point downwards and as close to their sides as possible. But should a contretemps of this description occur the parties could on no account allow it to pass unnoticed. One or both would at once demand satisfaction, and the challenge was rarely refused. The high sense of honour which prevailed among men of this class forbade them to shrink from the consequences of such an encounter. So much by way of introduction. The episode I am going to describe arose in precisely this fashion. The parties to the duel were a *rōnin* and three *samurai*, as I have already said. The *rōnin* was rather shabbily dressed and was evidently very poor. The sheath of his long sword was covered with cracks where the lacquer had worn away through long use. He was a man of middle age. The three *samurai* were all stalwart men and appeared to be under the influence of *sake*. They were the challengers. At first the *rōnin* apologized, but the *samurai* insisted on a duel and the *rōnin* eventually accepted the challenge.

"By this time a large crowd had gathered, among which were many *samurai* none of whom, however, ventured to interfere. In accordance with custom, the combatants exchanged names and swords were unsheathed, the three *samurai* on one side facing the solitary opponent with whom the sympathies of the onlookers evidently lay. The keen blades of the duellists glittered in the sun. The *rōnin*, as calm as though engaged merely in a friendly fencing bout, advanced steadily with the point of his weapon directed against the *samurai* in the centre of the trio, and apparently indifferent to an attack on either flank. The *samurai* in the middle gave ground inch by inch and the *rōnin* as surely stepped forward. Then the right-hand *samurai*, who thought he saw an opening, rushed to the attack, but the *rōnin*, who had clearly anticipated this move, parried and with lightning rapidity cut his enemy down with a mortal blow. The left-hand *samurai* came on in his turn but was treated in similar fashion, a single stroke felling him to the ground bathed in blood. All this took almost less time than it takes to tell. The *samurai* in the centre, seeing the fate of his comrades, thought better of his first intention and took to his heels. The victorious *rōnin* wiped his blood-stained sword in the coolest manner imaginable and returned it to its sheath. His feat was loudly applauded by the other *samurai* who had witnessed it. The *rōnin* then repaired to the neighbouring magistrate's office to report the occurrence, as the law required."

Mr. Yokoyama observed in conclusion that in feudal days, for obvious reasons, the art of fencing was more sedulously studied than that of jujutsu. Many skilful masters made their appearance from time to time, and endless stories are told of their wonderful prowess. The most famous fencers during the early days of Meiji were undoubtedly Messrs. Yamaoka Tetsutaro, Henmi Sosuko and Ueda Umanosuke. Among the then living celebrities may be mentioned Messrs. Takayama Minesaburo, Takuno Junshiro, Okumura Sakonda, Takano Sataro, Naito Takagi, Uchiyama and Takahashi.

CHAPTER VII

KARATE AND AIKIDO

I MUST confess that during my long residence in Japan and my membership of the Kodokan I never heard of either of these fighting arts. And yet their history probably antedates that of jujutsu, not to say judo, which latter is by comparison with both of them quite modern in its origin. From all the evidence which has within recent years percolated to the West, it seems clear that these two arts were in their physical attributes essentially combative and had little in common with what we should regard as sport, in which respect they must be sharply differentiated from judo, although their present-day exponents are at special pains to emphasize their ethical basis.

Seeing that as yet considerably more is known to the West about karate than about aikido, I shall give it precedence in what I fear will prove to be but a superficial description of its principal characteristics.

First then as to the name itself: *"Kara"* means empty and *"te"* means hand, i.e. to combat with empty hands, without lethal weapons. In this respect then karate resembles both jujutsu and judo. But as a purely "fighting art", designed to dispose of an enemy in the shortest possible time with no means barred, I think we must admit that it transcends them both in its deadly efficacy. And why this should be so will appear from the fact that a single karate technique, if executed in earnest, is capable of inflicting fatal injury upon its victim more surely and speedily than either jujutsu or judo. The reason for this is that by dint of long and constant practice and training the Karateka has so hardened his hands and fingers that he can with them split several planks and break a dozen tiles without any trouble. With the force of his blow he can plunge his fingers into the thoracic cage or the throat, hook or smash a rib and the larynx or with his fist break stones or even the back of a horse! Nor is that all. The expert karateka is virtually an acrobat and can with equal facility use his elbows, knees and feet to disable his opponent by terrific blows against vital spots in his body. To elaborate: In a recent article contributed to the *Kodokan Review* by one Funakoshi, a recognized exponent of the art, it is explained that from the head to the finger-tips there are a surprising number of parts of the body which can be employed in the techniques of the karate. For example, from the wrists to the finger-tips alone there are more than ten parts which are utilized to strike. The elbows, wrists, knees, feet (six points) are also much used. It may without lying be said that the human body is covered with natural weapons. It is unnecessary to say that in order to employ them effectively one must train assiduously. Thus the first of the things to study is how to clench the fist, to hold oneself in a natural posture of defence and attack, how to strike and to parry, etc. In some cases the little finger edge of a karateka's hand is hardened and calloused to such a degree as a form of protrusion of almost razor-like sharpness one blow with which, if applied to the victim's carotid artery or jugular vein, would suffice to kill him. It is reliably reported that some time ago a 4th Dan member of the Kodokan had the temerity to pit himself against a karate expert in a *shiai*, or contest, and that in less than two minutes the judoka was carried off the mat with several ribs broken and other minor injuries.

From these sensational facts we can infer what would be the fate of any Western pugilist opposed to a karate expert in the unlikely event of the legalization of conditions permitting the boxer to use his bare fists and the karate expert not only his bare fists but every other part of his body and extremities included in the karate natural armoury. The odds are that even before the gong had sounded for the end of the first round, the "subsequent proceedings would interest him no more", and that to his residuary legatees would belong the sad office of beseeching all listeners in polyphonic chorus couched in a minor key to "dry the starting tear for he was heavily insured". Or in more scientific jargon, we should be witnesses of a sort of catalytic process whereby a change in the composition of one body is effected by the contiguity of another body which does not itself undergo any.

What is the origin of karate? Who was its first creator? How was its technique perfected in the course of the centuries? To answer that question we can rely only upon tradition. Karate appears to have existed in China a thousand years ago in the period of Gen, Min and Shin, and before its appearance on the Japanese island of Okinawa, where it had its Japanese beginnings. Karate was also called Tode, To being the name of a Chinese emperor. It is true that at that epoch Japan was greatly influenced by China. However this may be, it was on the island of Okinawa that for the first time the technique of unarmed combat made its appearance. One of the reasons for the development of karate on the island was the establishment of the Kimmu government (meaning "without arms").

It is recorded that Napoleon was one day very much astonished to learn that there existed in the Far East a small independent kingdom where arms had for a long time been prohibited. This report had to do with the country of the karate, Okinawa, which was formerly called Ryukyu. Founded 500 years ago and grouping three mountains, it was styled "the Union of the Three Mountains", but it was the king of the mountains of the middle (Shopashi) who succeeded in taking in hand the three regions of the island and who prohibited the wearing of all weapons. The peace lasted 300 years until the day when, in the fourteenth year of Keisho, the terrible and powerful Clan Tozuka overwhelmed the island after having been for a moment repulsed. The new government completely disarmed the inhabitants and prohibited even the possession of arms at home. Methods of combat without weapons were then elaborated and developed to the maximum and "Chinese boxing" was methodically studied and perfected. The names given to describe these methods varied, the principal ones being okinawa-te, tode and karate. The use of atemi, or methods of attacking vital spots in the body, surpassed other methods of combat with the naked hand because the assailant could utilize the different parts of his own body, the fist, elbows, knees, feet, etc. as side-arms in combat at mid-distance. In feudal days every combat method was held secret and this tendency on the island of Okinawa was strengthened by the fact that it was hidden from the Tozuka regime. But notwithstanding all these considerations, the facts cited above do not entirely explain why nothing in writing remains in the form of archives, nor why everything associated with the art has been kept so rigorously secret until almost our own days. There is some old literature on

KUNIMIYA AND UMEGATANI ABOUT TO CLOSE

Umpire in the background

PORTRAIT OF THE AUTHOR
Showing pectoral abdominal development due to Judo practice

jujutsu but there is none on karate. And however numerous were the traditions concerning this art those who knew it never divulged their knowledge; they bequeathed it orally to their descendants as a precious heritage. This custom of keeping secret the teaching of karate lasted a long time, and even after it had been made public many of the old masters continued jealously to guard their special techniques.

Mr. Funakoshi relates that a short time after he had openly taught karate, Mr. Ogawa, then Minister of Education, assisted at a ceremony of the art. After further inquiry he recognized its educational value and had it incorporated into the course of physical education of the training colleges and prefectural lycées. Thanks to this event the century-old custom of keeping this art secret was abandoned and a new era dawned for karate. In 1923 Mr. Funakoshi was invited by the Central Secretariat of Physical Education of Okinawa to go to Tokyo where karate was completely unknown, to give a demonstration at the National Athletics Championships. Its success was resounding and after the demonstration none other than Dr. Kano informed him through the intermediary of a common friend that he wished to study the art. This was not then possible because Mr. Funakoshi had to return to Okinawa immediately after the Championships. But Dr. Kano having insisted, Mr. Funakoshi agreed to give a demonstration at the Kodokan. In due course he demonstrated the karate kata (Forms) several times before about a hundred of Dr. Kano's pupils and explained the basic principles of the art. There then followed a perfect deluge of detailed and technical questions and Mr. Funakoshi was amazed by the deference and interest shown by the questioners.

During the heroic epoch of judo, karate had been regarded as in the nature of an obstacle to its progress, and there had remained in the minds of the students of both arts a little contempt for the other. Today the situation seems to have changed and among objective and clear-headed judoka a wholesome respect for karate as a fighting art *par excellence* has been engendered. Indeed without decrying the merits of judo as a high-class sport and even as a fighting art, one may question whether in the latter respect its methods, even were atemi included, would prove to be so effective as those of karate for the reasons already adduced. And apart from atemi, it must be recognized that a very big proportion of the

prolific judo techniques can with safety to the assailant be practised only on the mats of the dojo and may therefore be classified
as purely conventional. On the other hand, if attempted on hard
ground against a tough customer of the Rocky Marciano "killer"
type, perhaps possessing a respectable knowledge of wrestling,
they might turn out to be decidedly risky to him. Did space
permit cases in point could easily be cited, but for the necessarily
restricted purposes of this superficial study I must leave that task
to intelligent judoka among my readers. However, it may be noted
that one great advantage which the karateka enjoys over the
judoka in a genuine life and death struggle is that he does not need
to close with his opponent in order to overpower him and that
being virtually an acrobat he can freely employ hands, fingers,
fists, elbows, knees and feet to rain his lethal blows from every
conceivable angle and altitude upon his victim, and that in most
cases a single terrific blow on the mark would suffice to render his
victim's insurance policy negotiable.

From what has been said it should be evident that as a sport
and therefore for the purpose of public exhibition, karate is not
qualified or at all likely to challenge judo in its popular appeal.
Obviously only experts can safely demonstrate karate in public
since every blow in its repertoire must be halted by the assailant
a fraction of an inch before landing on the chosen spot in the victim's body. Moreover, only spectators possessing some prior
knowledge of the art would be interested in a demonstration of
this character. Judo does not labour under any such limitations,
and thanks to the spectacular nature of its methods a judo tournament will always attract a crowded house. On this account
there need be no serious rivalry between these two arts.

My knowledge of aikido is equally second-hand because I have
never yet had the good fortune to witness a demonstration of the
art. Nevertheless I am aware that like karate aikido is considered
almost solely as a fighting art, whereas nowadays the votaries of
Kodokan judo are prone to lay much more stress upon judo as a
high-class sport. In aikido there are no competitions. Grades are
conferred upon the recipient on the basis of knowledge of techniques, style and speed. These always correspond to real value in
actual combat and to very great efficacy. As in judo, however, the
grades reflect a communion more or less close between mind and

body and it is admitted that a prior knowledge of judo renders the study of aikido easier and progress therein more rapid.

The reader should be warned that the word aiki itself is not an antonym for the kiai nor even a synonym for it, although respiration plays an important part in its exercise as also does development of the *saika tanden* (lower abdomen). In this context *"ai"* means grouped, assembled, etc. and *"ki"* feeling, consciousness, etc. Thus aiki is not the force liberated by the occult kiai shout described elsewhere in these pages but is rather the accumulated force, unity of thought and action, the grip of consciousness. Whereas in judo the practical principles may be summed up as (1) disequilibrium; (2) construction of movement and (3) termination, in aikido they are (1) contact; (2) pain and (3) disequilibrium and, if necessary, throw.

It is recorded that more than 700 years ago there existed to the north of Mt. Fuji a school of *"Budo"*, the ancient martial arts. This school specialized in the teaching of so-called aikijutsu which was kept secret and disclosed to only a few disciples, for the most part nobles of ancient lineage. This art had originated from kenjutsu, or swordsmanship, and little by little it had become an arm of combat superior to jujutsu. When the late Dr. Kano created his new method, which he called judo, almost all the older jujutsu schools rallied to the Kodokan. But the schools of aikijutsu or aikido preserved their independence. Nevertheless Dr. Kano, who recognized the value of aikido in real fight, sent a special mission composed of certain pupils to study aikido, and these graduates are said to have taught this form of defence to the *yudansha* of the Kodokan.

It is quite on the cards that before these lines meet the eyes of my readers much more will have become known about aikido in this country through actual demonstrations of the art given by authorized Japanese experts.

By way of a footnote to the foregoing, I make no excuse for quoting an extract from an intensely interesting despatch contributed to the London *Daily Mail* of 15th March, 1955, by its brilliant New York correspondent Don Iddon, in the series entitled "The Great Deterrent", being the record of his impressions of his exclusive visit to the United States Strategic Air Command Headquarters, near Omaha, Nebraska, which afford incidental evidence of the growing importance which the United States armed forces attach to practical knowledge of Japanese unarmed lethal methods. Thus in his description of the type of men serving at SAC he writes:

> "They are very fit and have to undergo rigid physical and psychological tests. Every airman here knows the balancing and throwing techniques of judo, the *striking and kicking methods of karate*, the holding and take-down skills of wrestling, and the club and knifing intricacies of police fighting. They are, in fact, Commandos. General LeMay insisted upon an expert team of instructors and sent to Japan for jujutsu specialists."

One would fain hear an authoritative assurance that steps are being taken in this country to train our fighting men along similar lines in these really indispensable arts of offence and defence so as to be prepared against various contingencies in the sphere of treachery and Fifth Column espionage. Starry idealism to the contrary notwithstanding, let us take to heart the aphoristic reminder:

> "Thrice is he armed that hath his quarrel just,
> But four times he that gets his blow in fust."

And to the foregoing the following metric couplet ought usefully figure as a rider:

> "Life never revisits the foully slain
> When once they've been cut through the jugular vein."

CHAPTER VIII

POST-WAR EXPANSION OF JUDO

THE expansion of judo has become world wide, moreover, considering that judo is essentially a dynamic and not a static art this process has been attended by a continuous increase in its techniques and therefore in the terminology of the art under the skilled guidance of leading Japanese *yudansha*. I need not say that it is no part of the purpose of this book to enter into a technical description of these developments which would usurp the functions of a textbook. I shall therefore confine these supplementary comments to a somewhat cursory review of the more striking manifestations of this truly epic expansion.

The death of Dr. Jigoro Kano, the distinguished founder of the Kodokan and creator of judo, which took place on 4th May, 1938, on board the Japanese steamer *Hikawa-Maru* while on his way home from an International Olympic Committee meeting in Cairo, was a grave if not an irreparable loss to the art. This great man was born on 28th October, 1860, at Mikage, Hyogo Prefecture, so that at the time of his demise he was seventy-eight years of age, although according to the quaint system of Japanese chronology whereby a child is deemed to be a year old when born, he was seventy-nine! I personally, as one of his earliest foreign friends and disciples, shall ever lament his loss, cherish his memory and recall with gratitude the immense debt I owe him for his never-failing solicitude on my behalf and his sage counsel during my strenuous novitiate.

It is for me no less sad to have to record the premature decease of another great friend and teacher in the person of the redoubtable Sakujiro Yokoyama, a name to conjure with in the annals of judo, who died some years before I left Japan in 1917. Then as recently as 1953 the death occurred in the late seventies of another famous pioneer, personal friend and instructor, Shuichi Nagaoka 10th Dan, who when first I met him was Professor of Judo at the palatial Butokukai in Kyoto. Many years before the last war and at the

81

age of about sixty but looking far younger, Nagaoka visited this country and with his invincible *waza* staggered all beholders. On the other hand it is consoling to note that another old friend and early instructor of mine whose name has already been mentioned in these pages, Kyuzo Mifune, today 10th Dan and Chief Instructor of the Kodokan, is still very much alive and astoundingly active on the mat despite his three score years and ten. I was privileged to dedicate to him my *Manual of Judo* and to receive from him a special message and his photograph both of which are reproduced in the Manual. The recent publication of his classic work entitled *Judo Kyoten: Michi to Jutsu* (*The Canon of Judo: The Way and the Art*) has been hailed with acclamation by judoka the world over. It bids fair for some time to remain the last word on the art.

Reverting to the main theme: Whereas in my day, as stated elsewhere, the pupils of the then Kodokan totalled about 13,000 including not more than 1,200 black belts, today Dan holders alone in Japan number more than 200,000. The new Kodokan, officially styled the Kodokan Judo Institute situated at 1–1 Kasugacho, Bunkyo-ku, Koishikawa, Toyko, was completed in December 1933 and apart from very superficial damage almost miraculously escaped unscathed the tremendous Allied blitz which laid waste about 60 per cent of the Japanese capital. The new Kodokan is a three-storeyed concrete structure covering an area of 1,376,25 tsubo (1 tsubo equals 6 feet by 6 feet). The ventilation and lighting system are ideal and the building is equipped with various modern conveniences which greatly facilitate the practice of judo and are a far cry from the comparatively primitive amenities provided for us at the old Kodokan. In those days we were content, both winter and summer, after working up a healthy perspiration on the mats, to pour icy cold water over our bodies from a well in the yard outside. The area for practice at the new Kodokan is 500 mats as compared with half that number at the old Kodokan.

In my day the number of foreigners studying at the old Kodokan might have been counted on the fingers of one hand; today they must run into four figures. Understandably most of these pupils have been drawn from the ranks of the Allied forces of occupation, and as might have been expected the majority

have been G.I's. But a growing number of foreign women, mostly
American, have since the war been awarded lower Dan grades at the
new Kodokan. And this fact prompts me to mention that in my
day I never saw a woman judoka at the old Kodokan, although it
was recently recorded in the present-day Kodokan monthly
bulletin that a certain Mrs. Kinko Yasuda 7th Dan, now eighty-
three years of age, began to take jujutsu lessons at a local dojo
and later studied under Dr. Kano, but I never had the good
fortune to meet this remarkable woman pioneer in the flesh. I
recall, however, that at the Yokohama dojo of the Tenjin Shinyo-
ryu school of jujutsu where I made my youthful debut, as recorded
elsewhere in these pages, there was just one girl pupil. Today things
are very different. The elementary judo movements are taught as
group exercises in the schools to both male and female pupils, and
at the Kodokan itself women *montei*, or disciples, attend as a
matter of course but practise separately in the vast 500-mat dojo
and are never pitted against male judoka in actual contest,
it being recognized that, with very rare exceptions, and grade for
grade, women are no match for men on the judo mat.

The Japanese Judo Federation, which today groups together
all the Associations of Black Belts in Japan, was founded after
the war in 1949 in accordance with the wishes of the American
army of occupation to recreate all the organizations in a democratic
form. Following the surrender of Japan and the assumption of
virtually autocratic powers by General MacArthur, a ban was
imposed upon the practice of judo. Later this shortsighted measure
was relaxed but judo teaching was restricted to the Kodokan
whose premises, as already stated, had amazingly escaped the
almost wholesale devastation inflicted on the capital by Allied air
attack. The seat of the Japanese Judo Federation is at the Kodokan whose President, Mr. Risei Kano, only son of the late Dr.
Jigoro Kano, is also President of the Federation. Although today
in Japan there are no separate judo schools as such, the Associations of Black Belts have their own dojo, as also have the
universities and the police. Certain instructors or Shihan also
have their own private dojo but all of them teach the judo of the
Kodokan. In this context mention should be made of the splendid
400-mat dojo of the Tokyo Metropolitan Police known as the
Keishicho Taiikukan, where the daily attendance of *yudansha*

is often larger than at the Kodokan itself and where on exceptionally high standard of technique prevails.

Two important innovations since my day are the annual All-
Japan Judo Championships and the East versus West annual
competitions. The former are staged in May and the latter in
October. The scene of the All-Japan Championship tournament
is the spacious Kokugikan Sports Palace of Tokyo and the occasion
never fails to attract an enormous crowd of both sexes and all
ages. Yet another exemplification of the truth of the hoary Latin
tag *"Omnia mutantur, nos et mutamur in illis"* is that admission
to the tournament is by tickets the prices of which vary widely in
much the same way as in the West. Thus the 15,000 seats of
the Kokugikan are retained in advance and the phenomenon to
which we Westerners have long been inured of speculators offering
seats at three or more times the official price has become a commonplace on these occasions. Could the dignified judo pioneers of
my day have had an apocalyptic vision of this remorseless and
corrosive process of commercialism in the sphere of their beloved
art they would probably have run the risk of an apoplectic seizure.
More ominous still: Aping the practice of wrestling "fans", when
the final contest is over admirers of the successful judo contestant
evince their enthusiasm by showering a rain of cushions towards
the ring. How far the presence of thousands of foreign troops
on the erstwhile sacred soil of Dai Nippon should be held
responsible for what those early pioneers would undoubtedly
have condemned as vulgarization it is not for me to say beyond
commenting that my own personal experience of overseas military
service in the war of 1914–19 convinced me that the impact of
these alien elements upon the civilian population of the occupied
country can never be conducive to the inception of a new
"Kulturkampf". The East-West competitions share with the All-
Japan Championships the suffrages of the crowd. Kyoto is the
centre of the West and Tokyo of the East.

I do not feel qualified to hazard an opinion on how the
Japanese judo stalwarts of today would compare with the legend-
ary figures of the Meiji era, not all of whom were known to me, e.g.
the truly fabulous Saigo who had never been thrown although he
was a lightweight. Nor do I think such speculations come within
my "terms of reference". Nevertheless, judging from the spectacu-

lar achievements of several recent Japanese champions when opposed to the best the West could pit against them, I feel fairly certain that the record since my day has been one of steady progress all along the line concurrently with the elaboration of fresh methods and the improvement of old ones to which I have called attention elsewhere. It is no part of my task to inflict upon my readers a wearisome catalogue of names in this connexion, and to do so might even appear invidious. Those more particularly interested, for the most part doubtless members of the younger generation actually practising the art, can always obtain detailed information under this head from the pages of the periodical bulletins issued by nearly all the leading judo organizations in this country, elsewhere in Europe and America. However, when I say that touring Japanese high-ranking Kodokan judoka regularly throw in unbroken succession a minimum of ten of the best Western Black Belts pitted against them in as short a time as three minutes and under and have been known in one instance to throw, one after the other, as many as forty and in another twenty opponents, some idea will be forthcoming of the wide margin still existing between Japanese and Western standards. The aptness of the sporting adage that "a good big 'un will always, other things equal, beat a good little 'un" is also corroborated by the fact that nearly all Japan's latter-day champions have been heavyweights. This trend has not unnaturally given rise to a movement in favour of the introduction of weight categories in championship contests, and although the movement has not so far been encouraged by the Kodokan and would seem to be alien to the original spirit in which the art was conceived by its great founder, the late Dr. Jigoro Kano, it is certainly gaining ground outside Japan, and has already been adopted in the United States and elsewhere.

Turning our gaze to the West: One of the most striking developments of judo since the foundation of the Kodokan more than seventy years ago was the formation in 1951 of the International Judo Federation of which Mr. Risei Kano, Dr. Kano's only son, is the first President. The International Judo Federation has superseded the earlier European Judo Union and to it most judo schools in Europe are affiliated. In this country the British Judo Association was founded in 1948 as a central body for the purpose, *inter alia*, of regulating the status of judoka practising in Great Britain so as to verify their right to their ostensible grades and to wear the variously coloured belts allotted to those grades. In this way it is hoped to obviate the danger of bogus claims being established to grades to which unknown claimants are not entitled. The goal set by the British Judo Association is to extend its membership so as to include all judo clubs functioning in this country. In pursuance of its aims it has instituted a Register of Black Belts (*yudansha*) to whom corresponding certificates are issued.

The acknowledged central judo organization in Great Britain is the Budokwai founded in 1918 by Gunji Koizumi 7th Dan, to whose pioneer vision and unflagging energy judo largely owes its impressive spread and "naturalization" outside Japan. The Budokwai's new headquarters in Gilston Road, South Kensington, with a 100-mat dojo, are probably the finest and most spacious in Europe.

The war with Japan inevitably retarded the progress of judo in the West because it put a temporary stop to the entry of Japanese instructors into the belligerent countries. In this respect Great Britain was the chief European sufferer. France and other continental lands which had not declared war against Japan were more favourably situated, while in the case of the United States, although she had fought against Japan and had indeed played the leading rôle in defeating her, the presence on the Pacific Coast and elsewhere of many Japanese–American citizens, among whom were some skilled *yudansha*, greatly helped to prevent a catastrophic slump in the standard of proficiency. Moreover the re-admission of competent Japanese judo instructors into the United States ante-dated their re-admission into Great Britain, and it was only after the visit to this country in 1951 of a Kodokan delegation headed by its President, Mr. Risei Kano, that arrangements were effected for the engagement of a high-ranking Japanese *yudansha* to act as judo technical director of the Budokwai. It is therefore to be hoped that if this practice can be continued and extended to other leading judo clubs in this country, the standard of skill will steadily improve and contribute to the eventual restoration of our international teams to their pre-war eminence. But it will not be easy to overtake France's great headway in this sphere. Even in 1953 she had no fewer than 500 judo clubs with a membership of some 150,000, an astonishing score! To quote a great Austrian savant Dr. R. A. Baudisch whose friendship I am privileged to enjoy, it may well be that the French and generally the Romanic race, with their temperamentally conditioned capacity for reflex action, quick as lightning, possess exceptional qualifications for advancement in judo. And doubtless too, in the case of the Japanese, their ability to react almost instantaneously to external impact so that "not a hair's breadth" intervenes between action and reaction, as Zen puts it, may help to explain their undisputed supremacy in judo and other martial arts.

I cannot leave this subject without adding a short account of the spread of judo in the Antipodes, more particularly Australia. Somewhat egotistically perhaps I am tempted to do so because the undisputed pioneer of this movement is a distant connexion of my own in the imposing person of Dr. A. J. Ross of Brisbane, acknowledged to be Australia's leading exponent of the art and from all available evidence one of the world's best. Dr. Ross went to Japan with his parents when only nine years old, and began to take an interest in judo at the age of fourteen. I myself was privileged to give him a little coaching in those early days. He gained the grade of shodan at the Kodokan while still in his late teens. Subsequently he emigrated to Australia where he entered the medical profession and although in due course he established one of the biggest practices in Brisbane he still found time to participate actively in both judo practice and contest wherein he holds an unbeaten record until recent ill health necessitated retirement from the mat at the age of sixty. His unquestioned technical skill has been helped by an exceptionally powerful physique. The "Doc", as he is affectionately dubbed by his numerous pupils and admirers, stands nearly six feet tall and in his prime scaled fifteen stone. He has been Hon. Chief Instructor to the Brisbane Judo Club since he founded it in 1928, and Hon. Chief Examiner in theory and practice for the Australian Council of Judo since its inaugural meeting also in 1928. It may well be doubted whether any modern non-Japanese judoka has won his spurs in such a hard way as Dr. Ross. Many years ago he toured the country with a theatrical firm and took on all comers. His open challenge specified that whereas he would use only judo throws and holds his opponents would be free to resort to any method, even biting, scratching, gouging and kicking, and he never lost a match on those terms. And ever since he has maintained his offer to accept any challenger, irrespective of size, age, ability or profession, with the same result. During the last war, with the rank of Captain, he was adviser to the Commonwealth Government on unarmed combat and in the training camps of Queensland gave demonstrations to thousands of soldiers. He holds the grade of 3rd Dan confirmed by the Kodokan. Dr. Ross is the author of a very useful manual on judo which has been adopted as the official textbook of the Australian Council of Judo. Thus the name of Dr. Ross is indissolubly linked with the inception and development of judo in Australia.

CHAPTER IX

FENCING, WRESTLING AND SWORD-DANCING

FENCING, wrestling and sword-dancing are branches of physical culture in Japan which assume such a distinctive guise as to deserve a special chapter to themselves, even if it be only a short one.

The Japanese term their form of fencing *kenjutsu* or *kendo*, literally "sword-art" or "sword-way", and as practised in Japan it appears to be a genuine national growth. The weapon used in practice is a stick called a *shinae*, made of three strips of bamboo bound tightly together, with a small round gourd and a hilt large enough to accommodate both hands. Its length is usually four feet. The Japanese style of fencing is two-handed, and although at the present day the police and military are armed with a light, single-handed weapon, not unlike the European sabre, the old *escrime* continues to be taught to the police in preference to our Occidental methods. It was also a matter of common knowledge that during the Russo–Japanese war of 1904–5 many Japanese officers substituted for the original blades of their service swords the far keener and more trenchant blades taken from ancestral weapons in their families' possession perhaps for several generations. It was doubtless felt that this exchange was more in consonance with what is known as "*Yamato-damashii*", or the ancient Japanese spirit, and would therefore infuse additional strength into the swordsman's every blow designed to reduce the stature of some Muscovite foeman by a head!

The principal native schools are the Shinkage, Shinto, Yagiu, Ono-ha-itto and Nito-ryu, the last-named being practised with two swords, one for each hand, as invented by the famous Miyamoto Musashi during the seventeenth century. In practice the performers are protected by masks and breastplates of strong lacquer, and by gauntlets. In practice striking at the legs is forbidden, and the decisive points are the head, both sides, the right arm and throat, the latter being virtually the only thrust permitted.

A good *kenjutsu* bout is quite exciting. It is interesting to watch the combatants as they move with cat-like agility this way and that, with occasional fierce rushes and noisy impact of the sticks, both men giving vent to hideous yells at frequent intervals, especially when a hit is claimed. The umpire often sits in a chair nowadays and gives his decisions with a placidity which nothing can disturb. When the issue is doubtful he usually says laconically, *"Mo ippon"* ("One more bout") and the champions sail in afresh. A peculiar feature of the Japanese method is that either combatant is at liberty to cast aside his weapon and try to close with the other. If he succeeds in throwing his adversary and disarming him, he is declared the winner.

Japanese fencers are undoubtedly skilful, but *kenjutsu* never appealed to me in the same way as judo, and it appears to lack the subtlety of the French and Italian rapier play, although I preserve an open mind on this point and am ready to be convinced to the contrary. In actual fighting one good cut with the "sword of old Japan" would certainly settle the contest, and the heavier weapon might conceivably bear down the lighter, while for the rest the value of *kenjutsu* as an exercise is unquestionable. Japanese who are addicted to the art can, as a rule, be identified by the abnormal development of their forearms. Perhaps the only foreigner who ever took up *kenjutsu* seriously was the late F. J. Norman, formerly of the Indian Army, a cavalry officer and expert in both rapier and sabre play. Norman was for some years engaged as a teacher at the Etajima Naval College and while there devoted his attention to the Japanese style to such good purpose that he speedily won an enviable reputation among the Japanese, and engaged in many a hard-fought encounter. Some few other foreigners have practised and doubtless do practise *kenjutsu* for the sake of exercise, but I am not aware that any one of them has won distinction in Japanese eyes. Japanese women rarely practise *kenjutsu*; the equivalent in their case is commonly the use of the *naginata,* a species of lance or halberd which was greatly in vogue among their sex in feudal days.

The *sumotori,* or fat wrestlers of Japan, are so well known and have been so often described that I shall make my reference to them very brief. To foreigners their exaggerated obesity would appear to be the very last qualification in the world for athletic exercises. They vary greatly in size, the smallest being not more than 5 ft. 4 in. in height or thereabouts, and the biggest considerably over 6 ft. and weighing as much as 300 lb and over. Fat as these men are it would be a mistake to conclude that they are therefore incapable of exerting tremendous strength. True, their wind is as a rule comparatively poor, but then the bouts are nearly always brief and, of course, all the competitors are at the same disadvantage. But they are actually very powerful fellows, and their fat has been hardened by continual beating and butting at wooden posts until it becomes almost a weapon of offence in itself. An ordinary man would go down like a ninepin beneath a swinging blow from the huge stomach of a Japanese wrestler. A little incident which really occurred during my stay in Japan, in the garden of a Japanese hotel at Miyanoshita, the celebrated Japanese mountain health resort, will help to substantiate these statements. The famous Taiho (literally "big gun" or "cannon"), the contemporary champion, a mountain of beef, though burdened with less abdominal hamper than many of his rivals, and something like 6 ft. 6 in. tall, was stopping for a few days at this hotel when he chanced to meet a foreign friend of mine who spoke the Japanese colloquial quite fluently. In the course of conversation Taiho asked my friend whether he knew of anybody in the hotel who would kick him in the stomach. The requirement was a novel one and my friend was taken by surprise, but just at that moment a young American tourist wearing a pair of toothpick shoes, then the fashion, drew near the couple and when Taiho's petition had been made known to him, undertook with significant alacrity to kick him as often as and wherever he pleased. As soon as this understanding had been arrived at Taiho assumed a posture with his legs slightly bent and his hands resting lightly on his knees. The young American drew back for a convenient "take-off" and at a given signal bounded forward like a chamois, and at the psychological moment planted his right trilby fairly and squarely in the centre of the wrestler's stomach. The result hardly coincided with his expectations. A footballer of some pretensions, he had confidently looked to see his victim collapse in agony upon the greensward. What actually happened was that

Taiho gave his ponderous abdomen a heave forward and the young American a second later found himself flying through space and landed flat upon his back several yards away. I have not heard that he has ever again tried to oblige a Japanese wrestler by kicking him in the stomach.

As a further illustration of Taiho's colossal strength I may mention that on another occasion with one hand grasping the waist of another foreign friend of mine who weighed a good 180 lb, he lifted him clean off the ground and held him thus suspended for a few seconds. I rather doubt whether even Sandow in his heyday could have duplicated this feat.

The limbs of these men, too, are extraordinarily supple, as even a tyro may convince himself by watching the manner in which each competitor before the bout will raise his massive legs alternately until the knees are almost level with his chin, these stereotyped motions being regarded as a survival of the steps which the 800 myriad members of the Japanese Pantheon are said to have practised before the cave of the Sun-Goddess Amaterasu in order to entice her out and so restore light to a world which had been plunged into darkness by her retirement. I have also seen some of these men do what we in England and America call the "split" and that "without unwholesome strain".

Lord Redesdale, in his *Tales of Old Japan*, explains that the wrestling arena is supposed to be formed of "sixteen rice-bales" in the shape of one huge bale, supported by four pillars at the four points of the compass, each pillar being painted a different colour, thus, together with certain paper pendants, making up five colours, to symbolize the "Five Grains"—the name of the autumn festival. The repertoire of the art comprises forty-eight fair falls, to wit, twelve throws, twelve twists, twelve lifts, and twelve throws over the back. If but as little as a foot of one of the contestants projects beyond the boundary of the ring, its owner loses the bout. It will therefore be realized how important a factor avoirdupois must be, other things equal, in a struggle of this description.

The umpire at these contests is an important functionary who must be thoroughly versed in all the mysteries of the art. At one time he wore a sword with which to commit *harakiri* should he be so unfortunate as to render an erroneous decision. Today the etiquette of the position is less exacting.

The wrestlers may be said to constitute a class apart, their unusual stature and their retention of the old-fashioned cue head-dress making them conspicuous objects in a crowd of their far more diminutive countrymen and women. They wrestle naked save for a *fundoshi*, or tight-fitting loin-cloth. The periodical matches held in Tokyo and at other places attract thousands of spectators, the greatest contests of the year in my day being conducted in a ring within the enclosure of the Ekoin temple. At the close of each bout it is an extraordinary sight to see the air suddenly darkened by a shower of hats, coats, umbrellas, and other articles of clothing which are pitched into the arena by the excited backers of the winners, and are subsequently collected by the champion's pupils to be restored to their owners on the following day in return for pecuniary gifts which vary according to the generosity or means of the individual. During the wrestling season many Japanese patrons of the ring become completely demoralized; they virtually cease to attend to business, and spend their days in watching the matches and betting on the results. Popular wrestlers, too, are often in great demand among geisha and other professional women who are not ashamed to purchase their favours at a ruinous figure. For the most part these men are low, vulgar fellows, with the appetites and tastes of animals. The champion of my day, one Hitachiyama, was an exception to this rule. By birth he belonged to the *shizoku* class and had had the benefit of a middle-school education. His abnormal measurements and tremendous strength naturally diverted his mind to the profession, and he speedily forged to the front. Many years ago he visited the United States with his disciples and gave an exhibition before President Theodore Roosevelt; but he did not pit himself against any of the American or Western champions so that the question of superiority as between East and West still remains undecided and conjectural.

The wrestling guilds are continually on the look-out for new blood in the shape of exceptionally well-developed children to adopt and train up in the profession; and seeing that a good wrestler can earn far more than an ordinary man belonging to the same social grade, the parents of burly offspring are, as a rule, only too glad to hand them over to the guilds.

During the spring of 1902 an enterprising Japanese went to Yokohama and in the unsavoury purlieus of the region commonly and descriptively known as "Bloodtown" collected a number of so-called foreign wrestlers whom he engaged to tour the country and to compete against the Japanese *sumotori*. The company comprised Englishmen, Americans, a Chinaman, a Swede, and a negro. The Swede was the champion and a really big and powerful man though by no means a chicken. Some of the others, however, were distinctly weedy and thin in the underpinning, and the contrast between their pallid bodies and spindle shanks and the dark skins and massive limbs of the Japanese hardly kindled within my breast a spark of racial pride. I attended some of the matches at Shizuoka and had the pleasure of seeing the big Swede win more than once. The negro, with his rolling eyes and thick lips, was regarded by the crowd in the light of an immense joke and allowed to win every bout. The big Swede was a very different proposition, and when on one occasion he hurled his adversary against a pillar of the arena and smashed a collar-bone there was a riot and the police had to be called in. It should be added that the Japanese wrestlers were not by any means first-class.

Another Japanese accomplishment cultivated by both amateurs and professionals is sword-dancing (*kembu*). The performer wears the *hakama* (loose trousers with many folds in the front, a sort of divided skirt) and a handkerchief tied round the head (*hachimaki*). The dance is actually the pantomimic recital of a story, the words of which are supplied by a companion who chants them with such fervour as to seem at times in imminent peril of bursting a blood-vessel and thus of dying a premature death. Nevertheless the dance grows on one, and an expert often displays great skill in drawing and handling his dangerous weapon. The *kembu* is very popular, and when given in public members of the audience signify their appreciation with an entire absence of self-consciousness surprising to an Anglo-Saxon. The dance is typically Japanese and should be seen by visitors to the country. Ignorance of the words of the song—not infrequently unintelligible to the uninitiated Japanese himself—necessarily detracts from perfect enjoyment of these exhibitions.

The art of drawing the sword which figures in the *kembu* might also be classed as a branch of fencing. It is termed *ihai* and is well worth seeing. An expert will perform some amazing feats, one of which is to pull the weapon from its scabbard with both hands tied. All these movements are carried out with lightning-like rapidity, and in watching them one can better appreciate the character of those spacious days when he who succeeded in first drawing his sword "had the drop on" his more deliberate adversary just as effectually as the "bad man" out West with his six-shooter.

Having regard for all these evidences of a disposition to live the strenuous life, I cannot share the pessimistic forebodings of some Japanese publicists who see in the future of the race nothing but physical and moral calamities. There can be no doubt that the substitution in the schools of benches and desks for the old-style method of squatting has helped to increase the stature of the youth of Japan; and the partial adoption of foreign diet should likewise add to the vigour of the race. Even in my day the introduction of meat into the army and navy and the reduction of the quantity of rice consumed by the troops had materially lessened the number of cases of beri-beri (the Japanese *kakke*) which was formerly a perfect scourge.

CHAPTER X

THE ESOTERIC ASPECTS OF BUJUTSU

IN Mr. Basil Hall Chamberlain's classic work *Things Japanese*, under the heading of *Esotericism*, there occur the following observations worthy of being quoted as an introduction to the subject:

"When an Englishman hears the word 'esoteric', the first thing, probably, that comes into his head is Buddhism, the second name of Mr. Sinnett or Mrs. Besant. Matters stand somewhat differently in Japan. Not religion only but every art, every pastime, here is or has been esoteric—poetry, music, porcelain-making, fencing, football, even bone-setting, and cookery itself. Esotericism is not a unique mystery shrouding a special class of subjects. It is a general attitude of the mind at a certain stage, and a very natural attitude, too, if one takes the trouble to look into it. Sensible men do not wear their hearts on their sleeves for daws to peck at. Why should an artist do so with his art? Why should he desecrate his art by initiating unworthy persons into its principles? Nor is it merely a question of advisability, or of delicacy and good taste. It is a question of possibility and impossibility. Only sympathetic pupils are fitted to understand certain things; and certain things can only be taught by word of mouth, and when the spirit moves one. Moreover there comes in the question of money. Esoteric teaching of the lower arts may be said to have performed in old days the function of our modern system of patents. The institution of guilds belongs to the same order of ideas. Such are, it would seem, the chief headings of the subject considered in the abstract. Fill them out, if you please, by further reflection and further research; and if you wish to talk to your Japanese friends about esotericism, remember the fascinating words *hiden*, "secret tradition"; *hijutsu*, "secret art"; and *okugi* "inner mysteries", which play a notable part in Japanese history and literature."

So far so good, but the talented author concludes by saying:

"Viewed from a critical standpoint, Chinese and Japanese esoterics well deserve thorough investigation by some competent hand. We ourselves do not think that much would be added thereby to the world's store of wisdom. But we think that a flood of light would be shed upon some of the most curious nooks and crannies of the human mind."

Much, of course, depends upon the individual definition of wisdom, as to which opinions necessarily differ. Of Chinese esoterics I know nothing, and of Japanese esoterics generally very little; but of that branch of Japanese esoterics which belongs to what may generically be styled *bujutsu*, literally "martial arts", though the Japanese terminology has a far wider and more comprehensive scope than its English equivalent, I may justly claim to know something—little enough, no doubt, from an expert Japanese standpoint, but probably more than any other living foreigner. And when I speak of knowledge, I mean theoretical rather than practical knowledge, since even among Japanese specialists the number of those who in the arts of judo or jujutsu, *kenjutsu* (fencing), *tessen* (use of the iron war fan), *naginata* (lance exercise), *kyujutsu* (archery), swimming and allied accomplishments are able to make any practical use of esoteric knowledge is exceedingly limited. That things were very different during the feudal era, when the samurai's skill in fence or wrestling, for example, might at any moment furnish his only safeguard against sudden death, I personally am fully persuaded. What I know at first hand of the feats that are possible in an era of so-called enlightenment (Meiji) among the chosen few, men whom I prefer to regard as the true aristocracy of the nation, predisposes me to lend credence to stories of ancient prowess which to the average foreigner, or even to myself when I first arrived in Japan, might appear simply mythical and fanciful. Confining my dictum then to "martial arts" and connoting by that expression individual skill in the use of individual weapons, both natural and artificial, I do not hesitate to declare that Mr. Chamberlain's pronouncement calls for qualification. I might go even farther and assert that in what concerns the fundamental and most vital principles of the art of individual self-defence and of attack we Occidentals have everything to learn from that small circle of the elect whose members in Japan have succeeded in preserving and one can but hope of perpetuating some remnant of the marvellous occult powers of the old-time masters. The question of a proper terminology in writing of matters which are entirely foreign to the average Western mind necessarily presents no small measure of difficulty. I hasten to add that apart from the one subject which I have selected for consideration in the following pages, I disclaim any special scientific and philosophical knowledge. What is more, I am writing not for the specialist in any branch of inquiry but for the general reader, and in choosing my expressions I am guided solely by the desire to make my meaning as clear and lucid as the nature of the topic will permit. So much by way of explanation is apparently called for in a hypercritical age in order to anticipate, and if possible to disarm, the objections of the favoured few that the definitions employed or the language generally used in this book are not "scientific". When, therefore, I speak here of occult powers I have no wish to hark back to the most precise and exhaustive etymology of the word; my intention is to represent thereby something supernormal rather than supernatural, which latter term ought by this time to have become obsolete.

Another point which likewise calls for emphasis is that the eulogistic appraisement which I can conscientiously apply to the true *bujin* of Japan, the man who enjoys esoteric knowledge but never abuses it to the detriment of society, is by no means intended to apply to the everyday Japanese for whom I entertain no unusual respect or admiration. Indeed it may help to convince the sceptical that hyperbole, or what looks like hyperbole, in the former case is not the outcome of hasty judgment or of an unworthy wish to strengthen "local colour" and "human interest", if I say candidly that fairly protracted intercourse with the ruck of Japanese has not infrequently intensified my wonder that *bujin* of the type I shall hereafter describe should belong to the same race. The *bujin* of this type—rare enough even in Japan—embodies the efflorescence of the very qualities which the average Japanese appears to lack. Some of these qualities the average Japanese may possess in part, while others he possesses in a far less marked degree than the average Englishman or American. I have found too many Japanese "slack"—no other word quite does justice to the sort of characteristic I have in mind—unreliable, sadly wanting in the sense of responsibility, unpunctual, and very far from ascetic. There is also in many Japanese a strain of cruelty which reveals itself in strange indifferences to the sufferings of animals, and in Japan it is no infrequent sight to see adults looking on laughingly and smiling while their young charges are inflicting deliberate torture upon some stray kitten or puppy. Whereas, too, the Japanese fighting-man is as hard as nails and far more capable of enduring physical pain than his Western contemporary, the average Japanese of sedentary habits will absent himself from his daily work for some slight ailment which an English or an American schoolboy would laugh at.

An intelligent Japanese would be the first himself to admit that the native nature is inclined to run to extremes. This tendency helps to explain many startling contrasts and contradictions in the race itself and in the terms which an unprejudiced foreign observer can find in his heart to employ with reference to that race for in almost one and the same breath he may conceivably display withering contempt and dislike for one class of Japanese and unbounded respect and admiration for another, while to the uninitiated listener both abuse and eulogy may appear exaggerated. The truth is that both are justified. Intellectually, morally and physically we find the two extremes exemplified. I am disposed to ascribe this fact to climatic influences more than to any other single factor. In spite of occasional lucid intervals, the climate of Japan must be pronounced enervating and depressing, in consequence of its extreme humidity and the violent atmospheric fluctuations to which the country is subjected as the result of its geographical position. It follows, therefore, that only those endowed with more than the average share of physical and mental vitality feel any natural inclination to "get out and hustle", as our American cousins sometimes phrase it; the more usual penchant is for tea, cigarettes, if nothing stronger, and the *dolce far niente* generally. Those, then, who yield to the soporific blandishments of the climate are bound to become flabbier and flabbier, physically, mentally and morally, as time goes on; while conversely, those who, through heredity or other causes which we need not stop to analyze here, remain proof against the temptation to pursue the line of least resistance inevitably grow stronger and stronger in precisely the same attributes. The habits of resistance and surrender both develop with what they feed on, until at one end of the line we find the *iro-otoko*, the debauchee, the rake, the libertine—in a word, the moral and physical degenerate and invertebrate—whilst at the other we find the *bujin* (fighting-man) the real jujutsu and *kenjutsu* expert, the highest exemplar of the adage, *Mens sana in corpore sano*. Thus it comes about that if a generalization is insisted on, I should be apt to say that the Japanese fighting-man belonging to the élite I have attempted to describe is a cut above the best of the Occidental product, whereas the Japanese "rotter" is perhaps just a little more of a "rotter" than his Occidental prototype. But of course, as already insisted, generalizations are always dangerous, and I should prefer to avoid comparisons and simply to invite a valuation of the Japanese *bujin* on his merits. In any event, I trust that I have succeeded in making it fairly clear that my estimate of the Japanese *bujin*, whether he be exoteric or esoteric, cannot rightly be extended to the Japanese people as a whole.

We have now reached a stage in this inquiry where we may profitably pause to examine the more concrete aspects of both ancient and modern Japanese esotericism in so far as these concern *bujutsu*. In what respect, it may be asked, can the powers of a Japanese esoteric of this class be differentiated from those of an Occidental fighting expert of the past or present? A real master of fence in feudal days, if opposed to an enemy of marked inferiority, could do several things, and of these I shall mention three. In the first place, he could exert a species of mesmeric force at will to such good purpose that he himself would instantly become invisible to his antagonist whose gaze would be helplessly fascinated by the point of the expert's sword, which in turn might be multiplied to seem like half a dozen points all equally real to the expert's prospective victim who, quite irrespective of his inferiority in the art of fencing, would not be able to anticipate the direction of attack seeing that he could not distinguish the true sword point from the false. In the second place, the expert could arrest the movement of his adversary's weapon in the very act of striking, preferably exactly at the moment when his would-be assailant had raised his sword above his head with both hands—the native sword being double-handed—with the object of delivering a downward stroke at the expert's head and shoulder. Paralyzed into immobility at such a juncture, the victim would be left with his entire body exposed to the expert's attack, and he would thus be placed completely at the latter's mercy. In the third place, if the expert wished to avoid unnecessary exertion or to spare the life of his foe, he could in a few minutes convert the latter's blood-thirsty rage into fatuous good humour and send him on his way laughing heartily at one of the expert's spurious valedictory jests. Analogously, we are told about the expert fencer who, unarmed and pursued by an enemy, snatched up a fan or a piece of paper and turning on his pursuer instantly convinced him that he—the expert—held a very business-like *katana*, or long sword, in his grasp. So much headway gained, it would be a comparatively easy matter for the expert thereafter to get the better of a foeman so inferior.

Recourse to this class of hypnotic, mesmeric, or odyllic force, call it what you will, also helps to explain why, minus any optical delusions, an old fencing-master attacked by the celebrated Miyamoto Musashi who flourished during the seventeenth century and usually fought with two swords, a short one and a long one, experienced no difficulty in worsting his antagonist with nothing more formidable than an ordinary paper fan. Of the feats above enumerated, I have been assured by perhaps the ablest then living exponent of the esoteric side of the martial arts that the conversion of an enemy's murderous anger into laughter and good humour is by far the most difficult.

On a par with these astonishing performances is a manifestation of magnetic influence by experts whereby birds can be made to fall from a tree to the ground apparently lifeless, and again instantaneously revived and put to flight. The exertion of this influence is usually accompanied or emphasized by the strange *kiai* shout, referred to in another chapter, though it may be opined that it is not the shout itself but the force behind dictating it that is really responsible for the phenomenon. On the other hand, it is a well-known scientific fact that a tone pitch which sets up vibrations in the surrounding atmosphere can accomplish remarkable concrete results. Thus the basso profondo "protodiakon" of a great Russian cathedral could break the window-panes were he to give full play to his terrific lung capacity within a confined space.

Under similar conditions he could crack the tympanum of a listener who chanced to be standing too near, or extinguish the flame of a candle. It is therefore a justifiable assumption that the peculiar timbre of the *kiai*, as uttered by an expert, may derive some portion of its efficacy from the atmospheric vibrations which it excites.

As a necessary rider to what has been said above, I should explain that the record of these esoteric feats relates exclusively to the past, and that I personally throughout my residence in Japan never heard of nor did I ever witness their duplication by contemporary experts.

But it must not be supposed that it is sufficient for the complete *bujin* to be an adept in all that pertains to the art of killing or disabling an opponent; he must know also how to restore a vanquished foe, if any life remains. To slay recklessly should be no part of the whole duty of a *bujin*. Of course it has to be admitted that just as in our own so-called days of chivalry certain highly humanitarian principles were often far more honoured in the breach than in the observance, so, too, in Japan, pre-eminently perhaps during the first half of the sixteenth century, the precepts of *bushido* and *bujutsu* were one thing, their application entirely another. Nevertheless, then as now the curriculum of the jujutsu dojo would not be complete without its course of *kappo*, or the art of resuscitation. Now that feudalism is a thing of the past, it is true that the *bujin* has less scope for the display of his aggressive spirit than in the more spacious days of Oda Nobunaga or of the Taiko Hideyoshi, unless he wishes to turn outlaw, and even then his term of voluntary activity is likely to be suddenly cut short, though thereafter he may "do the State some service" in an unrehearsed rôle. On the other hand, if the *bujin* may not gain merit by alternately crippling and restoring personal enemies, accidents met with in purely pacific walks of life are as common nowadays as ever they were, and in the long run a really earnest seeker after knowledge need never let his faculties atrophy through lack of practice.

Among the students of jujutsu and kindred arts themselves, it frequently happens that bones are broken or dislocated, sinews wrenched, and obstinate adversaries choked into insensibility, all of which conditions call for recourse to *kappo*. Here again, *kappo* may be, so to speak, both esoteric and exoteric, although according to the Kano system of judo, neither *kappo* nor *atemi* (method of attacking vital spots) may be taught to students below the *shodan* grade. Yet, as I shall have occasion to show more in detail in the next chapter, whereas in ordinary *kappo* consciousness cannot be restored to the patient without direct contact, a teacher versed in the *okugi*, or esoteric side of the art, can achieve the same result by the exertion of force of will, accompanied, as already explained, by the *kiai* (literally, "spirit-meeting") shout. Reserving for an attempt at fuller elucidation elsewhere the rationale of the process, it may be said here that, according to the *bujutsu* creed, the seat of occult force, as also of courage, is the *tan*, or gall-bladder. Technically this force is known as *aiki*, a term which is written with the same two Chinese characters as *kiai*, though with their order reversed. *Aiki*, however—the power which actually accomplishes these seeming miracles—is silent, the *kiai* shout being, shall we say, something in the nature of an auxiliary agent contributing to mental concentration upon the one object. Physically, as explained elsewhere, the practice of the *kiai* is supposed to have the effect of strengthening the region of the *saika tanden* (that part of the abdomen situated about two inches below the navel), and must thus bulk largely as a factor in the development of physical courage and occult power, much in the same way as the strengthening of the muscles and physique as a whole predisposes the subject to a life of greater activity than that of the sedentary clerk or student.

An index to the length of time this belief has existed in Japan is afforded by such words as *tanryoku*, meaning "courage", "spirit", "grit", "mettle"; *daitan*, literally "big gall-bladder"—i.e. "audacity", "impudence", "great personal courage", and some others. Perhaps unconscious deference to the same theory may be detected in the well-known Americanism "gall", implying impudence, a "cool cheek", as when it is said of a certain person that he has "an awful gall".

Concurrently with the development of the gall-bladder and *tanden* region generally, the abdomen becomes prominent—not necessarily fat but solid and muscular. The possession of a swelling chest is deemed of secondary importance. The part played by the brain in inspiring physical activity is not ignored, but just as concentration of will, according to Sandow's theory, is indispensable to the successful development of the surface muscles which are thus enabled to discharge increasingly difficult tasks at the command of the brain, so does this same concentration, when intelligently and persistently directed, operate upon the *tan*, the strengthening of which is supposed to increase one's capacity for the performance of acts of valour. By virtue of this developed *tan*, which has obeyed the impulse conveyed by a strong mind, an opponent inferior in this respect, although physically bigger and stronger, must give way—so the supporters of this theory contend. Thus during the Russo-Japanese war, as a prominent exponent of *bujutsu* once remarked to the writer, the Russians, in spite of greater weight and equally effective weapons, were invariably compelled to retreat before their smaller and lighter adversaries, and that, moreover, not alone in long-range actions but in hand-to-hand encounters. In the opinion of the above authority, this superior resolution of the Japanese was due to *tan* which is highly developed among the samurai (now known as *shizoku*) officers. The same Japanese also insisted that the courage required for the performance of *seppuku* (vulgarly *harakiri*) could be found only among those who had strengthened the *tan* to the necessary degree. But the importance of mental control is never really lost sight of. When, on the other hand, precedence is given only to physical strength, the ultimate result is bound to be highly disadvantageous inasmuch as the physical strength of an old man must as a rule be inferior to that of a young one who is equally assiduous in the pursuit of *bujutsu*; whereas the veteran *bujin*, skilled in the esotericism of jujutsu, can always in the end vanquish his more juvenile antagonist even though in exoteric wrestling he might be thrown again and again.

As bearing directly upon this phase of the inquiry I shall quote what Mr. Arima in his standard work on the Kano system of judo has to say about the cultivation of abdominal power as an indispensable feature of the expert's equipment.

"Judo being in itself one of the best and most interesting forms of exercise," he writes, "there would seem to be no need of subsidiary means to add to its merits. I, however, have had some valuable experience in a method of fostering abdominal power which served me full well in judo contests. One day while young I accompanied Viscount Tachibana and some of my schoolmates on an excursion. As we went along the Viscount pointed out to us the advantage of walking with the abdomen rather than with the legs. The words made such a strong impression upon me that I decided to begin the practice upon the spot. All through the excursion I laboured under this resolution, none of the fine views along the route having been noticed by me. In fact I became more exhausted than delighted with the day's journey. Not disappointed with the initial experiment I repeated the practice as often as I had opportunities with the result that since then I have never fallen behind anybody in the matter of walking, whether in a level or a mountainous country. A few years after our excursion the Viscount, in the course of conversation, said: 'Whether sitting, or standing, or moving, you must always take care that your lower abdomen is filled with strength. I have myself practised this method to this very day and, old as I am, I have become so corpulent, especially in the abdomen, that my old foreign clothes do not fit me.' This advice came in the nick of time, for then I was absorbed in the study of judo. I took up the suggestion in dead earnest, and after some time found that it helped me in preventing my body from becoming buoyant during a contest.

"An old book dealing with the preservation of health has the following about breathing: 'Stand or be seated upright and face the rising sun. Then breathe thirty times moderately deep, interlacing this seven times with deep breathing. Keep your eyes partly open while breathing, which latter must be deep and calm. Close your teeth and exhale slowly through the mouth, expelling the vitiated air as the fresh morning breeze expels mist. Inhale quietly from the nostrils and refresh your blood by filling your *tanden* (abdomen) with air invigorated by the sun's rays, after the manner of thirsty plants absorbing summer showers.' It is a recognized fact that by filling the *tanden* with air and strength we can best maintain our equilibrium in a judo contest, and this is perhaps due to the fact that the centre of our weight (centre of gravity) lies somewhere about the abdomen.

"Mr. Kikojiro Fukui, one of my friends, has also his own way of breathing. He says: 'Before meals, when your stomach is empty, seat yourself in a well ventilated place, stretch out your hands and put them on both sides of the lower abdomen with your thumbs at the back, and keep your head and body erect. Then draw in the air through your nostrils little by little until your lower abdomen is full. In so doing endeavour to swell the latter, assisting the operation with your hands. Remain in this condition until you can no longer bear it. Then exhale slowly through the nostrils, thus expelling all the air you can. Repeat the process for about five minutes at a time, gradually extending the length of time to twenty minutes as you get used to it. After a little while you will perceive your abdomen swell, followed by a development of the legs and trunk, finally culminating in the invigoration of your whole frame. Two months' exercise will probably convince you."

Additional instances of how this cultivation of abdominal power operates are given later, the object of this chapter being rather to furnish the reader with a bird's-eye view of the subject than to enter exhaustively into technical details.

I am, of course, fully aware that nothing short of ocular demonstration—and not always that—will satisfy a certain brand of mind that these things can be or that they have been. Some persons, for the most part Occidentals, are prone to cherish scepticism as a badge of superiority distinguishing its proud possessor from the common herd. I will not deny that scepticism is an excellent mental condition up to a certain point, but beyond that point it not infrequently degenerates into an obstinate disinclination to reject the outcome of careful inductive reasoning. Shakespeare makes Valentine say: "Home-keeping youth have ever homely wits"; and it is generally the case that capacity for belief is most highly developed in those who have seen most of the outside world. As far as I personally am concerned, I cheerfully admit that if before I went to Japan I had been told that there were Japanese then living who could produce the physical and quasi-physical phenomena which I have since witnessed with my own eyes, I should most probably have doubted the truth of these assurances. And it is because, as stated elsewhere, I have had ocular demonstration of phenomena which are inexplicable on the basis of generally accepted physiological, anatomical and psychological laws, that I tacitly accept more surprising stories from the record of the past, even though the *a posteriori* process may not be exhaustive. I give an account of these personal experiences, together with the views of an expert as to their causation, in succeeding chapters.

CHAPTER XI

THE ESOTERIC ASPECTS OF BUJUTSU
(concluded)

THE Japanese teacher to whom I am most largely indebted for
inspiration on the esoteric aspects of judo and jujutsu was not a
member of the Kodokan but a Mr. Nobuyuki Kunishige, a veteran
then well over sixty years of age belonging to the Shinden Isshin-
ryu school of the art. Mr. Kunishige was in those days the proprietor and director of a fifty-mat dojo called the Shidokan,
situated in the Shimbashi quarter of the capital of Japan, hardly
five minutes' walk from the station of the same name. I should
say that Mr. Kunishige taught fencing as well as judo, and was
besides an expert in the use of the spear and the iron fan, in
archery, swimming and horsemanship; in a word, he was a worthy
representative of the old samurai class which did not limit speciali-
zation to a single subject.

In person Mr. Kunishige would have been pronounced
decidedly large for a Japanese. His height was probably between
5 ft. 6 in. and 5 ft. 7 in. and his weight in the neighbourhood of
165 lb. though in his youth he was fully twenty pounds heavier.
Whenever he donned fencing or wrestling gear—and in spite of his
years he might often have been seen in action on the mats—one
could not fail to notice the abnormal development of his forearms,
this being the result of constant use of the fencing-stick from early
youth. As bearing upon what I have already said about abdominal
development, one interested in such matters would also remark the
generous proportions of the lower half of his torso, although it
would be erroneous to suppose that these were in any way
identical with mere obesity. His moral qualities, too, had stood the
test of years of comparative penury and were such as to render the
word *bushido* something more than vain and empty nomenclature.
In an age when the object of the majority was to turn everything
into hard cash, Mr. Kunishige had never been known to make an
exhibition of his peculiar powers for gain alone. For the edification

108

THE LATE NOBUYUKI KUNISHIGE

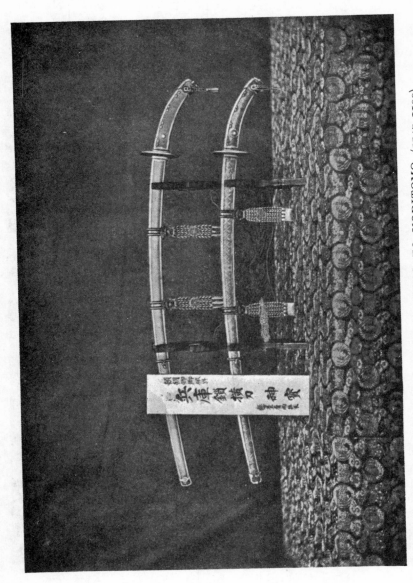

SWORDS FORMERLY BELONGING TO YORITOMO (1147–1199)

From the Shosozoin

of a private circle of friends and disciples he was generally willing to give a demonstration, but otherwise he exercised that branch of his art which concerned healing and resuscitation for the benefit of the suffering, and in those cases the charge was regulated by the financial ability of the patient, and was therefore, on occasion, nothing at all. At best it was pitched at a figure which would throw even a Russian feldsher into convulsions. In other words, pay or no pay, Mr. Kunishige would have deemed himself morally bound to respond to the call for succour.

My own acquaintance with Mr. Kunishige dated from the strenuous days of the war with Russia, when I represented a London daily in Tokyo, and devoted my leisure moments, those of them, at least, that were not taken up with rest and mental study, to the practice of judo. Occasional absences from Japan on professional pilgrimages had broken the continuity of our direct intercourse, but this had always been renewed when opportunity offered. and so when I finally decided to write this book I very naturally turned to my old friend and instructor for his understanding of the scope and meaning of judo or jujutsu, and Mr. Kunishige readily consented to satisfy my curiosity.

Thus it came about that on a freezingly cold evening in midwinter, the Japanese *kanchu*, I repaired to the chilly Shidokan in the company of a Japanese friend named Mr. Umezawa, a fine type of the Japanese gentleman and a splendid English scholar who had kindly agreed to make an extended note of the teacher's remarks and afterwards to furnish me with an English translation; for I may add that however fluently one may speak the colloquial, the detailed report of a lecture highly charged with Sinico-Japanese terminology is not a task to be approached lightheartedly even by a recognized japanologue, which I have never professed to be.

Mr. Kunishige received us in an upper room of the Shidokan, where he delivered his address to an audience composed not only of Mr. Umezawa and myself, but of a dozen or so of his Japanese disciples ranging in age from mere boys to young men between twenty and thirty. Mr. Kunishige took his stand behind a small foreign-style table on which a cheap kerosene-oil lamp gave out a feeble light. Mr. Umezawa and I were both accommodated with chairs at the same table, as guests of honour, and as a concession to our more sybaritic tendencies a couple of Japanese braziers were placed between our feet to sustain our circulation during the discourse. The members of the teacher's purely Japanese auditory simply squatted round the room in native fashion, with a heroic assumption of indifference to the disgracefully low temperature. These simple preparations having been made and the meeting called to order, Mr. Kunishige began his lecture a report of which I append, as far as possible translated literally from the original Japanese.

"In response to the request of Mr. E. J. Harrison," he began, "an enthusiastic student of judo, who, I understand, intends to write a book on our national art of self-defence with a view to introducing the latter to the foreign public, I venture to speak to you on the same subject, although I must confess that I do not consider myself fully qualified to undertake the task with full authority.

"First of all, I deem it necessary to draw a clear line of demarcation between judo (or jujutsu, as it is sometimes called) and *taijutsu*. The latter is a branch of judo and is, I regret to say, too often regarded as synonymous with the latter. It is this *taijutsu* that is generally taught in judo schools of the present day under the style of judo. *Taijutsu* is a part but not the whole of judo, for otherwise judo would lose its essential value and become an art hardly worth learning. The distinction between the two arts is this, that whereas *taijutsu* aims more particularly at physical culture, in which its main value lies, judo seeks to invest its exponents with power over life and death, within certain limits, its secret lying in the wonderful *aiki-no-jutsu* (The Japanese word jutsu, meaning "art", is usually by a colloquial corruption pronounced *jitsu*). *Taijutsu*, on the contrary, having for its primary object physical culture, does not include in its curriculum *ate* (methods of striking or kicking vital spots in the body in order to disable or kill an adversary) while the *katsu* (methods of resuscitation included in the overall system called *kappo*) employed in this branch of judo are also of the most simple description. A *taijutsu* contest ends when one of the parties is thrown to the floor. In judo or jujutsu the case is otherwise. Mere throwing does not determine either victory or defeat because even while being thrown down an expert can use *ate* in order temporarily to disable his antagonist by means of, say, paralysis of a joint or limb which will deprive him of fighting capacity. Moreover, *taijutsu* does not include *tsukide* and *keashi*, parts of *ate*, which properly belong to the sphere of judo. Nevertheless the two arts, judo and *taijutsu*, are closely related to each other. It is therefore advisable for students to begin with *taijutsu* as a preliminary course before entering upon the practice of judo.

"In learning judo the student should never lose sight of the necessity of developing the *shitahara* (literally, "lower-belly", i.e. the *saika tanden* referred to in previous chapters), since without a properly developed *shitahara* his art will lose no small portion of its efficacy. I shall say something more about the *shitahara* later on. In judo if your opponent tries to hit you, say, in the eye, you naturally defend yourself by stopping his fist before it reaches your eye, and in so doing you hit his hand on a vital spot (*kyusho*) to disable it. This act is what we term *ate* or *atemi*. This *ate* is an essential characteristic of the art of judo, and the great value of the latter rests in it. *Ate* may deprive an opponent of life for the time being, but it is by no means brutal seeing that it also provides its exponent with the means of restoring the fallen foe to life again by the application of *katsu* or *kappo*. In these possibilities lies its military virtue.

"The masters of some schools are inclined to separate judo and *seikotsu* (the art of bone-setting), but in my school *seikotsu* is treated as an integral part of judo for obvious reasons.

"Now the vital parts of the human body exposed to attack are the *jinchu* (immediately below the nose), *juka* (under the ears), *daino* (brain), *kono* (?occiput), *suigetsu* (breast-bone), *nyuka* (under the breasts), *ekika* (under the armpits) and *hihara* (the sides, both front and back). These parts are known in our school as the *kyukon* (nine organs). An *ate* aimed at any one of these spots affects the internal organs." (Actually only eight are given here; apparently one *ate* has been inadvertently omitted!)

I may interrupt Mr. Kunishige's recital here to state that the nomenclature of these vital spots varies somewhat according to the jujutsu school, and similarly some schools may recognize additional spots, not specified above, but speaking generally, as regards the more susceptible and fatal points in the human body, the leading schools are virtually agreed; the name may sometimes be different but the thing is usually the same. In my possession are charts clearly indicating the position of the principal vital spots and their particular connexion with nerve-centres and internal organs; but it is not the object of this work to give away information which might conceivably become dangerous in unscrupulous hands, the more so seeing that this information was given to me by a former teacher under the pledge of secrecy.

Continuing Mr. Kunishige said:

"A rib is especially liable to break when hit with force. *Katsu* is effective in repairing broken bones when properly administered within two hours after the infliction of the injury. With the help of *aiki* the art of *seikotsu* proves particularly effective in cases where the victim is being treated for *ate* applied to any one of the nine organs above mentioned."

It was at this point that the lecturer supplied several illustrations of the efficacy of *aiki* and *seikotsu* culled from his extensive experience, more especially the case of the setting of the upper vertebrae of a coolie named Suzuki who had fallen from the roof of a house and had been given up for dead by the ordinary practitioners.

"In such cases as this *katsu* alone is ineffective in restoring a man or woman to life. Thus the judo student should not neglect to learn the art of *seikotsu* to render *katsu* more efficacious.

"*Taijutsu* is effective against a small number of antagonists, but is of little use when one is confronted by many."

To substantiate this statement Mr. Kunishige told his hearers that quite recently an experimental contest had been arranged at the Metropolitan Police Station, where a *taijutsu* master was pitted against three policemen, his business being to throw each policeman three times in succession. The test resulted in the defeat of the master who was firmly held by his adversaries before he could fulfil the conditions. Mr. Kunishige went on to assert that with a proper knowledge of judo it would have been a comparatively easy matter to overpower even a larger number because the master could have disabled them one after the other by *ate*, and this, too, without inflicting any permanent injury, for he could have restored them just as easily.[1]

"If the student learns judo at all he should learn it thoroughly, i.e. until he has fully mastered *ate* and *katsu* together with *seikotsu* and *aiki* (the secret of judo.)

"All branches of Japanese martial arts have not for their prime object the killing of men; their ultimate purpose is to chastise wicked men. Military virtue is really identical with humanity, and martial arts aim at the attainment of this object. In judo we often have recourse to *ate* and it is therefore all the more necessary to learn *katsu* and *seikotsu*. Just as a sword is not necessarily a weapon intended to kill men so too *ate* is not solely designed to inflict injury.

"The essence of *bushido* is contained in the martial arts. A certain professor (Dr. Nitobe) recently published a work on *bushido* in which he says that *bushido* is a moral teaching which favourably compares with the moral doctrines taught in the various countries of the world; and he then proceeds to remark that *bushido* is independent of fencing, judo and other martial arts. I do not agree with this gentleman in the latter remark. In my opinion the martial arts are important parts of the structure which is termed *bushido*. Without the martial arts *bushido*, however noble and lofty it may be, must fade into nothingness. Loyalty and justice are the precepts of *bushido*, and the martial arts are the essential means of attaining the object in view. *Bushido* imposes upon men the sacrifice of their lives for the cause of loyalty and justice. But when an emergency calls upon us to die in defence of the State we can be of little service if we are ignorant of the martial arts.

[1]Personally I am inclined to qualify this statement. It would be easy for me to pick out half a dozen or more experts from the Kodokan who, without recourse to *ate*, could throw three inferior antagonists three times in succession, or even a considerably larger number. Nevertheless, in principle, Mr. Kunishige's contention is sound enough.

"Various opinions obtain as to the origin and development of bushido. Some ascribe the former to the advent of Buddhism, while others trace it to the introduction of the Chinese classics. I feel firmly convinced that bushido sprang up in pre-historic ages and that its origin may be traced back to the very foundations of this Empire. History affords abundant proofs of this contention. Together with bushido the martial arts sprang into being and have made the vast development which we witness today. Bushido surpasses religion and other moral teachings in that it gives prompt chastisement to the wrongdoer, while religion and moral teaching merely exhort men to abstain from doing wrong. Bushido calls upon men to rise to the succour of their fellow-creatures in danger from bandits, robbers and other evil-doers, even at the sacrifice of their lives. A person ignorant of the martial arts can do little to help others at the call of bushido (if he is ignorant of the martial arts). Thus far judo and bushido.

"I shall now proceed to give you a few hints which may be needful to the student of judo and martial arts (bujutsu) in general. As I briefly stated at the beginning of this lecture the student of martial arts should lay stress upon the shitahara. Here it is necessary to distinguish between the shitahara of the samurai and that of Zen—and by Zen is meant not only the Zen sect of Buddhism but all the adherents of that creed. The shitahara of Zen is the subjective culture of one's inner self while sitting in the zazen style; whereas the shitahara of the samurai requires both subjective and objective culture of oneself based upon a proper conception of loyalty and justice. By shitahara is meant the cultivation of mental immobility (kokoro wo ugokasanu). This cultivation is not so difficult to attain if you apply yourself thereto with thorough care. Never at any time should one lose sight of one's shitahara; sitting, standing, walking, or lying down, one should keep one's strength concentrated there. But in addition to constant watchfulness over their own emotions students must bear in mind the necessity for shinki (shin is "soul", "mind"; ki is also "soul", "mind", "temper", "humour"), for the training of the shitahara. Shin and ki at times separate from each other and at times are joined."

At this point the speaker gave a somewhat metaphysical explanation of the manner in which *shinki* may be controlled in order to eliminate the subject's consciousness of physical pain. Reducing this explanation to the simplest terms, it may be said that when your finger-tip is pinched you feel pain there because your mind at once travels thither; but if you could keep your *shin* detached therefrom you would no longer feel pain. To accomplish this object the *tanden* already referred to must be kept immovable, while your *ki* is, as it were, dismissed from your body, although you retain the power to recall it at a moment's notice. When you have reached this stage in your occult training you may be said to have finished a preliminary course of *aiki* and, according to Mr. Kunishige, this undertaking offers no insuperable difficulty.

"When you are really proficient in the martial arts," the lecturer went on, "you will arrive at the stage described by the old masters as *Furai muitsu* which may be likened to the facility with which the wind comes and goes without leaving any sign of motion. Still higher stages in *aiki* may be reached. I myself can practise only a small portion of the last named. But a man who has thoroughly acquired the art of *aiki* verges on the divine. The clairvoyance so much talked about nowadays is nothing but a part of *aiki*. But *aiki* can be acquired only by long and patient study, after one has attained the highest degree of proficiency in practical judo feats.

"In order to study the art of *aiki* one must learn the method of *shinki kiitsu* (*shin*="soul", "mind", "consciousness"; *ki*="turn of mind", "consciousness", "disposition"; *kiitsu*= "unity", i.e. the method of uniting soul and turn of mind). The old masters of my school have sayings to the effect that one with full knowledge of *aiki* can see in the dark, bring walking men to a full stop, or break the sword brandished to slay him, and these words can be accepted as true. I draw this conclusion from my personal experience in stopping bleeding from the nose and from the modern practice of clairvoyance. I believe that men can enter the divine realm through constant culture of their mental and physical faculties. But one who has not learned *shinki kiitsu* cannot grasp *aiki* even if taught. The student will do well to train his *shitahara* until he has

learnt to place his *ki* as his disposal without moving his *kokoro*
—mind, mentality, heart, thought, will, idea, etc. By mesmerism
one can place another under one's influence and compel him to
act as one suggests; but the art of *aiki* is even more certain in it
effect. Consequently great prudence is needed in the teaching
of this art because wicked persons could work untold evil and
endanger the safety of human society by its reckless exercise
I sincerely trust that those who study judo and other martial
arts will attach due importance to the doctrines of *bushido*."

Mr. Kunishige interspersed his address here and there with
quotations from the Japanese poets, but for foreign readers these
condensations of thought are of minor value.

CHAPTER XII

PRACTICE AFTER PRECEPT

AT the close of the lecture of which a summary has been given in the previous chapter the rank and file of the disciples retired, and Mr. Kunishige invited my friend Mr. Umezawa, myself and a few chosen spirits to drink tea over the *hibachi* (brazier). The cold was intense and both Mr. Umezawa and I, accustomed as we were to more luxurious superfluities, experienced no little difficulty in restraining our teeth from audible expression of our feelings. As a matter of fact, my poor friend contracted such a violent cold on this occasion that he had to take to his bed for several days, apropos of which he sent me a humorous postcard wherein he opined that the result in his case must have been due to an imperfectly developed *shitahara!* Be this as it may, while mentally we hung on Mr. Kunishige's words, physically we hung over the braziers and tried to imagine that we were warm. It would appear, however, that our abdominal power was scarcely equal to this *tour de force*, and so we continued to suffer on the one hand and to enjoy on the other.

Mr. Umezawa who, although a Japanese born and bred and the son of a *shizoku* who had worn the two swords in his day, had never before been inside a jujutsu dojo, evinced the keenest interest in Mr. Kunishige's exposition.

"I have heard from Mr. Harrison," he said, "about some of the remarkable feats you yourself can perform by means of this *aiki*. Would it be asking too much for something in the way of a demonstration of how this power acts?"

The teacher, with that almost instinctive deference to the Japanese custom which demands self-depreciation in these and similar circumstances, at once denied the possession of any extraordinary powers, but expressed willingness to undertake two or three experiments in the interests of our investigation.

It is necessary to say here that we were at this time sitting on the mats, the teacher and others in Japanese costume squatting in

117

bona fide Japanese fashion with their legs doubled up beneath them and those of us wearing foreign dress affecting the posture known in the vernacular as *agura wo kaku*, i.e. with the legs simply crossed tailor fashion. Neither style is specially calculated to improve the cut of one's inexpressibles; but the true native squat is simply perdition to the most resolute creation of the most conscientious tailor of either hemisphere, and no trouser-press extant can restore even approximate perpendicularity to a pair of knees which have been subjected for any length of time to the foregoing form of discipline. But it is not alone the inanimate texture of one's nether garments that suffers from the practice of squatting. The Japanese knee is astonishingly elastic and therefore capable of accommodating itself for hours at a stretch to this contracted position; but the Occidental knee is the victim of heredity, the product of centuries of hopeless addiction to some type of chair, whence it follows that—with very rare exceptions—foreigners, if they persist in their efforts to be polite by imitating their Japanese friends in this respect, have to be removed from native functions by an impromptu ambulance corps, owing to cramp in the legs. I have had more training than the average alien, but none the less would rather sit in a chair and listen to Japanese vocal music for two hours on end than squat in Japanese fashion for half that time *vis-à-vis* the most glamorous geisha from the Shimbashi quarter of the Japanese capital.

This seeming digression brings me to the point where Mr. Kunishige invited me to squat and face him. This I did as well as I could. He then instructed me to seize both his ears and to pull them as hard as I liked. Without more ado I obeyed. I am not exactly a weakling, but my most desperate efforts had no more effect upon Mr. Kunishige's facial expression than if they had never been. A Spartan might perhaps contrive to conceal the agony he was enduring beneath a mask of indifference but no Spartan known to history ever possessed ears which could have survived intact the tugging to which I subjected the corresponding organs of Mr. Kunishige. What is more, through all this pulling the teacher never altered his position on the cushion. At the end of a minute's exercise of this description I began to feel that in much the same manner and with about an equal prospect of making a dynamic or sentient impression might I exhaust my energies upon the Trafalgar Square lions or the Egyptian sphynx. Finally Mr. Kunishige asked, "Are you satisfied?" When I said I was he made a pass with one hand and simply observed, "His strength will now disappear", and with no external aid whatsoever leaned back on his haunches and dragged me after him still hanging on to his ears for all I was worth!

Similarly I was invited to push against Mr. Kunishige's broad chest with one or both hands; no efforts of mine could budge him any more than they could have budged Mount Fuji, whereas with his little finger placed lightly against my body he upset my equilibrium in a second, and I had no power to resist.

Again, I seized the teacher's right hand with both of mine and brought the strongest pressure to bear upon the upper joints of the four fingers. Once more it must be said that even the fingers of a Sandow could not resist such treatment for long without being disabled or broken, while the pain alone would compel surrender after a few seconds. Mr. Kunishige, however, let me work my will upon his joints with the most complete unconcern. While I began to go red in the face with my exertions he addressed Mr. Umezawa and calmly pointed out that if he were experiencing pain at the time his features must in the end disclose the fact, whereas his facial expression continued to be perfectly normal. Then when I could do no more but still continued to press, he made the same pass with his left hand and remarked, "His strength has now gone", and with scarcely a perceptible effort withdrew his right hand from my strenuous grip. Neither Mr. Umezawa nor I could remain proof against any of these experiments for more than a few seconds at the outside. Mr. Kunishige's very first pull at my ears made them crack ominously, and so with our finger-joints. The pain was simply excruciating.

Of an analogous character was an experiment in which he took a long sash used to confine the kimono at the waist, tied the two ends together and passed the loop thus formed round his own neck and that of a disciple of nidan grade. In this position he allowed the disciple to pull against him not only with both hands and neck but with the additional help of both hands which held the sash at his end on either side. Needless to say, Mr. Kunishige never stirred until once more, with the exercise of *aiki*, he began to lean back and with absolute ease pulled his opponent forward until his haunches left the mats and he tumbled forward against the teacher. After this it would surprise nobody to be told that it was for Mr. Kunishige a very simple matter to drag two of us round the room simultaneously in spite of our desperate struggles to return the compliment. The most striking feature of all these demonstrations was the comparative absence of stress and strain on the part of the teacher.

Two considerations effectually dispose of the—at best—remote hypothesis that Mr. Kunishige could have performed any of these feats through superior physical strength. One of these considerations is that he was, as previously stated, an old man—well over sixty years of age; the other is that he had duplicated these self-same feats against the strongest men in the empire in the persons of the huge *sumotori*, or professional heavyweight wrestlers of Japan. When it is added that 300 lb. avoirdupois is no uncommon weight for these "mountains of fat and muscle", as they have been aptly termed by an English writer, fuller comprehension of the nature of Mr. Kunishige's performance will be forthcoming, for his maximum weight at the time could not have exceeded 160 lb.

Shakespeare makes Bolingbroke say, "O! who can hold a fire in his hand by thinking on the frosty Caucasus?" Obviously the Caucasus had nothing to do with Mr. Kunishige's accomplishment of the prodigy mentioned by Shakespeare, for it may well be doubted whether Mr. Kunishige had ever heard of the Caucasus. Be this as it may, what is certain is that he actually picked up the glowing contents of a Japanese pipe and held them for several moments between his thumb and forefinger without sustaining any burn or apparently suffering any pain during the process.

Still more inexplicable, perhaps, measured by the commonly accepted standards of Western medical science and practice, was Mr. Kunishige's system of administering first aid, as adverted to in a previous chapter. As therein stated, the method of resuscitation employed in most schools, including the Kodokan, calls for direct contact with the patient. Not so with Mr. Kunishige or at least not necessarily so. It was a matter of common knowledge among the doctors of the district in which Mr. Kunishige lived that he had time and again restored to consciousness men and women given up for dead by the regular practitioners and that, too, to all outward semblance simply by means of a shout—the *kiai*, to wit—

but which I have already shown to be the vehicle of a more deeply
seated force called *aiki*, supposed to emanate from the *tanden*.
In one of these cases a coolie working on the new building of the
Department of Communications near the Shimbashi Station had
fallen from a great height and almost broken his spine. One shout
from Mr. Kunishige summoned back the waning life or—as Mr.
Kunishige himself would have said—infused into him some of the
life of the operator, and enabled him to rise to his feet, after which
the doctors had a chance to confirm the cure by recourse to more
concrete remedies. In many of these cases Mr. Kunishige made no
pretence to effect a permanent cure; what he did undertake to do
was to revive a patient who, if treated in the orthodox way, would
frequently have perished.

Here are two further illustrations of his gift which fall within
my personal recollection:

The male child of a neighbour was slowly dying in terrible
agony, and nothing the ordinary doctors could do appeared able
to alleviate the patient's sufferings. Finally Mr. Kunishige's aid
was solicited. He simply began to talk to the child in a quiet and
even tone of voice, explaining to him that both he and the speaker
were on their way to Ryogoku to see the firework display which
takes place annually on the Sumida river, and is known in Japanese
as the *kawa-biraki*, or "opening of the river". The child instantly
succumbed to Mr. Kunishige's hypnotic spell and was content.
All symptoms of pain disappeared and it was evident from the
child's delighted exclamations that he saw clearly the subjective
picture which Mr. Kunishige's peculiar power enabled him to
visualize. Thus Mr. Kunishige described the tramway ride to
Ryogoku, the arrival there, the vast crowds, the noise, the laughter,
the river, the strumming of the *samisen* from tea-houses on its
banks, and geisha-laden barges on its surface; and the child,
mentally speaking, passed away blissfully and painlessly amid
pleasant surroundings. In this instance, of course, the child was
doomed, and however much of a temporary stimulus Mr. Kunishige's power might have imparted to the waning faculties, it
could not have achieved a permanent cure.

In the second instance the subject was again a child, a girl who
was suffering from nasal haemorrhage of the most persistent and
violent type. Nothing that the doctors in the neighbourhood could

do had proved of any avail, and the situation had begun to look hopeless when a jinrikishaman who chanced to know of Mr. Kunishige's reputation advised the parents to carry the child to him. As a last resort this was done. The child was still conscious and could obey instructions. She was placed on the mats at a little distance in front of the operator who fixed his eyes upon her, emitted the *kiai*, and swept down his arm. On the instant the flow from one nostril entirely ceased, and that from the other was reduced to a slow dribble. A second *kiai* removed even these traces of the trouble, and the cure was complete. From that day onward the child was never again bothered with bleeding from the nose. As a matter of fact, this branch of the art was very commonly practised by Mr. Kunishige. Chance collisions, falls and blows in jujutsu exercises frequently result in "bloody noses", if not "cracked crowns", but with Mr. Kunishige at hand to stop the ruddy flow the pupils thought nothing of such trifles.

A young student friend of mine named Miyachi, a *shodan* of the Kodokan, lived with Mr. Kunishige for some time as his *shosei*, i.e. a young man who is furnished with free board and lodging by a senior in return for certain services. Before Miyachi entered Mr. Kunishige's domestic circle he had had little or no belief in the esoteric claims of these teachers of the old school, and so when on one occasion he too found his nose bleeding profusely he felt more amused than otherwise when Mr. Kunishige volunteered to cure him in the usual manner. However, he knew better than to raise any objection and so complied literally with the teacher's directions. The result was that he was cured in a few seconds. Describing his sensations to me, he said that when Mr. Kunishige concentrated his gaze upon him his expression was simply terrifying, and that when the *kiai* was uttered he felt as if a thin stream of cold water had started to run upwards from the tip of his nose to his forehead, after which the flow of blood disappeared. Evidently, then, faith in the efficacy of Mr. Kunishige's system was not in any sense a condition antecedent to these applications, and in this respect the system must be sharply differentiated from the affirming and denying of Christian scientists.

I have been here dealing less with approximate first causes than with concrete phenomena, so to speak, but it may be surmised that we have in all these experiments a more elaborate and perfect system of mesmerism than Western operators have yet succeeded in developing.

Diaphanous and anaemic doctors, who had been amazed and bewildered witnesses of Mr. Kunishige's ability to resuscitate where all the resources of the *materia medica* had utterly failed, had implored him to explain how it was done. To all such entreaties Mr. Kunishige had replied that with the best will in the world he could not impart the necessary information to any purpose until the student had undergone a hard preliminary training in jujutsu, in the absence of which the most adamantine abdominal muscles evoked by deep breathing would be of little avail. Apropos, Mr. Kunishige loved to narrate with many appreciative chuckles how many years ago at Kyoto he fell foul of one of the priests of the Zen sect, which inculcates deep breathing as an essential concomitant of its system of mental concentration, the benefits of which, so far as they go, not even Mr. Kunishige would have cared to deny. Indeed some of the most famous men in Japanese history, ancient and modern, including Togo, Kodama, Oyama, and many others, would willingly bear testimony to the debt they owe to the practice of *Za-zen*, as the particular method of sitting for hours at a stretch in profound meditation, which constitutes one of the most notable practices of this sect, is designated. The important point is that meditation is not the be-all and the end-all of mundane existence, and it was in connexion with this phase of the subject that Mr. Kunishige and the priestly advocate of Zen came to verbal blows.

"Yes", said the former, after listening politely and attentively to a long disquisition from his antagonist on the virtues of the system, "that is all very well as long as you remain squatting upon your three-by-three platform with no one to bother you. There you can develop your *shitahara* to enormous proportions free from rude and sacrilegious interference; but the moment you descend from your perch and run up against a *bujin* who has developed his *shitahara*, not by constant squatting but by constant movement, where are you?"

And Mr. Kunishige showed him as he had showed me how by a simple touch with a single finger he could topple him over. Needless to say, the sacerdotal disciple of *Za-zen* waxed exceeding wrath over this attack and illustration and departed in high dudgeon.

I am nothing if not eclectic, and in telling this story I have no wish to run down *Za-zen* of which, in fact, I treat sympathetically elsewhere in these pages; but facts are facts, and one cannot prepare oneself for the storm and stress of a world which is largely objective by endeavouring to elucidate abstract and concrete phenomena by means of purely subjective processes and independently of actual experience. Judo, jujutsu, and their essential *okugi* and *hiden*, or esoteric doctrines and practices, have just this superiority over too many Occidental forms of intellectual and physical training that they are both subjective and objective; their theory and practice go hand in hand, and—within limits—the student is not asked to accept as axiomatic any theory or principle which cannot be at least approximately demonstrated as true. For this reason, then, I maintain that if Japan had given nothing else to the world than this she would be deserving of recognition and appreciation from the Occident and the rest of the Orient.

I have heard it raised as an objection to judo that it tends to make young men brutal. Here too we must be very careful about our terminology. As to what constitutes brutality much depends upon the point of view. Your peas, potatoes, prunes and prisms brand of old lady would doubtless regard ping-pong as brutal; and the vanguard of the mollycoddle brigade may even be heard protesting that football is brutal because players get damaged occasionally; and that boxing, wrestling and, in short, nearly all physical exercises into which the factor of personal rivalry enters are for analogous reasons brutal. Candidly, to use an expressive Americanism, I have no use for such persons and for such arguments. Acquiescence in their implications and acceptance of their logical consequences would in the course of a few generations deprive the world of all its blood and bone. Or if such theories are to be applied only by an effete West—although I hasten to add that I have no belief in the possibility or probability of any such disastrous consummation—then we shall simply by hastening the day which is talked about *ad nauseam* by neurasthenic degenerates, when the Orient will make us its easy prey. If, again, by brutality is connoted a type of personal character which inclines its fortunate possessor to make light of hard knocks and injuries sustained by others because he is wont to make even lighter of similar

SEKI'S RESIDENCE IN SHIBA, TOKYO

THE AUTHOR WRITING THE FIGURE "ONE" IN JAPANESE
FOR SEKI'S EXAMINATION

temporary inconveniences when sustained by himself, then I will freely and cheerfully admit that judo is a brutal sport, and the only piece of advice I can offer to those who think that mankind ought to be packed in cotton-wool and kept "this side up with care" for fear of breakages is the good old Shakespearean one, to wit, "That he which hath no stomach to this fight, let him depart".

But because the judo student never makes a fuss but looks on almost coldly even when a good comrade is sometimes removed from the arena with a broken collar-bone, a snapped knee ligament, or a temporary concussion, it does not necessarily follow that he is not sympathetic. It may be said that his very coolness the better qualifies him for the task of administering first aid, and in no case are the most indispensable steps for the immediate relief of the victim of one of these misadventures neglected. The would-be reformer who sets out by trying to abolish pain by avoiding danger is starting from the wrong end. Judo does not teach the student to invite danger gratuitously. What it does teach him is how he can best bear himself when danger comes his way. Thanks too, to the physical and moral training which it gives to its best disciples, experiences which would be unbearably painful to the mollycoddle type of young man are positively and literally pleasurable to the student of judo. Thus it can be demonstrated that up to a certain point even pain is subjective and a matter of individual temperament, and a perfectly logical concatenation brings us to the conclusion that pain can be most effectively dealt with by making the subject almost impervious to it, just as one may avoid the sting of the nettle by grasping it firmly. This means that if pain cannot be abolished its area at least can be sensibly circumscribed. It comes to this, then, that to be candid, no form of physical exercise capable of conferring all-round development can be devised so as to be entirely free from the element of danger to life and limb; for I decline to agree that the solitary tussle with a pair of spring-grip dumb-bells or a collection of rubber strands is sufficient for this purpose, although as a subsidiary and an auxiliary means to the same end it may be heartily recommended within reason.

If this elementary and fundamental proposition be accepted—and it must be accepted—we may pass on and declare that the perfection of physical development, which I hold to be a noble end in itself, cannot be attained without acceptance of these risks to life and limb. The abominable horrors of vivisection, which constitute a foul blot on the escutcheon of our ramshackle "civilization", are the inevitable outcome of this fear of pain for the human. True, both the boxer and the judoka inflict pain even as they endure it; but they do not inflict it upon a helpless and an unwilling victim, as is the reprehensible habit of the votaries of our atrocious blood sports, but upon a free agent who finds enjoyment and exhilaration in exercising both his physical and mental faculties in escaping the infliction of punishment and in silently grinning and bearing it when it proves to be unavoidable. All this has nothing to do with the very proper and necessary steps which society sees fit to take for the reduction of accidents in avocations included in the struggle for existence, though analogous considerations are certainly applicable to the socialistic movement which seeks to eliminate competition and volubly decries the so-called "profit motive", both of which are among the most potent incentives to improvement in many spheres; but it has everything to do with the question of physical-culture in its broadest sense. Let those who prefer something less strenuous map out their own line of conduct, but let them also refrain from vexatious and officious interference with those who would feel that they had not lived without the football charge, a rousing bout with the mits, the fullest exercise of all the physical and many of the mental faculties in the struggle for a fall on the padded mat or the Japanese *tatami*. I have nothing but sympathy with those who through no fault of their own cannot participate in these mimic frays, and equally I have nothing but contempt for those who, because they are either unable or unwilling themselves to participate therein, would fain prevent others from doing so. The remedy for these gentry and bogus wiseacres is a good squelching by the very methods which are for them *anathema maranatha*.

I should add to this chapter the comment that although during my own fairly long residence in Japan, Nobuyuki Kunishige was the only Japanese I ever met in possession of what I have ventured to call occult or supernormal powers, and therefore able to give *inter alia* a true demonstration of the *kiai*, it does not necessarily follow that among the many thousands of present-day exponents of the Japanese martial arts there may not be some who could, if they wished, duplicate or even better the experiments described above. Indeed my attention has been called to a letter written as recently as 1954 by an American named R. E. West (3rd Dan) who studied at the new Kodokan immediately after the cessation of hostilities, to R. W. Smith of Oak Harbour, Washington, and in part quoted by him in the January 1954 issue of the *London Budokwai quarterly Bulletin Judo*. I shall confine my excerpt to the passages describing the writer's experiences with a Mr. Matsuura, 7th Dan (now deceased) and with a former President of the Kodokan named Jiro Nango, also deceased. Thus he relates that one afternoon while alone with the former,

"he demonstrated to me the ability of mental telepathy or something similar, in this manner. Sitting on his knees with his back to me and his hands together, he made his mind blank of all conscious thought. The idea was that I was to remain behind him for as long a time as I desired. Then with all the speed and power I could muster I was to grab him by the throat and pull him over backwards. I sweated it out for may be two or three minutes without making a move. Then I put all the power and speed I could into the effort. My next step was to get up from my back where I had landed in front of him. His explanation was that the action was not conscious, but rather sprang from the seat of reflex control, the *tanden*, or second brain. These things are not taught in the Judo College.

"My next experience came after I had donated money for the repair of the Kodokan. Jiro Nango (deceased) but then President, called me to his office. He was small and old and was the nephew of Kano. He was also one of Kano's first students. He thanked me for the gift, praised my ability and understanding of judo as unusual in an Occidental, then he asked whether I had any questions. I said, 'Yes, I would like to know how to develop the *tanden*'. He expressed surprise at my knowledge of its existence and said that it was not part of the regular Judo College teaching but that he would give me a demonstration of its effectiveness. Thereupon we removed our shoes and sat on our knees facing each other on the floor. At the time I weighed 175 lb. and considered myself quite strong. He weighed about 130 lb. and was old. We placed our right hands on each other's chest. At my own option I was to attempt to push him over backwards. I shoved hard, then harder, and finally with all my strength. He didn't move. Then he shoved back and I went over. He then stated that only by the power residing in the *tanden* could this be accomplished.

"Later, I questioned Mr. Koji Kikuchi about these extra powers. He was 6th rank and a College Professor at Meiji University. He said that a few could attain them. Also that in his youth he had spent two years in a Zen monastery attempting to acquire knowledge, but that he could almost reach the goal but not quite, and so gave it up. I asked him whether Dr. Kano had these powers. He said he didn't know but that he might have. I asked him whether there were many men in Japan who were able to do these things. The reply was, 'Very few'. Only a few could attain certain things. In closing regarding this, Nango was hard to throw normally because of excellent *tai-sabaki* (turning movement in judo), but when he utilized the power of the *tanden* he was impossible to throw."

CHAPTER XIII

MORE ABOUT KIAI

In previous chapters I have dealt incidentally with the part played by the mysterious force known as *kiai* and *aiki* in the production of certain phenomena connected with the martial arts, in the broad Japanese sense. The subject, however, is of so much interest and importance, since in the development of the *kiai* lies, so to speak, the kernel of military efficiency, that I have been induced to investigate a little further and to seek the views of a native specialist as to the real meaning of *kiai*. As luck would have it, while I was pursuing my own independent inquiries from Japanese teachers, a book entitled *The Art of Kiai* (in Japanese, of course), by one Kumashiro Hikotaro, was published in Tokyo, and to this source I am indebted for much valuable material reproduced in the following pages with the kind help of Mr. Umezawa who has made an excellent synopsis of the more salient points.

According to this authority, *kiai* may be described as the potential power which governs the course of human life, and the source of the energy inherent in the human race—the energy of all energies, in short. The existence of *kiai* and the ability to control it have been recognized from time immemorial, although heretofore that ability has been associated with the martial arts and regarded as a sort of monopoly of the samurai class, to which the common people might not aspire. This conception is nevertheless erroneous, for the presence of *kiai* may be detected in all human activities from politics down to chess! For the matter-of-fact Occidental the most important aspect of the inquiry must be some indication of the method by which power to make use of *kiai* can be acquired, and with the co-operation of Messrs. Hikotaro and Umezawa I hope to place the curious reader in possession of a few general instructions the efficacy of which he will be at liberty to test for himself.

As briefly pointed out in previous chapters, the word *kiai* is a compound of *ki*, meaning "mind", "will", "turn of mind", "spirit", etc. and *ai*, the contraction of the verb *awasu*, signifying "to unite". As this combination naturally suggests, it denotes a condition in which two minds are united in one in such a manner that the stronger controls the weaker. Psychologically it is the art of concentrating the whole of one's mental energy upon a single object with the determination to achieve or subdue that object. Physically it is the art of deep and prolonged breathing as will be explained more in detail hereafter. Its practical application is, so to speak, to gain a start over an opponent with whom one may chance to be face to face. *Kiai* is also sometimes spoken of as *aiki*. Although the two are one and the same thing when construed in a broad sense, yet they admit of distinction when more narrowly interpreted. Briefly *kiai* implies the active side of one's mind, whereas *aiki* has to do with its passive state. In other words, the former represents a condition in which one's *ki* or mental energy is actively concentrated upon the object in view, whereas the latter indicates a state in which this mental force is quiescent. For practical purposes there is no need to distinguish between the two. They stand to each other in much the same relation as active to latent heat. *Kiai* is thus the motive power which prompts man to an action with the strong resolve to carry it to a successful issue; it is the force which furnishes the impulse to take advantage of opportunity.

We may consider first the utility of *kiai* as applied to the martial arts. *Bushido* has its basis in mental (?moral) rectitude, and the latter is the essence of *kiai*. When one's mind is unjust *kiai* will prove of little avail. Martial arts are divided into many branches but *kiai* is the life of all; without *kiai* they cannot be carried to perfection. In the opinion of the Japanese fighting man it is not the mere concrete art, if such an expression is permissible, that enables one to win the victory; it is in *kiai* that the secret of success lies. The combatant who secures the lead over his antagonist will win, and it is not actually the art of fencing or wrestling but *kiai* that gives the combatant the power to secure that lead. Thus the late Yamoaka Tesshu, the most skilful fencing-master of his day, reveals the secret of the art of fencing in the following words: "Do not fix your mind on the attitude your rival assumes nor have it riveted on your own attitude nor on your own sword.

Instead fix your mind on your *saika tanden* (that part of the belly situated beneath the navel) and do not think either of dealing a blow at your opponent or of the latter's dealing a blow at you. Cast aside all specific designs and rush to the attack the moment you see your enemy in the act of brandishing his sword over his head".

Jujutsu (literally "soft art"), as its name implies, is based upon the principle of opposing softness or elasticity to hardness or stiffness. Its secret lies in keeping one's body full of *ki*, with elasticity in one's limbs, and in being ever on the alert to turn the strength of one's foe to one's own advantage with the minimum employment of one's own muscular force. "The soft conquers the hard", is a saying which expresses the idea of the proper use of *kiai*. Not only in fencing and jujutsu, therefore, but in all other branches of the martial arts *kiai* must be intelligently exerted if one wishes to attain the best results.

We may next consider *kiai* in connexion with the respiration. When one expels the air from the lungs one feels one's muscles and bones relax, while when one fills the lungs and abdomen with air one is conscious of the opposite phenomenon. In expelling the air one loses vigour, whereas in inhaling one gains strength. In the language of Japanese esotericism, the latter condition is called "fullness" (*jitsu*) and the former "emptiness" (*kyo*). To attack emptiness with fullness is a sure means to victory. If in the act of striking one of the combatants has his lungs full of air and the other's lungs are empty, the former is sure to win. Such, at least is the theory. Regarded in this light *kiai* may be deemed synonymous with the act of breathing. The phrase often used by Japanese fencing masters, *"Kiai wo kakeru"* (to utter the *kiai*) means to fall upon one's foe with a shout at the exact moment when the foe has exhaled his breath. The secret of *kiai* breathing lies in filling the *saika tanden* already described, instead of the chest, as we Occidentals are wont to do. What may be called deep abdominal breathing is spoken of in Japanese as *fukushiki kokyu*. There are many methods of breathing in this manner, but one of the simplest is thus described:

"Take a piece of cotton cloth about six feet long, fold it twice and pass it twice round the stomach just below the lower ribs, and fasten it tightly in that position. Then try to inhale the air deep down into your stomach. Repeat the process three or four hundred times a day, or even two or three thousand times, if you can get use to it. In so doing keep your body soft, hold your shoulders well drawn down, your back bent forward, and sit in such a manner that the tip of your nose hangs over your navel (or *saika tanden*). Accustom yourself when sitting to press the seat with your hips, as it were, and when walking to project your abdomen beyond your feet. These directions may be difficult to fulfil literally, but the idea is to regulate your movements as if you had the above-mentioned object always in view. When facing an opponent, whether in a standing or a sitting posture, look him steadfastly in the face, but do not omit even for a moment to have your mind's eye directed to your *saika tanden*, i.e. take care to breathe as already instructed and in this way you will not be disturbed by foreign objects."

What is termed *munen mushin* (literally "without idea and without mind") is an essential factor in *kiai* and can be acquired by regulating one's breathing. In this context the celebrated Buddhist priest Takuan may be quoted. He writes in his famous work *Kitsuyoshu*:

"*Munen mushin*—that is, the name of Buddha. When you open your mouth wide to expel the air you get *na*, and when you shut your mouth to inhale the air you get *mu*. When next you open your mouth you get *a*, and when again you close it you get *mi*. When again you open your mouth you get *da*, and when again you shut it you get *butsu*. Thus the thrice repeated exhalation and inhalation is equivalent to the Buddhist invocation '*Namu Amida Butsu*', which is symbolical of the letters *a* and *um*. The sound *a* is produced by opening the mouth and the sound *um* by shutting it. It may therefore be said that in the state of total absence of mind (*munen mushin*) you are always repeating the name of Buddha, even if you do not pronounce it aloud."

It will thus be seen that the secret of Buddhism is embodied in this *a um*, i.e. the art of regulating one's breathing.

Next to deep breathing the most essential physical condition of the art of *kiai* is the regulation of one's posture. The first desideratum is to keep the body soft, pliant and elastic, like rubber. To achieve this condition, again, it is necessary to concentrate one's vigour in the *saika tanden*, while keeping one's chest empty. The posture has an important bearing upon the breathing and the two must be studied concurrently. The second point to be observed is to keep the mouth closed and the chin well drawn in towards the throat. In the system of *za-zen* the student is taught to keep his ears on a line with the shoulders and his nose on a line with the navel. Here we have precisely the position required. If you keep your mouth shut and your chin drawn back, the principal muscles of the throat are made taut and the spinal column is straightened. The latter in turn gives proper vigour to the lower abdomen. The effect which one's posture exercises over one's body and mind is great. Physically the correct posture stimulates the circulation of the blood and invigorates the muscles and other organs. The mental effect is no less considerable. In the training of both the samurai and the Zen priests it has been taught from the earliest times that the mouth should be closed and the air inhaled through the nostrils so as to impart strength to the lower abdomen, or *saika tanden*. Maintenance of the posture described refreshes the mind and imbues the subject with a dignified air which is also an important factor in the art of *kiai*.

There is an old saying in the *Budo*, or "Way of the Warrior", which runs, "First, eyes; second, alacrity; third, courage; and fourth, bodily force". In *kiai*, too, great prominence is assigned to the eyes for two reasons, the first being the necessity of cultivating clear and rapid vision, and the second the help these organs give in the assumption of dignity already alluded to. Accordingly the habit of looking straight into things must be assiduously practised. The celebrated philosopher Mencius says that "the eyes are the best standards by which to judge men. When one's mind is dark the eyes are dull. Hear a man speak and look at his eyes; he cannot conceal the secrets of his soul". The eyes are the mirrors of the mental state, and few men or women with guilty consciences have clear and bright eyes. The student of martial arts and of *kiai* must therefore cultivate the habit of looking straight and steadfastly into the face of their *vis-à-vis* and of regarding every other object in the same manner without blinking.

What is called *nigiri-katami* (literally "grasping tight") signifies closing the fingers firmly with the thumb beneath. It is said that this practice will instil vigour and courage into the body and enable one to preserve presence of mind in the most trying circumstances. In all the martial arts the Japanese are prone to attach far more importance to the body below than above the waist line. It is advisable to put more strength into one's feet than into one's arms and hands. When one is startled one is sometimes deprived of the use of one's lower limbs and compelled to remain stock-still. In studying the art of *kiai* the feet must be carefully trained. A good plan is to stamp hard from time to time, to leap from side to side with the hands and arms held close to the waist; while in walking care should be taken to place the weight of the body upon the toes rather than upon the heels.

A celebrated Chinese philosopher of the Ming dynasty said: "If the mind be kept one and undivided it will accommodate itself to ten thousand varied circumstances. That is the reason why a superior man can keep his mind empty and undisturbed." These words explain the psychological aspect of the art of *kiai*. By the oneness and indivisibility of the mind is meant the unification of mental force which is an essential factor of *kiai*. The mind (*kokoro*) must always be kept in readiness to meet emergencies which may at any moment arise. Not only must you train your mind in the manner above described, but care must be taken to cultivate the habit of making good use of the mental force of your opponents. To bring your opponents under your control it is necessary to deprive them of their mind—that is to say, to distract their attention and subdue them to your own advantage. The celebrated Buddhist priest Takuan said: "Mind makes *ki* a vehicle to convey it far and wide in its active operation." Mind controls *ki*, but the latter may sometimes influence the former. When *ki* is quiet, mind also remains quiet. Mind lies hidden in one's innermost soul; *ki* operates externally to carry mind to the goal one has in view. In the art of *kiai* it is very important to cultivate and train the *ki*. In fencing and other martial arts stress is laid on the concord of mind (*ki*) and force (*chikara*).

By way of illustration let us suppose that you desire to obtain something nice. That is what in this cult is styled *kokoro*, or mind, more literally, heart. In order to get that something you stretch out your hand, or your hand reaches the object in obedience to the commands of your *kokoro*. That is what the Japanese call *ki*. When your hand reaches the object and you grasp it and draw it towards you, we have a manifestation of force, or *chikara* in Japanese. Without the help of each one of these factors nothing can ever become your own. *Kokoro* (mind) dictates action to *ki*, and *chikara* (force or strength) executes the behest of mind. The art of *kiai* deals with the cultivation of this *ki*. When *ki* is dull and weak there can be no great force to carry out the orders of mind. We Europeans say, "A strong mind in a strong body"; *kiai* implies the making of a strong body by means of a strong mind. *Kiai* hardens the entire frame rendering it invulnerable to attack, in theory at least.

Our Japanese author has so far explained that the art of *kiai* can be acquired through the culture of one's mind. At this point he quotes a few old sayings and cites a few practical examples to reveal the secret of the art and to demonstrate what it can accomplish. The following verses explain the secret of *kiai*:

"I have no parents; I make the heavens and the earth my
            parents.
I have no home; I make *saika tanden* my home.
I have no divine power; I make honesty my divine power.
I have no means; I make docility my means.
I have no magic power; I make personality my magic power.
I have neither life nor death; I make *a um* my life and death.
I have no body; I make stoicism my body.
I have no eyes; I make the flash of lightning my eyes.
I have no ears; I make sensibility my ears.
I have no limbs; I make promptitude my limbs.
I have no laws; I make self-protection my laws.
I have no strategy; I make *sakkatsu jizai* (literally "free to
            kill and free to restore to life") my
            strategy.
I have no designs; I make *kisan* (taking opportunity by the
            forelock) my designs.
I have no miracles; I make righteous laws my miracles.
I have no principles; I make adaptability to all circumstances
            (*rinkiohen*) my principles.

I have no tactics; I make *kyojitsu* (emptiness and fulness) my
    tactics.
I have no talent; I make *toi sokumyo* (ready wit) my talent.
I have no friends; I make my mind my friend.
I have no enemy; I make incautiousness my enemy.
I have no armour; I make *jin-gi* (benevolence and righteous-
    ness) my armour.
I have no castle; I make *fudoshin* (immovable mind) my castle.
I have no sword; I make *mushin* (absence of mind) my
    sword."

The secret of winning a contest lies in this, that you do not
think of winning the contest but rather think of the way in which
you may not lose the contest. You are defeated, says our author,
because you attempt to win the contest. If you are not defeated
the victory must always rest on your side. I may qualify this
observation by saying that in judo, at any rate as far as friendly
competitions are concerned, there is the draw to be reckoned
with in which neither side wins or loses, but presumably in a
fight to a finish one or other of the combatants will, in nine cases
out of ten, be defeated.

Senno Rikiu, who taught the tea ceremony in Hideyoshi's day,
was an expert in the art of *kiai*. Hideyoshi used to remark to his
retainers "You watch Rikiu making tea, and note that his entire
body is full of *kiai* leaving no room for attack." Kato Kiyomasa,
Hideyoshi's famous general who played the most important rôle
in the invasion of Korea, chancing to hear this high compliment
paid to Rikiu by his master, made up his mind to watch for an
opportunity to humiliate the *kiai* expert. One day he accompanied
his master to Rikiu's house and detecting what he regarded as a
good opening raised his fan level with his stomach on the very
point of hitting Rikiu with it. No sooner, however, had he lifted
the fan than Rikiu turned to Hideyoshi and calmly remarked,
"Your Excellency has a praiseworthy retainer in Kiyomasa," and
then he fixed upon Kiyomasa a steady glance which deprived the
renowned warrior of breath. We are told that in this case Kiyomasa had actually found an opening for attack, but his mind was
relaxed the instant he thought of his coming success, and thus
Rikiu secured a lead and overpowered him with *kiai*.

Yagyu Matajuro was a son of the celebrated fencing master Yagyu Hida-no-Kami, who was the tutor to the Tokugawa Shoguns in feudal days. He incurred the displeasure of his father and was turned out of the house. Matajuro repented of his misconduct and made up his mind to amend. Accordingly he studied the art of fencing under a well-known master for a number of years in rather difficult circumstances. He attained great proficiency, and returning to Yedo (the present Tokyo) called on one Okubo Hikozaemon with a plea that the latter should use his influence with Matajuro's father to remove the ban of disinheritance so that he might in due course succeed his father as fencing master to the Shogun. Hikozaemon was very fond of the wayward son of his old friend, and readily consented to act as intermediary in order to effect a reconciliation. At the same time he asked Matajuro to give him a demonstration of his skill in fence, for he knew that an assurance on this point would carry more weight with the father than anything else. Matajuro at once consented and proposed that somebody should be called in to act as his opponent, but as there was nobody else in the house at the time he finally told Hikozaemon that he would give him a demonstration of *kiai* instead. So saying he looked out into the garden where he saw a few sparrows perched on the branch of a tall pine-tree, and fixing his steadfast gaze on the birds gave utterance to the *kiai* shout, whereupon the sparrows fell to the ground insensible. When he relaxed the *kiai* the birds regained consciousness and flew away. Hikozaemon was struck with admiration on seeing this wonderful feat and had no difficulty thereafter in effecting the young man's reconciliation with his father as promised. This particular feat is known in the Japanese fencing schools as *toate-no-jutsu*, or "the art of striking at a distance".

Yamamoto Kausuke, a celebrated strategist who served Takeda Shingen prior to Hideyoshi's invasion of Korea, was one day passing through a mountain forest when a pack of hungry wolves suddenly made their appearance and surrounded him. On the impulse of the moment Kausuke intended to cut the animals down singly, and to that end placed his hand on the hilt of his sword, but on second thoughts refrained, as he concluded that it would be a disgrace to the honour of a samurai to use such a weapon against these animals. Instead he calmly clenched his fists with the thumbs held underneath the other fingers, in the so-called *nigiri-katami* style mentioned in a previous chapter, and coolly passed through the pack of wolves. The wolves appeared to be taken aback by the composure and dignified air of Kausuke and took to their heels.

Many anecdotes are told of the wonderful feats performed by experts in the art of *kiai*. The grasping of red-hot irons without visible injury to the hands and other performances of this description are ascribed to the practical application of *kiai*, which exerts itself not only between living men but equally upon inanimate objects through a delicate psychological process.

Our Japanese author makes a closing reference to the *kuji goshin-hō*, or method of protecting one's body by means of the nine ideographs, which occupies a very important place in the teachings of the secret Shingon sect of Buddhism. This method is, in fact, none other than a part of *kiai*.

The *kuji*, or nine ideographs, comprise *rin, hei, tō, sha, kai, jin, retsu, zai* and *zen*, and the method of practising the art may be explained as follows:

Rin: Close both hands, and then release and stretch out the index fingers one against the other. Bring the connected fingers close to your breast and repeat the word *rin* three times. Then lift the closed hands above your head and there separate them.

Hei: Close the little and ring fingers and then stretch out the middle fingers one against the other. Put the index fingers underneath the middle fingers and repeat *hei* three times, and then separate your fingers.

Tō: Bring your open hands close together so that the tips of the fingers touch each other lightly, and repeat the word *tō* three times.

Sha: Bring your open hands together so that the finger tips touch each other closely, and repeat the word *sha* three times.

Kai: Intersect firmly the ten fingers and fold them tightly, but leaving the two index fingers stretched out erect and one against the other. Repeat *kai* three times.

Jin: Intersect the ten fingers inwards so that they are folded well within the palms, and then repeat *jin* three times.

Retsu: Close your left hand with the palm turned to your right. Release the index finger, extend it upwards; place the thumb over the lower joint of your middle finger; bring the hand close to your breast; seize the tip of the index finger of your left hand with your right hand and repeat *retsu* three times.

Zai: Stretch out the fingers of both hands and connect the tips of the index fingers and thumbs so as to form a lozenge, and in this manner bring them close to the face and repeat *zai* three times.

Zen: Close your left hand with the palm turned upwards, bring it close to your breast, and there cover it with your right hand with the fingers extended. Repeat *zen* three times.

After going through the above forms in rapid succession intersect the fingers of both hands, lift them above your head, and repeat *wō* three times, after which you are at liberty to unloosen your hands.

This process, it is believed, will annihilate the forces of evil and danger and thus guard one's body against all possible perils. This art was widely practised by the samurai in the old feudal days. We may assume that its efficacy lay less in some occult virtue inherent in the ideographs cited than in the habit of mental concentration and continuity which might be fostered by constant repetition of these formulas. I accept no responsibility but merely reproduce them to complete what at best is but an imperfect survey of a highly interesting subject.

CHAPTER XIV

THE ZEN CULT IN JAPAN

USE and abuse are inseparable from all physical and intellectual activities, and the Japanese cult of Zen is no exception to the rule. But, on the other hand, that it embodies a great deal of very practical value to the student is a statement hardly likely to be gainsaid by those who have had the opportunity of investigating its claims and of noting the many illustrious Japanese who do not hesitate to attribute their successful achievements to the moral and intellectual qualities engendered by its cultivation. The roster of Zen adherents is strikingly comprehensive. Whereas in the past the Zen propaganda may be said to have been confined to the higher classes, the nobility, the priesthood, and the samurai, in these more democratic days efforts are not spared to bring its alleged benefits within the reach of the commonalty so that while on the one hand you are likely to be duly impressed by the knowledge that Togo, Oyama, the late General Kodama and scores of other notables are or have been disciples of the Zen cult, you may on the other at any moment be startled to learn that your office-boy is in quest of mental concentration in the same quarter.

As a method of moral and intellectual culture Zen has from time immemorial been studied in Japan among the samurai class, to which latter circumstance, no doubt, may be ascribed the common belief that the secrets of all branches of the martial arts cannot be acquired without a thorough knowledge of Zen. It is, however, open to question whether Zen has really anything to teach the samurai under this head. I may remind the reader that my old judo teacher, Mr. Kunishige, was inclined to treat with ridicule the excessive claims of the more fanatical Zen disciples whose zeal disposes them to undervalue knowledge of the martial arts *per se* in a world from which it is impossible wholly to eliminate the appeal to physical superiority, not to say violence. It should, of course, be added that (*vide* chapter on *kiai*) among Japanese fighting men the connexion between the spiritual and the

140

"NŌ" DANCE, STYLED "MORI HISA"

A GIRL "NŌ" DANCER

physical in development of the highest offensive and defensive efficiency is more consistently insisted on than in other parts of the world.

No doubt the proneness of the Japanese masses to associate Zen with skill in the martial arts was in no small measure due to the intellectual superiority of the Buddhist priests of old over the average samurai. As in the West, book-learning in the Japanese Middle Ages was virtually a monopoly of the priesthood, for the samurai were for the most part too constantly engaged in the internecine strife which prevailed at that epoch to find leisure for the pursuit of letters. But although their intellectual inferiority seems to have been admitted, they would not so readily yield to the priesthood in the matter of moral worth. As a code of ethics *bushido* probably exercised considerable influence over the minds of the more refined types of *bushi*, and it may therefore be surmised that the practice of attending the monasteries in order to receive instruction from the monks of Zen was adopted by the samurai less as an acknowledgement of their ghostly tutors' mission to reform their conduct or of the value of Zen as an aid to their beloved martial arts than as an admission of the intellectual predominance of the priesthood of that day. It is an undoubted fact that contemporary works on the secrets of the martial arts are written in the somewhat vague and ambiguous style affected by the Zen priests. But this circumstance cannot rightly be held to prove that knowledge of the secrets of the martial arts was due to Zen but rather that the samurai authors, who had been taught composition by the Zen priests, quite naturally copied their teachers' style when they sought to express themselves in literary form. In this way, then, the belief grew up that the secrets of the martial arts could be ascertained only by means of Zen learning. Still, the fact cannot be denied that Zen has largely influenced the Japanese masters of the martial arts right down to our own days. With the downfall of feudalism popular interest in Zen witnessed a temporary decline which has given way to an extraordinary revival among all classes of the people.

At the time of writing these lines there were in existence over twenty associations, composed of noblemen, politicians, medical men, scholars, bankers, business men, students—in short, all sorts and conditions of both sexes—whose special object was the study of Zen. Lectures on Zen were delivered on fixed days in many of the Buddhist monasteries, and were attended by large gatherings of enthusiasts eager to penetrate the mysteries of the cult. Japanese friends of mine who have at one time or another listened to these discourses admit that replete as they are with citations from the Buddhist sacred writings they are apt to tax the intelligence of men of ordinary literary culture and that their profound meaning eludes the grasp of those who are not well versed in Buddhism. In the following pages I make no pretence to furnish a complete exposition of the Zen doctrines; all I can do is to lay before my readers a general outline of its more distinctive features. For a more detailed and authoritative survey of this important subject I would refer the curious to the brilliant and erudite works of Mr. Christmas Humphreys, Q.C., founder of the Buddhist Society, London, in 1924. Among his many books is a special volume devoted to Zen Buddhism.

ZEN AND ZENSHU

Zen must not be confounded with *Zenshu* which is simply one of the numerous sects into which Buddhism split up after the death of Siddhartha, the Buddha. As is well known the Buddhist teaching falls into two broad divisions which the Japanese term respectively *Daijo* (*Mahayana*, or esoteric Buddhism) and *Shojo*, or exoteric Buddhism. Denominational strife is so bitter that even the claims of *Mahayana* are denied by many, while the followers of *Mahayana* look upon *Shojo* with profound contempt. The controversy continued after the transmigration of Buddhism to Chinese soil where schism became more marked than ever. *Shojo* alone was composed of twenty or more sects each of which slavishly adhered to a particular sermon out of all the sermons preached at different times and places and to different classes by Siddhartha during the fifty years of his life. The *Zenshu* is of comparatively later origin.

The history of Buddhism tells us that when Siddhartha was preaching his gospel at Ryozen one of the devotees presented him with a bunch of flowers called *konparage*. Siddhartha simply laid the gift on his head and pinched the blossoms without uttering a

word, to the bewilderment of an assemblage which is said to
have numbered 80,000. With a solitary exception not one of the
disciples understood what the teacher meant. This exception,
Makakayo, is said to have looked up into the teacher's face and to
have smiled a smile full of significance. The incident is referred to
in Buddhist writings in a phrase which the Japanese render
"nenge misho", meaning literally "pinching the blossoms and
smiling", and conveying the great truth that "Buddha alone can
impart (knowledge) to Buddha" (*"Yui Butsu yo Butsu"*). What
was unintelligible to the multitude was quite clear to Makakayo. To
avoid misunderstanding I ought frankly to add that Siddhartha's
action in pinching the blossom conveys no more to me than it did
to the vulgar herd. We are further informed that Siddhartha was
very pleased when he noticed the smile and declared that he
would transmit to Makakayo the great secret of the Buddhist
doctrine. After the death of Siddhartha, Makakayo's influence
predominated. He became Siddhartha's successor and was
regarded as the fountain-head of Buddhism. Makakayo was
succeeded by Ananda who in turn gave place to Stona Washu,
and so on until the famous Dharma made his appearance in the
twenty-eighth generation. Until then the belief had remained
free from denominationalism. Dharma, in compliance with the
will of his predecessor, paid a visit to the Middle Kingdom during
the reign of the Emperor Wu of the Liang dynasty, and there
found that Buddhism had been allowed to split up into many
sects which were incessantly engaged in controversial warfare,
then at its height. With a view to restoring harmony Dharma
preached his famous *"Furyu monji"*, literally, "No scribe in
writing", by which he meant that the truths of Buddhism do not
lie in the words of Buddhist books nor can they be committed
to writing; they must be communicated direct from heart to
heart. This teaching of Dharma gave birth to yet another sect
which has since become known under the style of *Zenshu*, or Zen
sect. By *Zen* is connoted the great and fundamental truth of
Buddhism which is by no means a monopoly of the Zen sect but
actually the common property of all Buddhist believers. For this
reason Zen should not be confounded with the Zen sect on account
of identity of nomenclature.

WHAT IS ZEN?

The next question which arises is, What exactly is Zen? The task of furnishing a lucid and sufficiently comprehensive reply has baffled many an eminent teacher of Buddhism. Collating the best available authorities I shall attempt to explain the modern conception of its most vital traits. As already stated, Zen is supposed to denote the fundamental truth which pervades all the sects of Buddhism. The word zen is a contraction of the Sanskrit zen-na which is rendered "silent meditation" (jo-ryo). It describes a state of mind free from all worldly passions and concentrated on the examination of one's inward self. Thus Zen has for its prime object the cultivation of the ability to bring mental perturbation under immediate control. Zen is the pure product of India. It was widely practised by the Brahmins long before Siddhartha saw the light and it seems that in his early days the great teacher himself practised the Brahminical form of Zen. This circumstance gave an impulse to the development of Zen to a degree undreamed of by the Brahmins. When Siddhartha founded his system he included Zen in the formulæ of religious austerities to be observed by his followers as a practical means of dispelling illusion and arriving at a clear perception of the Great Truth. Zen therefore claims the highest place in all the austerities prescribed by Buddhism.

ZEN AND ZA-ZEN

The word Za-zen is used to denote the practical method of observing these austerities. The first word Za in the foregoing compound is defined in one of the Buddhist scriptures as "total absence of passions amid all external influences". Apart from this philosophical definition it may be stated that the word Za (to sit) means the posture assumed in sitting. Za-Zen may therefore be described as the manner of sitting when engaged in the practice of Zen austerities. The formula known as Kekka fuza is described in the scripture named Fukun-za-zen-gi and is generally followed by those who practise Zen. This formula is rendered:

"After assuming a squatting posture place your right foot on your left thigh and your left foot on your right thigh. The place your right hand on your left foot and join the palms of both hands with the thumbs erect. Sit upright; do not lean either to the right or left or backwards or forwards. Keep your ears on an even line with your shoulders and your nose in a vertical line with your navel. Keep your mouth firmly closed, lip to lip and teeth to teeth, the tongue well drawn up towards the palate. Keep your eyes open. Sanitary rules should never be neglected when these austerities are being observed. A Buddhist work entitled *Za-zen Yojin-ki* conveys a warning in this regard which reads: 'See that your garments are well washed, for dirt is injurious to health and may prove a hindrance to your religious culture. Insufficient clothing, food and sleep are also causes of failure. Do not eat raw foods or anything that is tough or impure since gastric troubles may arise from this source. Nor should you become addicted to high living which is not only injurious to health but excites the desires unduly. Take food not because of its flavour but merely to sustain life. Do not practise *Za-zen* immediately after meals but allow an interval to elapse before doing so!' "

These lines, written as they were many centuries ago, convey wise counsel as true in these days of medical advancement as in the infancy of science.

The primary object of Zen being, as already explained, to get rid of or subdue one's worldly passions in order to obtain a clear perception of the Great Truth, its directions should be observed at all times and in all places. The prescribed formula of *Za-zen* should not be regarded as the only way of attaining the desired goal, while on the other hand it must not be discarded as useless. On the contrary, the teachers of Zen maintain that this formula is the surest and easiest means whereby ordinary mortals can acquire mental tranquillity. The disciple is warned against merely slavish adherence to the formula which, in too many cases, is manifested by persons who take up the study of Zen for the sole purpose of being in the fashion.

ZEN AND ITS CULTURE

Assuming Zen to be the realization of true Buddhism, there is no royal road to its culture. Zen can be acquired by faith, the followers of the cult contending that only through implicit belief in Buddha is it possible to develop the mind in the right way.

In the Zen priesthood the novices usually begin their studies with avowal of the Strong Determination known as the Four Great Desires (*Shi-daigan*) viz.:

"Innumerable is the populace, but I declare my intention to save it in its entirety. Inexhaustible are our worldly passions, but I avow my intention to destroy them all. Countless are the Scriptures, but I avow my intention to learn them all. Insuperable is Buddhism, but I avow my intention to attain it."

The novice must first gain a clear perception of the Great Truth before venturing to teach others the road to salvation. Gratuitous loquacity is frowned upon. Says one celebrated sage: "Don't carry your learning on the tip of your nose; keep it rather buried deeply within your *saika tanden*." Again, "Commit no evil, do only good, and preserve the purity of your heart and will." If your mind be pure and your daily conduct fair and just, then without the least overt attempt to be so you will be at one with Buddha. Buddhism demands a stoicism of its own. If, say the sages, you keep aloof from mundane fame and the lusts of the flesh and are inspired by a firm resolve to attain the Great Truth, the gates of stoicism will be opened to you. By dint of perseverance you will be able to become a transcendental man in whom the ego emerges into stoicism. True stoicism implies the entire abandonment of the ego and the advent of the mind into the Great Truth of the universe. This, we are told, is the true doctrine of Buddhism and Zen culture has for its object the elevation of the mind to this pitch of lofty transcendentalism.

The mysterious connexion between Zen and the esotericism underlying not only the Japanese martial arts but the more harmless and essentially aesthetic accomplishments comprising flower arrangement (*ikebana*), the tea ceremony (*cha-no-yu*), and the fine arts generally, has been admirably analyzed in a small volume entitled "Zen in the Art of Archery", by a German scholar named Eugen Herrigel, printed originally in German but an excellent translation of which by R. F. C. Hull was published by Pantheon

Books Inc of New York in 1953 together with a valuable introduction by the veteran Japanese Professor Daisetz T. Suzuki, reputed to be the greatest world authority on the subject. In his introduction Professor Suzuki points out that

"one of the most significant features we notice in the practice of archery and in fact of all the arts as they are studied in Japan and probably also in other Far Eastern countries is that they are not intended for utilitarian purposes only or for purely aesthetic enjoyments, but are a means to train the mind, indeed to bring it into contact with reality. Archery is therefore not practised solely for hitting the target: the swordsman does not wield the sword just for the sake of outdoing his opponent; the dancer does not dance just to perform certain rhythmical movements of the body. The mind has first to be attuned to the Unconscious. If one really wishes to be master of an art, technical knowledge is not enough. One has to transcend technique so that the art becomes an 'artless art' growing out of the Unconscious. In the case of archery, the hitter and the hit are no longer two opposing objects, but are one reality. The archer ceases to be conscious of himself as the one who is engaged in hitting the bull's eye which confronts him. This state of unconsciousness is realized only when, completely empty and rid of the self, he becomes one with the perfecting of his technical skill, though there is in it something of a quite different order which cannot be attained by any progressive study of the art. What differentiates Zen most characteristically from all other teachings, religious, philosophical, or mystical, is that it never goes out of our daily life, yet with all its practicalness and concreteness Zen has something in it which makes it stand aloof from the scene of wordly sordidness and restlessness."

The author himself, who underwent a six-year course of instruction in archery under one of the greatest Masters of this art, emphasizes at the outset that

"by archery in the traditional sense, which he esteems as an art and honours as a national heritage, the Japanese does not understand a sport but, strange as this may sound at first, a religious ritual. And consequently by the 'art' of archery he does not mean the ability of the sportsman which can be controlled more or less by bodily exercise, but an ability whose origin is to be sought in spiritual exercises and whose aim consists in hitting a spiritual goal, so that fundamentally the marksman aims at himself and may even succeed in hitting himself.''

None the less, despite what superficially regarded might to the "realistic" Western mind seem immersion in a welter of abstraction, the author of the book in question was before the end of his instruction afforded ocular proof that the "spirituality" of Zen underlying the art of archery could at call be translated into the "actuality" of hitting a tangible target and that too under conditions in all probability never hitherto imposed in our more matter of fact West. The master's demonstration was so astounding that I feel justified in quoting the author's description of it.

"The practice hall was brightly lit. The Master told me to put a taper, long and thin as a knitting-needle, in the sand in front of the target but not to switch on the light in the target-stand. It was so dark that I could not even see its outline, and if the tiny flame of the taper had not been there, I might perhaps have guessed the position of the target, though I could not have made it out with any precision. The Master 'danced' the ceremony. His first arrow shot out of dazzling brightness into deep night. I knew from the sound that it had hit the target. The second arrow was a hit, too. When I switched on the light in the target I discovered to my amazement that the first arrow was lodged full in the middle of the black, while the second arrow had splintered the butt of the first and ploughed through the shaft before embedding itself beside it. I did not dare to pull the arrows out separately but carried them back together with the target. The Master surveyed them critically. 'The first shot', he then said, 'was no great feat, you may well think, but because after all these years I am so familiar with my target-stand that I must know even in the pitch darkness where the target is. That may be so, and I won't try to pretend otherwise.

But the second arrow which hit the first—what do you make of that? I at any rate know that it is not "I" who must be given credit for this shot. "It" shot and "It" made the hit. Let us bow to the goal as before the Buddha!' "

SOME CELEBRATED ZEN PRIESTS

Below I cite some concrete examples of celebrated priests whose names adorn the pages of religious history on account of their assiduous cultivation of their mental faculties.

Shoyo Daishi was the son of Lord Kuga Michichika Naidaijin. He was a precocious child. At the age of eight he lost his beloved mother and it is recorded that the sight of the thin and constantly vanishing streak of smoke from the incense burned by her death-bed moved him to deep meditation on the evanescent nature of human life and inclined him towards Buddhism. A few years later he was distressed to learn that he was to succeed to the headship of the illustrious house of his father, for worldly pomp and glory held out no charm for him. At thirteen he secretly left home and entered a monastery at the foot of Mount Hiyei in the suburbs of Kyoto. Arrived at man's estate he proceeded to China to prosecute his studies. While staying at a famous monastery at Tondo-san he chanced one day to be out walking in the vicinity of a Buddhist temple, where he noticed an old man engaged in the work of spreading mushrooms on the ground to dry in the burning sun, the month being June and the heat excessive. Shoyo Daishi was moved to compassion at sight of the veteran's frail form bent and decrepit with age. Approaching the old man he accosted him and asked:

"Why don't you get somebody else to do the work for you?"

"Another man is not myself," was the curt reply of the old man who did not so much as turn his head in the direction of the first speaker.

"You had better wait until the sun goes down and it gets cooler." ventured the young priest. "You may injure your health."

The old man promptly answered, "I have no time to wait."

These words greatly impressed the young priest, as they forcibly demonstrated recognition of the mortality of mankind. All men

must die one day or other. If we have something to do we should
do it now while we are alive and able to do it. We have indeed no
time to wait, as the old man said. Shoyo Daishi bore this precept
in mind and thanks to years of study and application in course of
time he became celebrated. It should be added that Shoyo Daishi
is the posthumous name of this priest who during his lifetime was
known as Dogen. The name Shoyo Daishi was conferred upon
him as recently as 1880, after the manner of Japan. He lived from
1200 to 1253. The word "Daishi" (*vide* Papinot) means literally
"great master" or "saint" in Sinico-Japanese, and is an honorific
title added to the posthumous name of certain bonzes considered
as the holiest or most learned, the practice being imported from
China. According to the same authority, it was the Emperor
Seiwa who first conferred this title in 866 upon the celebrated
bonze Sauche (Dengyo Daishi) and upon Ennin (Jikaku Daishi).

Another celebrated priest, known posthumously as Josai
Daishi, studied under Tettsu Daishi when young. One morning his
teacher put to him and fellow students for exposition the phrase,
"Ordinary mind—it is Buddhism." While his fellow students were
puzzling over this seemingly paradoxical utterance Josai alone
said, "I understand." When asked how and what he understood
he made the famous reply, "A black ball ran rolling in the pitch
black night." It is gratifying to be told that these words may be
interpreted to signify that in the midst of profound darkness there
exists never-ceasing activity. Analogously the Great Truth of
Buddhism lies where the ego has emerged into stoicism. The truth
can be taught in the natural walks of life, and not in the assumption of knowledge and vain conceit. Josai's teacher was evidently
pleased with this answer, and pressed him to say something more
about it, when Josai added without hesitation, "When I meet
tea I take tea, and when I meet rice I take rice." This additional
reply still further pleased the teacher who there and then predicted
that his young pupil was destined to spread the doctrine of his
sect widely through the world. I must again remind the reader that
I am not personally responsible for the cryptic character of many of
these Zen pronouncements. I am simply acting the rôle of a medium
of communication.

The expressions *kōan* and *sanzen* may fittingly be quoted in this
context. The former means the practice of *Za-zen* and *kōan* (liter-

ally, "public exposition") is a commentary on the words and deeds of the famous Buddhist teachers. The *kōan* is couched in the briefest possible terms so that copious annotation is needed to elucidate its meaning. The most popular compilation of the *kōan* is the *Hekiganshu* of Setchu Zenshi, with notes by Engo Zenshi. This is perhaps the oldest publication of its kind extant. The *Shoyo-roku*, compiled by Wanshi Zenshi, with notes by Mansho Zenshi, is a later publication but no less valued by Zen priests.

As a sample of the kind of thing Zen enthusiasts are supposed to be capable of digesting I will quote from the *Hekiganshu* a *kōan* with accompanying annotation thereon. The *kōan* reads, "*Dharma kakuzen*" which, when literally interpreted, means "The clearness of Dharma." The annotator on this *kōan* writes as follows: "Emperor Wu of the Liang dynasty asked Dharma, 'What is the first principle of Buddhism?' to which Dharma replied, 'No Buddha.' The Emperor again asked, 'Who is it that sits opposite me?' Dharma said, 'Don't know.' The Emperor failed to catch the point. Dharma left the Emperor and, crossing the river (Yangtse), went to the Shobin monastery where he sat still facing the wall for nine years." One feels greatly tempted to add that such a proceeding was the minimum reparation he could make for his exasperating ambiguity which, if the truth were known, served as a convenient cloak for ignorance in those days as now. However, the fact remains that the *kōan* are looked up to by Zen priests as instruments by means of which the ego can be eradicated in order to gain a clear perception of the Great Truth. While, therefore, Zen in its highest form aims at transcendentalism, *Za-zen* may be styled the vehicle which carries the disciple to the desired goal.

The most enviable results of *Za-zen* are to be seen in a physical and mental composure apparently proof against internal and external impact. The habit of assuming the posture described earlier in this chapter and of remaining thus plunged in profound meditation for hours together, either at home or in special apartments in certain monasteries, is said to confer upon those who have cultivated it successfully the power to preserve an imperturbable coolness in the face of the most imminent peril. We are told, for example, that disciples of Zen and *Za-zen* among the officers who fought during the Russo-Japanese war never for a moment lost their absolute calm in the midst of an inferno of shot and shell.

If these contentions can be substantiated, then, as already remarked, *Za-zen* assuredly has its bright side. The least desirable aspect of the cult, on the other hand, must be pronounced a species of intellectual priggishness nothing less than irritating to the Occidental. I have met Zen students in my time who quite unconsciously inspired me with a desire to kick them round the block. From this type of "intellectual" it is impossible to obtain even a remotely intelligible idea of what Zen and *Za-zen* are. To all your inquiries he replies in terms of stereotyped vagueness which, as already intimated, are a convenient, if not entirely impenetrable, mask for ignorance. One young man, pallid and anaemic, whom I once questioned on the subject, smiled a superior sort of smile and said, "I will illustrate. I clap my hands. Where has the sound gone?"

I sought to furnish an explanation on the basis of Western physics, but he would have none of it. It ought to be added that while he dismissed all my suggestions with an air of lofty contempt, he made no serious attempt to give me the Zen interpretation of the phenomenon. Chance encounters of this kind tend to breed the suspicion that the Zen disciples are wasting valuable time on the pondering of wholly useless problems which can have no bearing upon real life. A good deal doubtless depends upon the individual character of the Zen priests in charge of the courses of meditation prescribed for secular students. If these men are of high mental and moral character, the student will probably derive practical advantage from the discipline to which he voluntarily submits. Otherwise the consequences for the immature intellect can be only confusion worse confounded.

CHAPTER XV

THE JAPANESE EQUIVALENT OF THE YOGI

MANY writers on Japan have laid special stress upon the essential materialism of the rising generation and its devotion to Herbert Spencer. In the main this appraisement of the intellectual attitude of the student classes is not without justification. On the other hand, however, the point should not be lost sight of that Japan today is in a state of transition, mental, moral, political, and even physical. Intellecturally the student classes, young and old, are fickle in their allegiances, and for some time to come it will be impossible to expect the genuine naturalization of any foreign school of philosophical thought or the absolute predominance of any one school of purely indigenous origin, if such can be said to exist in the full sense of the words. Nor can it be declared that this nebulous subjective attitude is without its special value. Whatever its negative disadvantages it at least makes for the spirit of tolerance. The Japanese mind always has been and is today unusually susceptible to new impressions. Here, no doubt, we have another illustration of the law of compensations in that the Japanese mind has rarely shown itself to be creative in its manifestations, so that if, in addition to this defect, it were also loath to draw inspiration from the outside, stagnation would be its inevitable portion. The erratic contortions of the Japanese mind are in consonance with the Buddhist maxim which in Japanese reads tersely:

"Sho gyō mu-jō

Ze shō meppō,

Sho metsu metsu i

Jaku metsu i raku";

which Professor Imbrie has rendered:

All phenomena are impermament;
This is the law of becoming and perishing.
Becoming and perishing shall perish completely:
And the calm perishing (i.e. Nirvana) will be bliss."

In certain fundamentals, no doubt, Japanese character is a fixed quantity, but those who have had the privilege of witnessing the whole or only a part of the country's achievements during the Meiji era would be guilty of unpardonable presumption were they to predict the phases through which it is destined to pass during the next fifty or hundred years. It is not alone in Japan that the signs of ethical and economic unrest are insistent; almost everywhere it is the same. And while it may be true that Young Japan is still groping for a moral sheet-anchor I must protest emphatically against the exasperating and intolerable spirit of theological snobbishness expressed in the pages of a certain missionary publication to the effect that because the mass of the Japanese people is still "unevangelized" it is living "without God and hope in the world". These reflections may seem a trifle foreign to the subject which I am about to discuss and I venture the opinion merely for what it may be worth, but that opinion is that those who flatter themselves that the day will ever dawn when the Japanese as a whole will profess Christianity imagine a vain thing and are pursuing a will-o'-the-wisp. They will dabble in Christianity as they have dabbled and are dabbling in numerous other "anities", "isms" and "ologies"; but the sort of Christianity which will ultimately be evolved in Japan will have very little in common with its various prototypes of the Occident. The symptoms of schism are not wanting, but at the moment we are seeing only the beginning; the end is not yet and is never likely to be. Indeed it must be said that the calamitous post-war failure of denominational Christianity to substantiate in practice its claim to be regarded as a world religion and therefore exempt from the taboos and inhibitions of narrow nationalism in the hour of crisis is not calculated to impress the critical Japanese mind in its favour. So much for that.

My immediate purpose is to furnish a popular account of some phenomena which are not at all in keeping with the widespread idea that the Japanese are steeped in materialism or that their only salvation from materialism lies in Christianity. Already in previous chapters I have endeavoured to illustrate the rôle which a sort of transcendentalism plays in the otherwise physical processes of fighting with lethal weapons, from which it will appear that, whatever the materialism of one class of philosophical speculation in Japan, the Japanese mind has succeeded in "spiritualizing" the martial arts to an extent undreamed of by Europe and America.

Now, apart from the martial arts it is curious to observe that belief in occultism among educated persons is very real in Japan. Irrespective of the phenomena of the late Mrs. Mifune, the late Mrs. Nagao, and their numerous imitators and rivals, with which the West is familiar on its own account, closer inquiry reveals the presence in society of a type of occult operator called by the Japanese *sennin*—a word which I am inclined to render as "yogi" or "adept". While some of these yogi are known to pass their lives in the forests and mountains, cut off as far as possible from communion with their kind, there are others who, although they have attained a high degree of occult development by persistent introspection, are yet content to pass the rest of their lives in the busy haunts of men and even in pursuance of normal avocations, with the exception of periodical retirements for the recuperation of their occult faculties. It must be said, too, that while the Japanese yogi may not reach the heights which are supposed to have been successfully scaled by the Hindu mahatma, he has never sunk so low as the fakir who immerses himself in filth and practises abominations in order to cultivate the lower possibilities of *hatha-yoga*. How far removed is the Japanese *sennin* from the degradation of the fakir will appear from the following anecdotes which I have taken direct from Japanese sources.

In Nihon-bashi, the very heart of Tokyo, which is never free from the deafening clang of the electric tram, the raucous "honk honk" of the motor-car, the ringing of telephones, and the smoke of factories—emblematical of the triumphs of the century—there lived in my day a well-known Japanese yogi. If one crossed the tramline at Sandai-cho, turned to the west and proceeded a little farther up a narrow lane, one reached a hydrant round which were usually grouped a number of servant-girls engrossed in idle chatter. Immediately opposite the hydrant there used to stand a neat little house with a latticed front door over which was suspended a wooden name-plate bearing the unpretentious inscription "Miyagishima Tomekichi."

Most Western readers are prone to associate the conception of a yogi with a habitation in the heart of some mountain range, and to picture the yogi himself as an old man clad in primitive garments, his form attenuated to an incredible degree, and his snow-white hair and beard of a length and thickness calculated to baffle the ministrations of the most efficient safety razor. It may thus seem incongruous that a yogi should be found housed in the midst of such bustle. Moreover the very name of Tomekichi is more apt to suggest a carpenter or some other kind of artisan than a mystic possessed of abnormal powers. Nevertheless, these considerations cannot alter the fact that this particular Tomekichi, if report did not lie, had fully earned the title which he wore, as the following story proves:

A good many years ago this yogi heard by accident that a certain foreign missionary in Tsukiji, a district of Tokyo, was a great authority on miracles, and in order to ascertain his view on the subject the yogi paid him a visit. At the outset considerable difficulty was experienced on either side owing to the yogi's ignorance of English and the missionary's ignorance of Japanese, as he was a new arrival in the country; but by dint of eloquent pantomime, so it is said, the yogi succeeded in communicating to the missionary the object of his call. In the course of this original interview the yogi instinctively realized that the missionary differed from him in his understanding of a miracle. Eager to convince him of his error the yogi closed his eyes for a second as though seeking inspiration, but an instant later rose and at once proceeded to propound his views in fluent English, of which tongue a moment before he had had no knowledge whatsoever! The missionary was thunderstruck. The yogi continued his discourse for some time, now and then replying to questions put to him by the dumb-founded foreigner. At the close of his remarks the yogi sat down again and began to stare about him with an air of amazement, as though he had just awoke from a profound slumber, nor could he speak or understand a word of the language in which he had just been expounding miracles with such perfect ease. Once more his only recourse was pantomime. The surprise of the foreign

HOSHO SHIN
Impersonating "Benkei"

SCENE FROM "SAKURA–SHIGURE"

missionary beggars description. The yogi himself was quite unconscious of the miracle he had himself performed and shared the missionary's astonishment when informed of what had taken place. Another story told of Mr. Tomekichi is that, in compliance with a similar unconscious inspiration, he once conducted an argument with a famous Buddhist priest on a subject with which he was normally unfamiliar, and completely routed his antagonist.

At the time of writing Mr. Tomekichi was on the wrong side of fifty. He wore a beard, his hair was thickly streaked with grey, and his expression was somewhat stern. At one time he lived in seclusion, sustaining life on fruits, roots and leaves of young plants. During this interval he allowed his hair to grow without restraint. The people thought he had gone mad and efforts were made by his family to dissuade him from this course of action but in vain. However, in my day in Japan he lived much the same ostensibly as the rest of his fellows, if we except these occasional manifestations of occult power.

A glance at a map of Japan will inform a conscientious investigator that the plain of Musashino gradually rises from the boundary of Chichiku and Kai until it connects itself with a mountain range which stretches across the province of Musashi and Kai with an offshoot running into the province of Shinano in a northerly direction. This large expanse of country appears to be destitute of human habitation. Rising dominant above all rivals is the Kumotori-yama, its greatest altitude being 7,000 feet. Not far from Kumotori stands another mountain called Hakuseki which, though not so lofty as Kumotori, is considerably more precipitous; and at the summit of Hakuseki stands a Shinto shrine, twenty-four feet square and built of plain hinoki wood. The galvanized iron roofing of this edifice is not artistic or in harmony with the environment, but even this false note cannot detract from the impressiveness of the scene as a whole, for the shrine is situated in the midst of a thick and gloomy pine-wood which for centuries has never been touched by the sacrilegious axe. When the wind rises up from the valley below and soughs mournfully through the dense foliage of the ancient grove the effect is weird in the extreme and fully calculated to attune the human mind to a pitch at which belief in the possibility of supernormal forces becomes almost instinctive.

This mountain lies within easy reach from Tokyo. Alighting at Himadawada, the terminus of the Aone line of the Government railway, and proceeding along the hilly road for about fifteen miles on foot, the traveller comes to a country town named Hikawa. Beyond this point he must pursue a narrow and difficult track which skirts the bank of the Hihara river until he reaches the foot of Hakuseki. The ascent of the latter, which calls for two days of easy climbing, brings the traveller to the precincts of the Shinto shrine referred to. In point of antiquity the shrine has little of which to boast, its foundation dating from about ninety years ago. It was built by a simple peasant named Nagasaki Hichirozaemon, who believed he was obeying a divine injunction conveyed to him in a dream; but this peasant, in spite of his social status, was venerated as a yogi by those who knew him. Furthermore, although a peasant, Nagasaki could trace his lineage back to one Nagasaki Iyo-no-kami, a retainer of Imagawa Yoshimoto who for a time in the sixteenth century challenged the supremacy of Oda Nobunaga. One branch of the family settled down at Kitaniigata, a village in the Tsuzuki district of Kanagawa prefecture, where he prospered and was held in high esteem by the villagers. For many generations the members lived in an old house surrounded by dense woods which lent the premises a somewhat dismal appearance. It was here that Nagasaki Hichirozaemon first saw the light. He was a child of shy and retiring habits and did not mingle with boys and girls of his own age in rustic sports, preferring instead to spend entire days in seclusion and meditation in the darkest apartments of the house. This disposition grew more confirmed with increasing years. It is said that when asked by his father what he was doing on these occasions, he replied that he was holding converse with a Tengu, a supernatural being supposed to haunt high trees and mountains. The serious and placid tone with which he spoke left no room for doubt as to his sanity. In other respects, however, nothing remarkable happened until he reached the age of thirty, when one fine morning he startled his family and the rest of the villagers with the announcement that he had received a revelation to the effect that the country would soon be plunged into a condition of grave unrest, and that the gods had bidden him erect a shrine on the top of Hakuseki where he must worship, so that his eyes might be enabled to peer into the future.

The shrine was built accordingly. That this prediction was not an idle creation of his brain appears to be established by the fact that shortly afterwards the War of the Restoration broke out. His subsequent prophecies also proved to be remarkably correct. The Korean trouble of 1883, the attempted assassination of the then Russian Crown Prince by a mad policeman at Otsu, the Sino-Japanese and Russo-Japanese wars all occurred as foretold by the peasant prophet.

Just before the announcement of one of his predictions Nagasaki invariably retired to the seclusion of his mountain shrine. Again he would occasionally disappear and later return after several days' absence, his body covered with scratches. He would never disclose his whereabouts, but the accepted belief among the villagers was that he had been wandering among the mountains holding communion with the spirits.

Many years ago in the depth of winter when the snow lay thickly upon the hills, the peasant made his appearance at Hihara, at the foot of Hakuseki, and after staying there overnight began the ascent. Whenever he retired to the shrine a devotee of Hihara was wont to supply him with food sufficient to last him for the term of his sojourn, usually about a week. This particular winter, however, he stayed away much longer than usual until the devotee began to feel uneasy on the score of his safety since he knew that his stock of food must have been consumed. He therefore ventured to ascend the mountain and at the summit sure enough found the mystic safe and sound and in high spirits, betraying no signs of exhaustion, although he had gone without food for ten days.

The next anecdote on my list is far more in sympathy with the spirit of the age, for it concerns the supernormal gifts of a thoroughly up-to-date Japanese educationist, a Mr. Kaneda, Bachelor of Science and Principal of the Kitano Middle School. This gentleman, we learn, despite the respect and popularity which he enjoyed among his students, could not escape the lot of his colleagues in being saddled with a nickname. From a habit he had developed of thrusting out his chin when engaged in class he had been dubbed by the students *ago-no-kochō*, or "chin master". This weakness was said to be especially in evidence when he was demonstrating algebra. He was also known as *zōri-no-kochō*, or "straw sandal teacher", because he insisted that the scholars should wear this footgear in the classrooms in order to keep the floor clean. Finally, he was frequently styled "the Tengu teacher", and from this nickname a clue can be gained to the peculiar powers which had suggested its application.

During the early part of February 1910 Mr. Kaneda attended a scientific meeting held at the College of Science of the Tokyo Imperial University, when he demonstrated his wonderful mental power to the bewilderment of all the savants who were present. Briefly the incident occurred in the following manner: After the regular proceedings were over Professor Dr. Jimbo, Mr. Kaneda's old principal, and a few other professors sat round a table indulging in small talk, when a letter from a certain German scientist was brought in and handed to Dr. Jimbo. Dr. Jimbo broke the seal and found that the contents were written in Esperanto. After perusal Dr. Jimbo showed the letter to his former pupil and asked, "Have you studied Esperanto? I'm afraid you haven't, seeing that you have been in the country all the time."

"I haven't studied it," replied Mr. Kaneda, "but I can understand it if I see it."

The cool and confident air with which Mr. Kaneda uttered these words excited the curiosity of Dr. Jimbo and the other members of the party.

"What!" exclaimed Dr. Jimbo, "you can read it though you haven't studied it? What do you mean?"

Mr. Kaneda answered: "I am endowed with *jitsuryoku* (superhuman divine power) and by its aid can easily tell the meaning of a letter written not only in Esperanto but in any other foreign language which I have never studied."

"Superhuman power!" ejaculated Dr. Jimbo. "Humbug! Don't talk nonsense, my dear boy!"

"Give me a trial," rejoined Mr. Kaneda simply, "and I will tell you what the letter contains."

After glancing through the letter Mr. Kaneda explained its meaning without the slightest mistake. He further told the professor that in order to communicate his—the professor's—thoughts to him, he—the professor—need only enclose a sheet of blank paper because he—Mr. Kaneda—could read even unwritten lines! Leaving all present in a state of stupefaction the professor and Mr. Kaneda went out and walked some little distance down one of the

Hongo streets, when suddenly the professor bethought him that he ought to call upon a foreign lady friend and introduce his former pupil, Mr. Kaneda, as he had long promised to do. Mr. Kaneda, however, assured the professor that it would be useless for him to pay a visit that day because the lady was not at home. Dr. Jimbo, still sceptical, insisted, but sure enough on their arrival at the house they were informed by a servant that the hostess had gone out for the day, as anticipated by Mr. Kaneda.

A few days after this Mr. Kaneda called on Count Okuma at Waseda, but found that a large number of previous visitors were being turned away disappointed, the Count being indisposed and unable to receive. The trouble was a terrible headache. Mr. Kaneda handed his card to the footman who at once began to inform him that his master was too ill to see anybody, when Mr. Kaneda calmly interrupted him and said that he had called for the express purpose of curing the Sage of Waseda. The footman gazed at Mr. Kaneda in surprise, unable to understand on what grounds a schoolmaster could assume the duties of a physician, but in the long run ushered the caller into the presence of Count Okuma. The ensuing dialogue is thus reported:

Mr. Kaneda: "I hear you are ill. What is the matter with you?"

Count Okuma: "Nothing serious, thank you. I have only a bad headache."

Mr. Kaneda: "Then let me cure you."

So saying the visitor began to stare steadfastly into the face of the Count for a couple of minutes, and then said, "How do you feel now? The headache is gone!"

The veteran statesman, who at the outset was inclined to treat the experiment as a huge joke, suddenly realized that the pain had indeed entirely disappeared, and his astonishment was proportionately great.

"How on earth," he asked, "did you manage to effect so sudden a cure?"

"By my *jitsuryoku*," was the reply.

"Hum!" said the Count. "Whatever it is it is wonderful."

Mr. Kaneda went on to say that he had the potential capacity for curing all diseases. Smallpox was prevalent at the time, and he had the temerity to declare that he could cure any case if he came into contact with the patient, but it is not recorded that he actually gave a demonstration of the truth of this part of his claim. Giving rein to his humour, the visitor further assured the Count that if he cared to make use of his superhuman power he could resist the pressure of old age and live for 500 years. He made the remark apropos of Count Okuma's notorious contention that he would live to be a hundred and twenty-five. If the truth must be told, Count Okuma died at the age of about eighty.

Mr. Kaneda first demonstrated his *jitsuryoku* when he received an appointment as principal of the Miyo Middle School. His predecessor had been compelled to resign owing to strikes among the students, and when Mr. Kaneda entered upon his duties he found himself in a somewhat difficult position. Over half the old staff of teachers had followed the example of the former principal, and the students were behaving in a very unruly manner. After conferring with the school faculty Mr. Kaneda sent for the roll-call, on glancing at which he took note of some thirty names and ordered that the students answering thereto should be sent for. The order was promptly obeyed and when the students appeared he reprimanded them for the part they had played in the strikes. The students were no less surprised than the teachers on seeing their misbehaviour pointed out with absolute accuracy by a man who had only just entered the school and had never met them before. Hence his nickname of Tengu.

Mr. Kaneda had repeatedly foretold the winners of baseball matches and of other athletic sports among the pupils. In giving out marks it was not necessary for him to go laboriously through the examination papers; all he had to do was to look at the students' faces in order to ascertain the nature of their performance, and subsequent scrutiny of the papers by the other teachers had always shown his decisions to be correct.

In a very interesting book entitled *Senjitsu Shugyo Kidan,* or *The Story of the Study of the Arts of the Sennin,* the author, Kawamura Hokumei, tells the experience of a friend of his who devoted three years of solitude and austerity to the attainment of the powers of a *sennin* or yogi, and on the very eve of success was seduced by a trifling circumstance and returned to the bosom of our more prosaic civilization. The hero of this true story was one Ubunai Masataro, the son of a Shinto priest of the town of Nanbu. Ubunai was born in the first year of Ansei (1854). He was known as a precocious boy endowed with remarkable wit and resource which not infrequently won him the admiration of older playmates. It is told of him that one day, when he was barely six years old, he was playing with a number of comrades in a farmyard in which stood a peach-tree whose branches were heavily laden with ripe and tempting fruit. The boys naturally tried to gain possession of the fruit and had recourse to various expedients to effect their object but with little or no success. Finally Ubunai announced that he would get the fruit for them. He ran back to the house and there obtained a length of strong kite twine to one end of which he tied a stone. Then swinging the weighted line he easily made it fast to one of the branches which he pulled down until the fruit was within reach and his comrades had filled their sleeves.

The author furnishes the reader with numerous other trivial details of his hero's youth—of how he was an earnest student with a strong penchant for penmanship which he would practise until the small hours of the morning, brush in hand; how he had a phenomenal appetite which on one notable occasion led him to devour at a single sitting twenty-four bowlfuls of macaroni with twenty-four eggs. On the other hand he neither smoked nor drank. He was fond of the martial arts and gained considerable skill with the spear. When the War of the Restoration broke out, Ubunai, who was then about sixteen or seventeen years old, fought on the side of the Shogun and emerged unscathed. After the Restoration he obtained an appointment as teacher at a village school in his native province, where he soon won the esteem of his pupils, their parents and guardians. It was at this stage of his career that Ubunai began to entertain the idea of becoming a *sennin*. His mind once made up he set about the necessary preparations for a prolonged sojourn in a neighbouring mountain forest. His outfit included a pair of scissors, a penknife, some sheets of writing-paper, a pen and ink, a notebook, a collection of poems, a dictionary, matches, a watch, an oil-paper mosquito net, and some medicine. He decided to lay in a stock of rice and cooking utensils on the way. His preparations being complete, he paid a farewell visit to his father on a Saturday evening. The farewell was unspoken on Ubunai's side, and his father knew nothing of his resolve. Ubunai returned to the school late at night, but tired though he was with the long walk he could not fall asleep, his mind being a prey to strange reflections and emotions. Early on the following morning he set out on his journey to the mountain without taking a soul into his confidence, and the villagers never suspected his purpose. *En route* he reached the town of Morioka, where he paid a visit to his former teacher, Ida Keisho, under whom the author of this account was studying at the time. The same evening Ubunai invited the author and a few friends to dinner at a neighbouring restaurant and afterwards spent the night in the school dormitory. Early next morning he again set out with a heavy bundle on his shoulder, simply announcing that he was bound for a place about five miles away. The author did not see Ubunai again until three years had elapsed, when the would-be *sennin* reappeared at Morioka after abandoning his attempt. His experiences in the mountains he personally narrated to the author who shares them with the reader, as reproduced below. Ubunai journeyed to the town of Hashiba after leaving Morioka, and thence to a mountain forest on the borders of Akita prefecture. Selecting a suitable spot he pitched his tent and addressed himself to the adventure.

It did not take him long to exhaust his slender store of rice, which circumstance drove him to gather young roots and to catch fish in the mountain streams for food. His tent offered inadequate resistance to the elements, and in due course he built a log cabin in its stead. He had many dangerous encounters with bears, snakes and wolves, and more than once saved monkeys from the attacks of these enemies. Personally he counted among his friends a bear whose life he had saved and which later on during the first winter showed its gratitude by helping him to repulse the savage onslaught of a pack of hungry wolves which sought to rob him of his food supplies.

Whilst engaged in profound and prolonged meditation in his hermitage at this season he incidentally satisfied himself that the choice of diet constituted an all-important factor in the attainment of the powers of a *sennin*, and he therefore determined to change his mode of living in order to facilitate the desired transformation. He further tells us that at this stage of his experiences he became conscious of vast improvement in his health; the fears to which he had hitherto been a prey fell away from him and time sped on golden wings. Spring came round again, and then the anniversary of the memorable day in May when he quitted the paternal roof and the haunts of men to seek his mountain solitude. He was assailed by a thousand recollections of the past—though Ubunai was still little more than twenty-two—and found it hard to contend with his emotions. Nevertheless he never faltered in his resolve to pursue the course he had mapped out. He felt convinced that so long as he continued to eat fish and meat daily he could not hope to reach the desired goal, since these foods corrupted the blood and led to mental distraction which necessarily interfered with that deep introspection essential to perception of the Great Truth of the universe. He thereupon gave up fish and meat altogether and thereafter subsisted entirely upon chest-nuts and other fruits and herbs. Two months later, he tells us, he became conscious of a stupendous change at work in his physical condition. His skin grew appreciably whiter and his muscles gradually hardened. He lost all sense of fatigue no matter how hard he worked; his bodily movements became so agile that he was able to scale the most precipitous cliffs without difficulty and without any feeling of danger, and could wade through icy streams without incurring numbness of the feet. Moreover his hearing and vision grew abnormally keen. Thus he could hear an ant creeping on the ground or human beings talking six miles away. More than once he was startled by the sound of persons approaching, and would advance in the direction of the voices, thinking to meet the speakers any moment, only to realize that they were many miles off. Similarly he could readily and correctly name the shades of colour of the feathers of a small bird perched on a tree fully 200 yards away from him, and he could discern fishes swimming at a great depth. He continued to practise his austerities for several months longer, and by that time had brought his senses to a still higher stage of development. He could then identify odours for miles around. Last of all he became impervious to the extremes of heat or cold. In the summer, with-out any kind of artificial protection, he could endure the blistering rays of a sun which is almost tropical in Japan at that season; and in midwinter, without the smallest inconveniences, he could stand out of doors stark naked exposed to a blizzard. Thus he had spent three years and had almost reached the longed-for goal when something happened to divert him from the path he had chosen and to relegate him once again to the status of an ordinary mortal.

Ubunai narrates that one day when gathering chestnuts he chanced to meet two peasants who, the instant they caught sight of him, manifested signs of the liveliest terror. They trembled all over and falling on their knees implored him to spare their lives. Apparently they took him for what is known as a *yama-otoko*, or mountain man. In accents of profound humility and awe they promised him the customary offerings if he would be merciful. Ubunai paid no attention to these overtures but instead disappeared into the forest. When the next day he returned to the scene of this adventure he saw that the ignorant peasants had been true to their word and had left a tray bearing a big bowl of boiled rice and some other edibles dear to the average Japanese palate. It has already been stated that Ubunai in his youth had been famous for his prowess as a trencher-man, and when thus suddenly his nostrils were assailed by the delicious fumes of these long-forgotten delicacies his mouth began to water freely and he could not resist the temptation to eat. The consequences may be guessed. If such a confusion of "epitaphs" be permissible, the bowl of rice proved to be the Adam's apple in this case and Ubunai fell as irrevocably as our alleged first parents. He began to dwell on the folly of his present life of privation and to dally with the idea of abandoning his *sennin* ambitions in favour of the avocations of his ordinary fellow-creatures. The rest was easy. He forthwith bade adieu to his hermitage and made the best of his way back to the old homestead where he was welcomed with the fatted calf, metaphorically speaking. His parents were overjoyed to see him, and soon afterwards he again received a position as teacher in the village school where he resumed the humdrum existence common to that calling.

That levitation is among the more highly prized attributes of the adept or yogi in Japan could be shown by numerous stories. Perhaps the following narrative concerning the prowess of the Buddhist priest Yosho will suffice.

Yosho was a native of the province of Noto, a peninsula of Central Japan, the coast of which is washed by the waters of the Japan Sea. A precocious boy, Yosho at the age of eleven was sent by his father to the Shorengein monastery on the summit of Mount Hiei, not far from Kyoto, where he studied Buddhism under the supervision of the famous abbot Kunishi Risshi of the Tendai sect. The youthful Yosho early distinguished himself among his fellow-novices by his perseverance, deep devotion, and scrupulous observance of ritualistic details. After a sojourn of several years in the seclusion of the Hieizan monastery he departed, imbued with the determination to win for himself a place in the ranks of the *sennin*. As a preliminary step he ascended Mount Konpo, where he spent several months in a hermitage and immersed himself in profound meditation. He next entered the Muda temple, and there with redoubled ardour pursued his studies for the attainment of the desired end. As a Buddhist priest Yosho abstained from meat or fish as a matter of course; but he carried asceticism even farther and eliminated from his diet even cereals, vegetables and fruits. While practising prolonged fasts he subjected himself to various kinds of self-torture, and as the result of these persistent austerities eventually, it is said, attained a degree of occult development which raised him far above ordinary mortals. Then, realizing that the moment had come for entry upon a path destined to lead to yet higher stages in the development of a *sennin*. Yosho divested himself of his *kesa koromo*, or symbolic garb of a Buddhist priest, and hung it upon the branch of a pine-tree with a slip of paper containing a message bequeathing the garment to his disciple Enmei Zenshi of the Hyogen temple, as a keepsake. This done, he left the temple for an unknown destination.

Great indeed were the surprise and sorrow of Enmei Zenshi when he received this parting message. Wishing to see his teacher once again he set out upon the quest with nothing to guide him save his individual caprice. After wandering for several years among the plains and mountains he was almost on the point of discontinuing the effort in despair when he accidentally encountered a priest named Onshin whose retreat was on Mount Yoshino, and from this recluse obtained the amazing intelligence that he had recently seen Yosho, now a fully-fledged *sennin*, in more senses than one, engaged in the congenial occupation of soaring above Kitanomine! The priest Onshin furthermore communicated to Enmei an experience of his own which helped to demonstrate the heights of adeptship which had been successfully scaled by Yosho. Some months before Onshin's meeting with Enmei he had been mortifying the flesh in a certain remote quarter to such purpose that he seemed in imminent peril of collapsing entirely, when suddenly a handsome youth approached him and producing a whitish-looking substance, bade him eat it. The exhausted priest did so, and in an instant felt marvellously refreshed and invigorated. On inquiring the name of his benefactor he was told that he—the youth—was a disciple of Yosho and that the food just administered was a gift from his master. With these words the lad rose in the air and flew away like a bird! In the light of this information Enmei apparently came to the conclusion that if a mere disciple of Yosho could thus defy the normal laws of gravitation, he—Enmei—would be rather badly handicapped in chasing the master, and there and then abandoned further search. All this time, we are told, Yosho was in his mountain abode. One day he met a priest of the Tadaiji temple, to whom he stated that he had passed fifty years in the mountains, and with the help of the Buddhist sacred writings had acquired the power of flight through the air.

About this time the old father of Yosho was taken ill, and as is natural in such circumstances felt an overmastering desire to see his son once more before he died, their last meeting having taken place on the day when Yosho, then a boy, left for the Hieizan monastery. Whether by means of telepathy or some other mysterious faculty with which the *sennin* are endowed, Yosho learnt of his father's condition and—so the story goes—came hurtling through the air one evening, and perching upon the highest point of the roof, like some gigantic bird, began to recite a Buddhist prayer! The voice was speedily recognized by Yosho's father and brother, who both rushed out of the house, but although they looked fixedly in the direction of the voice, they failed to see their kinsman. The father begged him to come into the house and grant his parent a glimpse of him in person. Yosho refused but promised to come on the 18th of every month if his father would burn incense on that day. With proper observance of this condition by the father, Yosho made regular visits and from his position on the roof chanted sutras to his heart's content.

We are further told that at this period the Senkoin temple of Hieizan was in charge of the venerable abbot Jokan, who was in the habit of chanting the *Sonjodarami* (part of the Buddhist scripture) with such intense pathos that all who heard him were moved to tears. One clear moonlight night Yosho made an aerial trip to the temple and picking out a convenient beam in the ceiling squatted thereon and listened with pleasure to the abbot's singsong. Conscious of a witness the abbot inquired the name of the intruder, whereupon Yosho condescended to float down from the beam and allow himself to be ushered into the abbot's sanctum where the two holy men passed the rest of the night in profitable converse. When the bell for matins began to toll Yosho announced that he must go, but added that he felt rather stiff in the joints owing to the fact that he had not for many years communed so long with a mere mortal. To overcome the difficulty he asked the abbot to move the incense burner nearer to him, and the request having been complied with the *sennin* bird-man ascended on the smoke and was soon out of sight.

Myself a believer in the possibilities of occultism I have always insisted upon the necessity of subjecting all unusual claims to the test of the most cold-blooded investigation. For this reason I should not deem this chapter complete did I omit to say a few words about the so-called "fire-walking" ceremony, concerning which, as it is performed twice annually at one of the Shinto temples of the capital, a good deal has been written from time to time by enthusiastic foreigners. Of course one can speak only for oneself and my experience may not be that of others, but it is the experience of at least two of my male friends who agreed with me in pronouncing the thing we saw a puerile farce, though strange to say certain of our common acquaintances who also witnessed the "ceremony" at the same time carried away with them the impression of having seen something incapable of a normal explanation. Speaking for myself and friends, what we saw was not the spectacle of human beings walking over fire but over a spot where fire had formerly been. The preliminaries were all very impressive and equally wearisome. The bed of pine-logs and charcoal glowed luridly in the centre of the small courtyard of the Shinto temple as attendants fanned it vigorously and white-clad Shinto priests

chanted their incantations. As I eyed the tongues of flame and felt
the heat oppressive even from where I sat, I thought to myself,
"Well, if anybody walks through this fiery furnace without injury
I shall consider the case for occultism established beyond the
shadow of a doubt." But what really happened? The attendants
gradually relaxed their efforts to stimulate the fire and began instead to beat out the embers in the centre of the pile until, as time
went on, a path had been formed absolutely black as the ace of
spades, though banked on either side by dull-red masses of wood
and charcoal.

Only then did the priests, after a little more mumbo-jumbo,
venture to skip daintily over the path thus formed, after having
carefully rubbed the soles of their bare feet in a mass of salt at one
end of the almost extinct bonfire. Men, women and children then
followed the example of the priests, after the latter had dusted
them down in turn with the sacred *gohei* (paper cut in a peculiar
shape, fastened upon a stick, and placed in a Shinto shrine before
the *kami* as a sign of offering, supposed by the vulgar to represent
the spirit of the deity) and a double-shuffle in the salt-heap.
Even while stepping briskly along the narrow path I could not
help thinking what a gigantic piece of humbug the entire "ceremony" was, nor did it surprise me one whit to find that the pathway was just about as hot as any pathway of the same material
treated in the same manner ought to be, and that my feet were sore
and blistered at the close of the "ordeal". Perhaps I did not carry
away enough salt on the soles before I stepped on to the charcoal
bed, but in any case my experience was calculated to convince me
that whatever else the "ceremony" might be it assuredly was not
occult.

Another circumstance lending colour to this conclusion is the
fact that it is performed for money, every foreigner who attends
being charged in my day a minimum rate of one yen, then the
equivalent of about two shillings. To prevent misunderstanding
hasten to add that in my opinion the ceremony has been genuinely
performed in the past and may even have been performed in our
own day at other times and places; but as far as the priests of this
particular temple were concerned it was plain to me that they had
no power to duplicate the feats of their predecessors. Whether this

loss of power is due to the decline and corruption of Japanese religious belief I cannot say, but the fact seems to be clear enough. My previous chapters on the virtues of *aiki*, as exemplified by Mr. Kunishige, will furnish the reader with the grounds on which I base my belief in the possibility of a real fire-walking ceremony; and I can but regret that it has not been given to me to see it.

CHAPTER XVI

THE CULT OF COLD STEEL

IN some respects Young Japan moves slowly in spite of her thirst
for modern progress. Her courts and her codes have been modernized; murder is classified as a capital crime; but these facts and
definitions are alike powerless to change the popular point of view
in every instance. Modern Japan hanged the Korean assassin of
Prince Ito, but the people of Japan still persist in revering and
keeping green the memory of more than one political murderer of
the none too distant past.

On 12th April, 1910, for example, the good folk of the metropolis turned out in their thousands, arrayed in their spring best
to do honour to the names of the eighteen strenuous samurai of
the Mito clan who, on 24th March, 1860, fell upon the famous
Regent Ii Kamon-no-kami, or Lord Ii, as he was on his way to
the palace of the Shogun and had just reached the Sakurada
Gate in the very heart of Tokyo, the ancient Yedo. The Regent
was being carried in a *norimon* (palanquin) surrounded by his
retainers. On the bridge crossing the moat was the cortège
of the Prince of Kyushu; and coming along the road towards the
same point was the retinue of the Prince of Owari. Sir Rutherford
Alcock describes what followed in the following words:

"The Gotairo (Regent) was thus between them, at the foot
of the bridge, in the opening formed by the meeting of a
broad street which debouches on the bridge. A few straggling
groups, enveloped in their oil-paper cloaks, alone were near
when suddenly one of these seeming idlers flung himself across
the line of march immediately in front of the Regent's *norimon*.
The officers of the household, whose place is on each side of him,
rushed forward at this unprecedented interruption—a fatal
move which had evidently been anticipated, for their place
was instantly filled with armed men in coats of mail who seemed
to have sprung from the earth—a compact band of some

172

eighteen or twenty men. . . . The unhappy officers and attendants, thus taken by surprise, were hampered with their rain
gear, and many fell before they could draw a sword either to
defend themselves or their lord. A few seconds must have done
the work . . . when one of the band was seen to run along the
causeway with a gory trophy in his hand. Many had fallen in
the mêlée on both sides. Two of the assailants who were badly
wounded, finding escape impossible, stopped in their flight and
deliberately performed the *harakiri*, to the edification of their
pursuers—for it seems to be the law (so sacred is the rite or
right, whichever may be the proper reading) that no one may
be interrupted even for the ends of justice. . . . Eight of the
assailants were unaccounted for when it was all over; and
many of the retine were stretched on the ground wounded
and dying by the side of those who made the murderous onslaught. The remnant of the Regent's people, released from their
deadly struggle, turned to the *norimon* to see how it fared with
their master in the brief interval—to find it only a headless
trunk! The bleeding trophy carried away was supposed to have
been the head of Gotairo himself, hacked off on the spot.
But strangest of all these startling incidents, it is further
related that two heads were found missing, and that which was
seen in the fugitive's hand was only a lure to the pursuing party,
while the true trophy had been secreted on the person of another, and was thus carried off, though the decoy paid the penalty
of his life."

That Japanese of the Meiji Era, or Era of Enlightenment,
should under the highest auspices perpetuate the memory, not of
the illustrious victim but of the murderers, may seem more than a
trifle anomalous and incompatible with the then Japanese status
in the comity of nations. It was this very Ii Kamon-no-kami who
played a leading rôle in that remarkable movement against great
odds which culminated in the opening of Japan to foreign intercourse. Lord Ii became Prime Minister of the Shogun Iyesada in
1858, and later of the twelve-year-old Iyemochi. On 29th July,
1858, he signed the first treaty with the United States, and soon
afterwards signed treaties with England and France. These
treaties excited strong opposition among the Conservative ele-

ments throughout the country, and the Court party at Kyoto
demanded the expulsion of the barbarians. Lord Ii dealt resolutely
with the malcontents, and thus added fuel to the flames. The
opening of Kanagawa, the dispatch of an embassy to the United
States, and the treaty with Portugal all served further to exasper-
ate the anti-foreign party, and the assassination of the great
statesman ensued, as described above. The same spirit which
prompted the paying of homage to his murderers undoubtedly
operated to forbid the erection of a statue to his honour in the
capital, or the presence of the representatives of the Government
on the occasion of the unveiling of the statue eventually erected at
Yokohama to commemorate in a fitting manner the jubilee of the
opening of the port to foreign trade.

The precincts of the famous Yasukuni Shrine, also known as
the Shokonsha, or "Spirit Invoking Shrine" at Kudan, a picturesque part of Tokyo, was the scene of the celebration in honour
of the Mito assassins of the Regent, for it is here that by imperial
favour their names have been preserved in the form of *ihai*, or
ancestral tablets. The celebration was organized by the well
known Tokyo newspaper *Yamato Shimbun*, and invitations were
issued in the names of Count Hisamoto, Lieut.-General Baron
Miyoshi, and Mr. J. Haseba, President of the House of Representatives. In the morning a solemn service was held in the presence of
thousands of people, in strict accordance with the Shinto rite.
The shrine where the spirits of Japanese heroes are deified was
suitably decorated and in the compound of the shrine were several
tents for the accommodation of the surviving relatives of the
eighteen assassins, including such notables as Marquis Yamano-
chi, Viscount Matsudaira, Viscount Kaida and some others. The
shrine was visited by Prince Kitashirakawa, Prince Kuni, Prince
Asaka, Prince Takeda and many other dignitaries of the empire.

Later in the day the more popular portion of the programme
was performed with unusual zest, the proceedings including a procession of mounted samurai, fencing and wrestling matches,
stately and wearisome Nō dances, geisha processions and dances,
fireworks and dramatic performances. The procession of samurai
was of considerable historic interest as a faithful reproduction of
the manners, customs and costumes of a byegone age. The participants early assembled at Ueno Park and, forming a long line,

marched to Kudan Hill. They were armed with old-fashioned muskets, bows, swords, lances and other warlike paraphernalia of the Tokugawa era. After nightfall numerous electric cars were brilliantly illuminated, and unofficial homage to the opponents of the "open door and equal opportunity", as far as Japan was concerned in those rough old days, continued to be paid until a late hour of the evening.

The Shokonsha, where the ceremony took place, was erected in 1869 for the worship of the spirits of those who had fallen for the Mikado's cause in the revolutionary war of the previous year. Services are also held in honour of those who fell in the Saga troubles of 1873, the Satsuma rebellion of 1877, the China war of 1894-5, and the Russo-Japanese war of 1904-5, in which latter context it is curious to note that two or three foreigners, especially the commanders of the two transports which were sunk by the Russian Vladivostok squadron off Tsushima, are among the number of those thus apotheosized. The shrine is built in conformity with the severest canons of pure Shinto architecture, and is completely empty, save for a mirror, a European drugget, and a dozen cheap wooden chairs for the use of the officials who come to assist at the memorial services which are held here from time to time. As on the occasion mentioned above, these services are enlivened by horse-races, wrestling and other popular amusements. The enormous bronze *torii*, or Shinto gateway, which marks the approach to the shrine, was manufactured in the Osaka Arsenal and set up in December 1887.

This popular demonstration on behalf of bloodthirsty reactionaries may well prompt additional reflections on what in Japan may truly be styled the cult of cold steel and of political assassination. Old residents can readily recall the days when he who ventured beyond the confines of the foreign concessions and sought the purer atmosphere of the surrounding country virtually took his life in his hands. The land then swarmed with *rōnin* (literally "wave-men"), or unattached samurai who had foresworn allegiance to their lords in order to have a free hand in hunting down and slaying the hated alien, commonly but by no means flatteringly spoken of as *ketojin*, or "hairy barbarians". Even when these two-sworded gentry might no longer thus amuse themselves in their leisure moments, which were plenty, they never met a foreigner on the highway without treating him to a melodramatic scowl which would have put to shame an Adelphi stage villain.

Much space has been devoted to descriptions of the *katana*, or native sword, with which nearly all these crimes of violence were committed. The blade of this type of weapon is usually 2 ft. 89/100ths in. in length, made of soft, elastic, magnetic iron combined with hard steel. The *katana* was not usually worn alone but together with the *wakizashi*, or dirk, of about 9½ in. in length, with which the owner would, if necessary, commit *harakiri*, otherwise *seppuku*. The custom of wearing two swords is traced back as far as the beginning of the fourteenth century, and was abolished by an edict issued on 28th March, 1876, which went into effect from 1st January, 1877. And yet in 1871 or a little earlier Mr. Mitford, later Lord Redesdale, wrote in the introduction to one of his charming *Tales of Old Japan*: "The statesman who shall enact a law forbidding the carrying of this deadly weapon will indeed have deserved well of his country; but it will be a difficult task to undertake and a dangerous one. I would not give much for that man's life. The hand of every swashbuckler in the empire would be against him." The truth is—I quote Mr. Chamberlain's *Things Japanese*—"the edict was obeyed by *this strangely docile people* without a blow being struck, and the curio-shops displayed heaps of swords which a few months before the owners would less willingly have parted with than with life itself!" So hard is it to predict with anything like accuracy the mental and moral processes of the Japanese!

The Japanese sword has been called "the living soul of the samurai", and the etiquette connected with its handling was of the most minute description. A very trustworthy outline of the more important rules occurs in *Fu-so Mimi Bukuro: A Budget of Japanese Notes*, by the late C. Pfoundes, a Japanese scholar and investigator whose work is too little known, on the principle, no doubt, that a prophet is without honour in his own country. The volume mentioned comprises a series of articles contributed to the *Japan Mail* of Yokohama and republished in book form in 1875. From a copy in my possession I extract the following:

"To touch another's weapon, or to come into collision with the sheath, was a dire offence, and to enter a friend's house without leaving the sword outside a breach of friendship. Those whose position justified the accompaniment of an attendant invariably left the sword in his charge at the entrance or, if alone, it was usually laid down at the entrance. If removed inside, it was invariably done by the host's servants, and then not touched with the bare hand, but with a silk napkin kept for the purpose, and the sword was placed upon a sword-rack in the place of honour near the guest and treated with all the politeness due to an honoured visitor who would resent a discourtesy. The long sword, if two were worn, was withdrawn, sheathed, from the girdle with the right hand, and placed on the right side—an indication of friendship, as it could not be drawn and used thus—never by the left hand, or placed on the left side, except when in immediate danger of attack. To exhibit a naked weapon was a gross insult, unless a gentleman wished to show his friends his collection. To express a wish to see a sword was not usual, unless when a blade of great value was in question, when a request to be shown it would be a compliment the happy possessor appreciated. The sword would then be handled with the back towards the guest, the edge turned towards the owner and the hilt to the left, the guest wrapping the hilt either in the little silk napkin always carried by gentlemen in their pocketbooks or in a sheet of clean paper. The weapon was drawn from the scabbard and admired inch by inch, but not to the full length, unless the owner pressed his guest to do so, when, with much apology, the sword was entirely drawn and held away from the other persons present. After being admired it would, if apparently necessary, be carefully wiped with a special cloth, sheathed and returned to the owner as before."

Considering the exaggerated veneration in which the native *katana* has been held from the earliest times it is not surprising that the occupation of a swordsmith should in feudal days have been regarded as an honourable profession the members of which were men of gentle blood. In this context the following comment taken from Lord Redesdale's *Tales of Old Japan* may interest my readers:

"In a country where trade is looked down upon as degrading,

it is strange to find this single exception to the general rule.
The traditions of the craft are many and curious. During the
most critical moment of the forging of the sword, when the
steel edge is being welded into the body of the iron blade, it is a
custom which still obtains among old-fashioned armourers to
put on the cap and robes worn by the Kugé, or nobles of the
Mikado's court, and, closing the doors of the workshop, to
labour in secrecy and freedom from interruption, the half
gloom adding to the mystery of the operation. Sometimes the
occasion is even invested with a certain sanctity, a tasselled
cord of straw, such as is hung before the shrines of the Kami,
or native gods of Japan, being suspended between two bamboo
poles in the forge, which for the nonce is converted in to a holy
altar.''

In the hands of an expert swordsman the best blades will cut
through the dead bodies of three men, laid one upon the other,
at a blow. "The swords of the Shogun used to be tried upon the
corpses of executed criminals; the public headsman was entrusted
with the duty, and for a 'nose medicine', or bribe of two bus
(about three shillings), would substitute the weapon of the
private individual for that of his Lord.''

It is equally characteristic that the technical skill and imagination of many of the country's leading artists and craftsmen should
have been lavished upon the adornment of this deadly weapon.
Thus its various accessories were often cunningly wrought in
metals and alloys. Of these latter the best known are *shibu-ichi*
and *shakudō*, both formed of a basis of copper with varying
admixture of silver and gold. Specially noteworthy among these
articles, and dear to the heart of countless foreign curio collectors
are the *tsuba*, or guard, and the *menuki*—small ornaments
fixed one on each side of the hilt and held in place by the silk
cord which binds together the various parts of the handle. The
price of a sword by a famous maker would in feudal days, which
means well into the nineteenth century, reach a very high sum.
Thus a Japanese noble would be found girding on a sword the
blade of which unmounted was worth in our currency from £200 to
£300, and the mounting, rich in cunning metal work, would be of
proportionate value. Weapons of this sort were handed down as

heirlooms from father to son and became almost a part of the wearer's own self.

One blow dealt by an expert swordsman, if the enemy failed to ward it off, was usually sufficient to dispose of the business in hand. More than one foreigner has fallen a victim to the terrible "upper-cut" of the Japanese assassin. The Anglo-Saxon's understanding of the technical term "upper-cut", as applied to the "noble art", is a blow the starting-point of which is the striker's hip and the objective of which is generally the point of his opponent's jaw. Should he succeed in the laudable ambition of getting it in, his adversary, nine times out of ten, is so struck by the force of the argument that he quietly subsides. The Japanese upper-cut was based upon similar dynamic principles, and was even more effective in its results. The sword was drawn from the scabbard with a long, sweeping motion, but instead of losing valuable time by raising the weapon above the head for a downward stroke—a *nashi-ware*, or "pear-splitter"—the assailant continued the movement from left to right in an upward diagonal direction, his object being to slash his victim open from the right hip to the left shoulder. Of course the force of the blow might be insufficient to carry out this playful little intention, but unless parried early in the day it generally deprived the victim of all interest in the subsequent proceedings. Major Baldwin and Lieutenant Bird, both of H.M. 20th Regiment, were thus slain near Kamakura on 21st November, 1864, by two Japanese samurai; in the former case the blow was delivered with such tremendous force as to sever the spinal cord. These murderous attacks upon the intruding alien were dictated by what is known in Japanese as *jo-i* ("the barbarian-expelling spirit"), and it is many years since the last crime of this nature was perpetrated.

But although the sword is no longer worn save by military, naval and police officials, it would be incorrect to say that the taste for cold steel has entirely disappeared. Even today, when deeds of violence are committed, the murderer usually employs a sword or dagger where an American or European would in all probability prefer a firearm. Nor is the more disinterested and fanatical recourse to bloodshed a thing only of the past. There have been so far during the Meiji era, which commenced in 1868, no fewer than six political assassinations by Japanese. The first to fall was a noted scholar named Yokoi Shonan, who was slain on 5th January, 1868; the second was Omura Masajiro, Vice-Minister of War, who perished in September of the same year; the third was Hirosawa Saneomi, a Privy Councillor, who met his fate on 9th January, 1871; the fourth was the celebrated Okubo Toshimitsu, Prime Minister, who was attacked in his palanquin and fore-shortened, so to speak, on 14th May, 1878; the fifth was Mori Arimori, struck down in his own residence on 11th February, 1889; and the sixth was Hoshi Toru, whose sensational taking-off on 21st June, 1901, profoundly shocked the capital at the time. The details of this tragedy are so remarkable and characteristic as to justify their reconstruction from the local newspaper files of the day.

Hoshi Toru, one of the most powerful and corrupt politicians of Japan, was sitting in a room of the Tokyo City Hall on Friday afternoon, 21st June, 1901, after having attended a meeting of the council of which he was a member, when the door suddenly opened, and a man, entering quickly, approached him and said, as afterwards appeared, "Do you repent?"

To this Hoshi replied briefly, "Stand back!" when with a movement so rapid and unexpected that none of the other persons present could possibly intervene, the newcomer drew a short sword from under his Japanese garments and stabbed Hoshi no fewer than six times in almost as many seconds. The *Japan Mail* of that day records that the first thrust pierced the victim's right side and reached the lung; the second entered the left side; the third was on the back of the head and laid bare the brain; the fourth was through the back of the lungs; and the fifth in the stomach. After delivering the first blow the assassin held Hoshi up in order to inflict the remaining wounds, the sixth of which was a less serious cut in the shoulder. Immediately on being released the unfortunate Hoshi sank to the floor and expired within five minutes. The assassin offered no serious resistance and was quickly seized by the horrified witnesses of this desperate deed. He proved to be one Iba Sotaro, a man of about fifty, who had until then borne an unblemished character. His family had for generations acted as fencing masters to the Tokugawa Court, and his father, Iba Gumbei, was looked upon as one of the best swordsmen of his day. The assassin himself had been noted as a fencer, but with the dawn of the new era he had turned his attention to more profitable pursuits and had studied English and various branches of science to such good purpose that he was appointed tutor to Viscount Ogasawara. He later founded a school and threw himself enthusiastically into the work of teaching. Agriculture and finance were also among the subjects of which he made a speciality. He was honoured with several important offices in business and educational circles. It was, in fact, his connexion with the latter which had led to the growth of the strange conviction that upon him devolved the sacred duty of removing one whose influence he regarded as highly pernicious to political and public morality. This resolution was strengthened by the knowledge that his skill in fence was such as to ensure the successful accomplishment of his plan; and, indeed, none but a perfect master of his weapon could have inflicted upon Hoshi in the same brief space of time six wounds of the terrible nature already described.

On searching him the police found a *zankanjō*, or written statement of reasons for slaying a traitor and vindication of the assassin's deed, in which he set forth the motives of his crime. In this the writer explained that the elevation of a man so depraved as Hoshi to a position of such responsibility as President of the Tokyo Educational Society could not be contemplated with equanimity, and he—Iba Sotaro—had therefore determined to effect his removal.

"Nothing," he declared, "could be more serious than the fact that this felon should be in a position to demoralize and corrupt the administration of Tokyo and destroy the morality of the citizens . . . that he should bring misfortune and shame to all, from sovereign to subject, and that, while his accomplices in bribery and corruption were exposed and punished, he alone should show a brazen face and should continue with increased vigour his course of insatiate plunder, spreading the poison of evil to all classes and destroying the morals of youth. For many generations my family has acted as instructors of swordsmanship in Tokyo. I myself, indifferent as my accomplishments are, have devoted myself to the cause of education and have sought to promote the spirit of learning and of military science. I have also felt it my duty to spare no effort for the improvement of agriculture and of the manufacturing industry, though I am well aware that my abilities are an indifferent qualification for such a task."

The writer added evidence to prove that he had had no personal dealings with his victim and bore him no personal grudge whatever. He concluded:

"If I now brave the pain of parting from my wife and children—pain as cruel as that of being torn asunder—if I face the voice of public opinion, if I ruin myself for the sake of killing this finished villain, it is because I cannot endure to see such an arch rascal as Hoshi Toru pursuing with fresh vigour his evil courses, as President of the Tokyo Educational Society, teaching the youth to be corrupt and crooked, introducing demoralization and disorder into the administration of Tokyo, and bringing misfortune upon all from the Emperor downwards. Thinking men, I ask you to appreciate and sympathize with the sincerity of my sentiments."

A copy of the foregoing document had been posted to the *Nippon*—a leading native organ—before Iba proceeded to the fatal rendezvous, and he had also taken the additional precaution of divorcing his wife. The short sword with which the deed was committed had long been a precious heirloom in the assassin's family, and so great was the strength employed in driving it home that the point was actually broken.

I make no apology for quoting at some length a document of such extraordinary psychological and racial interest. Iba Sotaro was clearly a man of otherwise irreproachable moral character, the superior of his victim, and in full possession of his senses. The crime was inspired by purely disinterested motives and carried out with a perfect appreciation of the consequences. But let us try to imagine an analogous incident in London or New York. If, say, a man of comparable standing were to drop into the County Hall and in broad daylight cut down the Chairman of the County Council with a cavalry sabre subsequently explaining that he had felt compelled to act in order to make a terrible example of a man whose personal reputation left a good deal to be desired, we should be furnished with a case not by any means unlike that which I have attempted to describe. And when I add that public sympathy was freely extended to the assassin and that he was sentenced to penal servitude for life, it will be seen that there is still some little difference between the ethical standards of Occident and Orient.

No account of this sanguinary incident would be complete without a few words devoted to the character and career of the victim. Hoshi Toru was born in 1850 and was therefore fifty-one years of age at the time of his death. He early applied himself to literary pursuits and in 1872 was appointed superintendent of customs at Kanagawa. He earned an unenviable notoriety among foreigners by his action in issuing orders to the police to prevent them from making use of private landing-places. The affair was ventilated in the courts and the superintendent exposed to even more unfriendly criticism because in one of his dispatches he spoke of Queen Victoria as *Nyo-ō* instead of *Nyo-tei*. The former simply means queen whereas the latter term is the proper designation of an empress. Sir Harry Parkes, the "little tiger" of British Far Eastern diplomacy, exalted this discourtesy into a diplomatic question and the offender was forced to seek fresh occupation. In 1874 he went to London where he studied three years and obtained his diploma as a barrister of the Middle Temple. On returning to Japan in 1877 he went in for politics and in 1879 helped to establish the Liberal party. He also made one or two excursions into journalism of a somewhat advanced type until the Government discouraged further efforts by suspending his publication. Then a speech of his landed him in gaol for a season on the quaint charge—very common in Japan—of bringing officials into contempt, although it often appears to an impartial onlooker that a good many bloated Barnacles of the Circumlocution Offices of East and West need no extraneous aid in arriving at that delectable condition.

After his release he still persisted in his career of agitation and in 1887 was expelled from Tokyo under the provisions of the Peace Preservation Law. Two years later he benefited by the declaration of amnesty which accompanied the promulgation of the Constitution and so returned and was elected as Member of the House of Representatives for Tokyo prefecture and chosen President of the

House, an office which he filled in the most able manner. His next appointment was that of Minister to Washington, and it was while thus engaged, if tradition does not lie, that he made a special study of the American political "boss" with a view to introducing his methods as a private monopoly into Japan. He returned in 1898 and amassed wealth with such unprecedented rapidity as to encourage the belief that "boodle" was in no small measure responsible. He helped Marquis Ito to organize the Seiyukai and it was at a garden-party given at the Imperial Hotel, Tokyo, during 1900, to celebrate the occasion, that I first made the personal acquaintance of this extraordinary man. He was of large physique for a Japanese and credited with the possession of herculean strength, but his face was not by any manner of means prepossessing. Many of his more candid countrymen, indeed, were in the habit of instituting comparisons between Hoshi and the common toad, not at all complimentary to Hoshi. He seemed destined to arouse in the breasts of his contemporaries the extremes of two emotions—hatred and admiration—the former being exemplified by the *Mainichi* newspaper in a campaign of scurrilous abuse to which even the "yellowest" of "yellow" journals in the United States rarely descends in the heat of a party campaign. He was freely accused of every kind of bribery and corruption as a member of the municipal administration of the capital, but the courts exonerated him and he continued to wield despotic authority over the then Marquis Ito, as the *de facto* leader of the latter's new party until the sword of Iba Sotaro cut him off in the heyday of his triumph.

By a grim coincidence the two most striking figures on this memorable occasion fell at the hands of assassins, but as statesmen and patriots it would be an insult to the glorious memory of Prince Ito to search for points of resemblance. Prince Ito had his enemies and many of them, but while those enemies during his lifetime never scrupled to calumniate him whenever opportunity offered, it is a noteworthy fact that never once was he seriously accused of pecuniary improbity. In a position to have piled up millions had he wished, it is no secret that he died a comparatively poor man, and that more than once during his life his friend and master the Emperor paid his debts. It was at this same garden-party that I was introduced to the then Marquis Ito and Marquis

Yamagata, but strangely enough both these famous *Genro*, or Elder Statesmen, showed themselves absurdly reticent and neglected to make me the recipient of any State secrets. Some newspapermen who subsequently met the former, then a prince, appear to have been more fortunate in this respect. In one case at least it is recorded that the Prince, at some public function, drew the favoured foreign scribe into a convenient alcove and there, in obedience to that instinct which at times irresistibly compels confession, imparted to his flattered *vis-à-vis* his hopes and fears and ambitions for the future. His confidant showed the right spirit by declining to be equally communicative for the benefit of the general public, for he felt that he had been made the repository of weighty confidences the premature disclosure of which might shake the empire to its foundations. Thus we shall never know why a statesman notoriously prone to keep his own counsel should suddenly have taken it into his head to unburden his soul in a *tête-à-tête* with a foreigner. Perhaps were I a trifle more imaginative I could recall one or two momentous utterances for my special benefit on the occasion of my meeting with the Marquis, but somehow they seem to have slipped my memory.

Returning to Hoshi Toru. At the time of his assassination a correspondent writing to the *Japan Mail* described him as "a type of Tammany Hall with a cynicism which even the New York bosses would not dare to show publicly. And yet there was another side of his singularly complex character. He had many intellectual tastes. His private library contained no fewer than 100,000 volumes, and he read not only English but Latin, Italian, French and Spanish, and had begun to study German shortly before his death.

An anecdote which well illustrates his unscrupulousness in an amusing and less vicious light than usual was once told me by the late editor and proprietor of the now defunct *Japan Herald* of Yokohama, Mr. H. Brooke, who died very many years ago. Mr. Brooke, before he came to Japan, had had considerable political experience in the colony of Victoria, where he held for some time the portfolio of Lands and Works, and having made the acquaintance of Hoshi in the early days of the Japanese Liberal Party was invited by that gentleman to attend a convivial gathering of that body and to honour the assemblage with a speech. Mr.

Brooke, nothing loath, consented, and after the *sake* had been permitted to circulate freely rose to his feet amid acclamation. As he could not speak Japanese he had brought an interpreter with him, but Mr. Hoshi undertook to act in his stead and since Mr. Brooke was well aware that Mr. Hoshi spoke English fluently he unsuspectingly acquiesced in this arrangement. The *modus operandi* was for Mr. Brooke to reel off a few hundred words or so in a batch and then to pause while Mr. Hoshi turned them into the vernacular. Mr. Brooke knew full well that these newly fledged Liberals were not in good odour with the Government and that there were police spies in the vicinity eagerly awaiting a pretext for interference, and he therefore purposely refrained from giving utterance to any save the most conventional sentiments. Imagine, then, his surprise when, as Mr. Hoshi proceeded with his interpretation, the audience burst forth into thunders of applause. He remarked to Mr. Hoshi at the close of his oration that the enthusiasm displayed seemed out of all proportion to the merits of the speech, but Mr. Hoshi smiled deprecatingly and assured Mr. Brooke that they had esteemed it an honour and a privilege to listen to the views of so experienced a politician. They parted, and Mr. Brooke returned to the hotel with his interpreter who, on their arrival, addressed him as follows:

"I beg your parden, sair, but Mr. Hoshi made a false interpretation of your speech. He did not say what you said."

"What on earth for?" inquired Mr. Brooke, who had had his suspicions.

"He probably feared," rejoined the Japanese, "that if he made a radical anti-Government speech himself he would be arrested, but as the police spies do not understand English they thought he was translating what you had said, and so they would not interfere. Mr. Hoshi is a very cunning man!"

Mr. Brooke was of a choleric temperament, and when he realized how he had been used to serve Mr. Hoshi's turn he referred to the founder of the political party in periods not strictly Pickwickian. But his troubles were not yet over. His supposed speech, reproduced by the newspaper reporters from Mr. Hoshi's Japanese version, appeared the next morning in cold, ideographic type, and evoked from the editor of the *Japan Mail* of strong Japanese official sympathies a scathing criticism in which Mr. Brooke was roundly condemned for having thus taken advantage of his immunity from the laws applicable in these cases in order to deliver a political harangue of an inflammatory character! Mr. Brooke's only witness being his interpreter he chose to grin and bear the soft impeachment rather than make a fuss and confess how neatly he had been exploited by the ingenious Hoshi. Nor, so far as I can recollect, did he wear crape when he heard of Mr. Hoshi's tragic finale.

Perhaps I may be forgiven for including in this chapter a short account of quite an exciting personal experience which brought me far too close for my liking to the "sword of Old Japan". This experience befell me shortly after the treaty of peace between Japan and Russia, signed at Portsmouth, U.S.A. on 23rd August, 1905 and ratified on 5th November, 1905, brought to a close the state of war between those two belligerents. The terms of this treaty proved so unpopular in Japan that widespread rioting broke out by way of protest, more especially in Tokyo where huge mobs fairly ran amok and carried their depredations so far as to burn down many police stations in the capital. These happenings were naturally grist to the mill of an enterprising newspaper correspondent, as I then was, ever avid for a good "story" and so I kept a sharp look-out for further developments of this dangerous situation.

Then one day I spotted a gang of young bloods evidently heading in the direction of the offices of the leading Government organ called the *Kokumin Shimbun* (People's Newspaper), and so in duty bound attached myself to it. Far from resenting my presence the crowd welcomed it vociferously and so more or less in step and at the double we finally reached our objective. Meanwhile other groups of rioters had arrived from other directions and an angry howling mob had gathered outside the *Kokumin* building bent on setting fire to the premises for which purpose petrol-soaked masses of straw and other inflammable material were hurled through the ground-floor windows. It was evidently hoped in this way to destroy or damage the printing-presses on the ground-floor.

Then suddenly I heard the cry go up, *"Battō shita!"* meaning "Swords are drawn!" and almost simultaneously from an open doorway four thick-set Japanese clad in foreign garb and each brandishing a naked *katana* dashed out to repel the attackers.

Even today I can recall the truly sinister swish made by these icy blades as they cut through the air. The swordsmen were apparently members of the *sōshi* (literally "strong man") strong-arm physical force fraternity, more crudely swashbucklers, doubtless hired by the newspaper administration to defend the premises in case of a mob attack. The crowd stampeded back in panic at sight of these deadly weapons wielded savagely by the powerful arms of the defenders but not before their keen edges had inflicted some nasty wounds upon several in the front ranks. I noticed one man with blood streaming from a gash in the neck; another had a hand severed at the wrist as he raised his arm with an almost reflex action to ward off the blow; and a third seemed to have lost his nose! The four *sōshi* were slashing recklessly right and left and only the swift retreat of the crowd averted more serious casualties. As for myself, I don't mind admitting that the sight and sound of these swords of Old Japan caused a distinct subsidence in the region of my inadequately developed *saika tanden*. I realized only too well that my grasp of *aiki* was imperfect and so deeming discretion to be the better part of valour I bolted for dear life. Then in my hurried retreat I slipped on the kerb and fell on one knee expecting any second to become the recipient of the unwelcome attentions of one or more of the *sōshi* swordsmen. However, I got up and took refuge in a convenient alleyway from which point of vantage I surveyed the field of battle now in the undisputed possession of the four *sōshi* who swaggered to and fro still flourishing their blood-stained blades.

But worse was to follow. From an upper window an elderly Japanese looked out, took aim with a revolver and fired. The bullet pierced the brain of a young man in the front rank and he fell dead on the spot. Then soon afterwards a strong force of police arrived on the scene. Using their unsheathed swords they quickly got the situation in hand, drove back the crowd and cordoned off the *Kokumin* building, but not before the ground-floor had been partially wrecked. Thereafter martial law was declared and the troops were called out to reinforce the police. Before order could be completely restored throughout the capital many fatalities took place, but with these this record is not concerned. Incidentally, however, in due course the Japanese who had shot and killed the young man in the crowd was indicted for this act, but thanks

JAPANESE GIRL PLAYING THE GEKKIN

THE JAPANESE BOW

to the quaint workings of Japanese jurisprudence and although formally found guilty, the nominal sentence of a year's imprisonment passed upon him was postponed indefinitely!

In closing this incomplete chapter on political assassination I should say that in addition to the crimes actually consummated there have been numerous unsuccessful attempts, notably the attack on Count Okuma in 1888, when in consequence of popular excitement evoked by his treaty revision proposals a fanatic hurled a bomb at his coach and inflicted injuries upon his leg which necessitated its amputation, and the attempted murder of the late Tsar, then Crown Prince of Russia, by a mad policeman at Otsu.

CHAPTER XVII

THE ART OF NINSŌ OR PHYSIOGNOMY

It is certainly a trifle disconcerting, to say the least, when a friend to whom you have never at any time given an inkling of your intentions glances at you casually one fine day and then remarks, "Well, I see you are engaged to be married."

The foregoing is the epitome of a personal experience of long ago which I would not venture to inflict upon the reader were it not that it furnishes a convenient text for what is to follow.

In the absence of any previous intimation that my friend had taken up the Sherlock Holmes business in deadly earnest, I felt positively bewildered, the more seeing that the soft impeachment was well deserved—I *was* engaged to be married, albeit the last man in the universe, one might then have said, of whom any such step had been expected by his friends. Always ready to give credit where credit is due I admitted the truth of the diagnosis and added, "How on earth did you know? I haven't told a soul so far."

"I found out just this moment by means of *ninsō*."

"What the deuce is *ninsō*?"

"The Japanese term for their art of physiognomy."

"You don't mean to say that you can detect the fact of a man's engagement simply by looking at his face?" I asked incredulously.

"Exactly what I do mean to say," replied my friend, frankly enjoying my bewilderment. "What's more," he went on, "I see that you recently received news touching a financial deal of some kind and that the news was of a favourable character."

I began to feel light-headed—a state of being not difficult to encounter in Dai Nippon owing to climatic aberrations. "You're right again," I muttered feebly. Then, reassembling my scattered faculties, I said. "Look here, M———, I must know something more about this. Seems to me there's excellent copy in this *ninsō*. Who's your teacher? Can't you introduce me and induce him to furnish me with a general outline of how these results are obtained?"

"Why, yes, I think that can be managed," was the reply.

My friend then told me that the expert from whom he had been taking lessons was a young man named Seki, whose family had been in the *ninsō* business for at least 200 years. He lived in the Shiba ward of the capital and had a large clientele.

A few days later, having previously secured Seki's consent, we proceeded together to the Shiba residence and were at once ushered into the presence of the master. The house was a two-storied structure in Japanese style, well and strongly built, the substitution of a kind of porous cloth for the more usual fragile paper to all in the *shōji* (a window or door sash usually covered with paper) indicating clearly that the owner had ideas of his own and was not content to follow slavishly in the footsteps of convention. Such indications are distinctly refreshing in Japan, a land where century-old etiquette reigns supreme in many spheres despite the reputation the Japanese enjoy for progress. The reception-room on the ground-floor looked out into a pretty Japanese garden. A gigantic Fowler phrenological chart in one of the alcoves, or *tokonoma*, suggested that the owner was of eclectic bent and had not limited his field of inquiry to Japanese authorities alone.

Seki himself sat behind the regulation Japanese brazier with his back to the open *shōji* and garden, in such wise that while his own face remained more or less in the shadow all the available light impinged upon that of the client, male or female, who chanced to be squatting before him at the time at the other side of the brazier. I learned later that it was no unusual occurrence for Seki to anticipate the exact object of the inquirer's visit the moment he or she entered the room, often to his or her amazement and embarrassment, notwithstanding previous belief in the efficacy of his art. Another circumstance which could not fail to impress the foreigner was that no effort whatsoever was made by Seki to provide, or by his clients to demand, privacy. Thus nobody seemed to find anything objectionable in the disclosure and discussion of the most intimate details of his or her past, present and future, in the presence and hearing of strangers. It is dangerous to set an absolute standard of propriety, and personally I am not at all disposed to think any the worse of the Japanese on the score of their proneness to call a spade a spade. Neither my friend nor I was a tyro in the sphere of Japanese manners and customs, but

still we were obviously and unmistakably foreigners, so that the
willingness of a small army of Japanese men and women, representing numerous walks in life, to submit to open scrutiny before
us surely argues that anti-foreign prejudice is not quite so deeply
rooted and widespread as many would fain have us suppose.

Seki proved to be a young man not much over thirty, of highly
prepossessing appearance, of average height for a Japanese, clean-
shaven, with closely cropped hair. His eyes, exceptionally large,
bright and penetrating, were his most striking feature, and furnished an index to his profession. He received us with customary
Japanese politeness, ordered cushions for us to sit on, tea to drink
and invited us to look on while he proceeded with his examination.
He explained that this being the summer season, he was less busy
than usual, but still hoped that the list of callers might provide
us with some interesting data.

One of his first visitors after our arrival was a youth of nineteen
or thereabouts, who entered the room with a sheepish air. He had
hardly had time to take his seat in front of Seki than the latter
greeted him with the stern query, "What do you mean by running
away from home without informing your mother? You must
write to her at once and relieve her anxiety."

The wretched youth stared at his mentor with bulging eyes
and hanging jaw, and could find no word of denial, for the piercing
vision of the expert had accurately detected that which to the
uninitiated must have remained hidden, in the absence of
voluntary confession from the subject.

The next seeker after advice was a young married woman
accompanied by a female friend. Seki looked at her for a moment
steadily and then began: "I see you are having trouble with your
husband who has brought another woman into the house. You
have been in an interesting condition for three months. Well, you
are mostly to blame for your husband's conduct. You are too fond
of nagging and give him no peace. I advise you to change your
tactics and to submit, even if you have to live in the same house
with the concubine. You must try to win back your husband's
affection by kindness; prove to him that you are a better woman
than the other, and in that way you can win him back."

Not the kind of advice an Occidental fortune-teller would be
likely to give his client, but the Japanese standpoint on such

questions of domestic policy is not ours, and the Japanese social watchword is hardly *Place aux dames*! Seki was one of the most sympathetic Japanese of my acquaintance, but he did not pretend to rise superior to the practice of his ancestors in this regard, though I have had ample proof that if he thought the husband were wholly to blame for what had happened he would not have hesitated to say so. In fact, the complete indifference with which he told his clients, both the bad and the good, about their characters and prospects, making not the smallest attempt to flatter, satisfied me of his absolute sincerity and *bona fides*. The sceptical may wish to know why a line, a spot, or a shade of colour in the face of a human being should furnish an infallible clue to disposition, to past, present or future happenings in the life of an individual. I do not pretend to explain why this should be so, but at least when I am given conclusive proof of the expert's ability to discover these personal details, both known and unknown to the subject, I see no reason why I should not accept the expert's own voluntary explanation of the method by which he arrives at these staggering results. It is for the sceptic to offer a more plausible theory to account for the phenomenon.

The next client was a woman of twenty. She was visibly embarrassed beneath the physiognomist's steady scrutiny. "You are engaged," said Seki. "You will be married within the year. You will be well advised to try to remedy some defects in your character. You are too much of a gossip and scandal-monger, and unless you are careful the tie between yourself and your husband will be very thin. Your physique is not good. You are too fat. Your shoulders are too broad and your hips too narrow. I am sorry to say that your prospects are not likely to be very bright, but things may improve after your twenty-seventh year." It was patent from the girl's confusion that Seki had correctly gauged her weaknesses, while she had admitted the fact of her engagement. After she had withdrawn Seki turned to us and stated that in all probability her husband would die a year after their marriage.

A middle-aged woman came next. Seki glibly mentioned that she was married to her second husband and had a female child; that her husband was abroad, but that she would probably hear from him by the spring. He assured her that she would live to a good old age and had no cause for anxiety as to the future.

Nearly all these readings were coupled with useful advice on diet and hygiene. Seki, in addition to being a professional physiognomist, was a duly certified doctor of medicine, but on his own admission could invariably arrive at a more reliable diagnosis of an individual's physical condition by the study of the countenance than by recourse to the ordinary tools of a physician.

A young student wearing glasses was told that he would achieve worldly success throughout his career, but that he could not hope to enjoy good physical health.

A hard-looking man in his thirties had barely time to squat before Seki remarked: "Yes, I see you have been speculating and have come a cropper. You ought to know better. You are too fickle and never stick to any one thing for any length of time. You are also involved in domestic trouble."

All this was true. In every case, of course, the expert outlined the future and gave good advice, but he did not as a rule tell all he saw. He would not, for example, without very satisfactory reasons inform a client of an early death or grave disaster, unless he knew of means whereby either could be averted.

A young photographer whom we had brought with us to take pictures was given a free reading, and for the first time in his life It is no exaggeration to say that he was one of the most dumbfounded men in Tokyo before Seki was "through" with him. The fact that he was engaged in marriage preliminaries was speedily detected. "But," continued Seki with a smile, "what are you going to live on if you do marry? You haven't a cent and are not likely to earn much more for many years to come. You generally spend far more than you are able to earn."

The young man, with many blushes and chuckles, confessed that he was aspiring to the status of a Benedict without any visible means of support. Seki branched out into several other lines of inquiry which cannot be described in these pages, but as he proved invariably correct with respect to the past and present, we ourselves were confident that his predictions in their turn would be justified by the event.

In another case a mother submitted her five-year-old boy for inspection. Seki said by way of preliminary: "I take it that the boy's father is a naval or military man. Isn't that so?" The astonished mother admitted that it was. Further Seki, making no bones about it, described this sweet child as at once avaricious, destructive and cowardly, with a future in which coin of the realm would undoubtedly bulk very largely, as also the eternal feminine.

Several visitors submitted to the expert photographs of prospective brides or bridegrooms for reading of character. Admitting the reality of the art, it is obvious that in this branch of activity there lies wide scope for usefulness since the expert claims to be in a position to determine whether or not the contracting parties are of compatible temperament and whether, therefore, the proposed marriage will or will not prove a failure.

One male applicant was a naval officer in the Reserve, a man with a decidedly unpleasant face and manner. Seki examined the photograph of the girl this man was thinking of marrying and gave a highly favourable report. No sooner had the officer retired than Seki turned to me and observed: "That girl is far too good for a fellow like that. He will be sure to make her unhappy."

Sometimes a couple before marriage would apply to Seki for advice, and by means of his art he could often furnish useful indications of character which subsequently enabled the parties to avoid petty squabbles which in most instances were due to ignorance and misunderstanding of individual weaknesses. When man and wife were forewarned of their respective shortcomings it was far easier for them to steer clear of these pitfalls.

One of the most unsavoury cases on the list was that of a rough-looking man from whom the confession was extorted that he intended to sell a fifteen-year-old daughter into a life of shame. Seki "roasted" the blackguard unreservedly and warned him that nothing good would come of such a step, but it may well be doubted whether his words carried the desired weight.

As an elderly woman entered the room Seki looked at her and promptly said, "You want to ask my advice about adopting a thirteen-year-old girl; is it not so?" The woman in amazement stammered assent. Seki then told her that she had married half a dozen husbands, but that not one of them had been of any use to her in her business, and that she was now in financial difficulties in consequence. All these details were correct.

Another case which illustrates Seki's honest determination to disclose what he deemed to be the truth, however unpleasant, was as follows: Three Kagoshima men once called on him and one of the trio submitted his face for inspection. It was noticeable that as Seki looked him full in the eyes the subject blinked continually. Seki made several preliminary statements which showed that by means of his art he had correctly ascertained the client's antecedents. Incidentally he reproached him for having neglected to pay proper respect to the memory of his late father. Then came the dramatic denouement.

"I see you are a defendant in a law case," said Seki. "It's a criminal action, and I am sorry to have to tell you that no matter what steps you take you cannot get off with less than two years' imprisonment."

The unfortunate client gasped with astonishment and consternation. He admitted that the first statement was quite true, and explained the facts. It seems he was a lawyer who had drafted certain articles of association for a company in Kagoshima which had subsequently failed in suspicious circumstances. The directors had been arrested and their depositions had involved the lawyer in responsibility for his share in preparing the aforesaid articles. The object of the visit of the lawyer and his two friends was to solicit Seki's advice. If, in his opinion, the case was worth fighting they had money and were ready to go on with it; but if he assured them that nothing could be done to avert an unfavourable outcome they would then let events take their course. Seki reluctantly confirmed his former diagnosis that no action of their part would be of any use, and that the minimum penalty the lawyer could expect would be two years.

From what has been said it will be seen that Seki's modest reception-room was frequently the scene of tragedy as well as comedy, and that those who ventured to appeal to the oracle of *ninsō* had to be prepared to take the consequences. True, Seki did not always reveal everything he saw in the facial record; he exercised a wise discretion, but when, as in this case, he thought no good purpose would be served by reticence, he could be painfully frank.

Individual instances might be indefinitely multiplied but they would add little to our knowledge of how these results are achieved. On this point Seki was unexpectedly frank. Although naturally unwilling to disclose the details of his method he very kindly furnished me with a lucid general outline of the *ninsō* system together with a sketch of his own family and personal history.

The practice of physiognomy in the Seki family dates back nearly 200 years, while the majority of the male members of the family had also studied medicine, the subject of this sketch being a fully qualified practitioner and a student of the then well-known Tokyo physician, Dr. Takagi. Nevertheless, in the Seki family medicine has been, so to speak, only a side line and it has been an imperative tradition generation after generation that the male head of the family should devote himself mainly to the investigation and practice of *ninsō*. If we are prepared to admit that *ninsō* is an art and not a superstition, then it is evident that every succeeding representative of the family must benefit appreciably by the mass of accumulated knowledge and experience transmitted from his forefathers; in other words, it is not difficult to believe that even in the absence of a scientific theory these keen-witted and observant Japanese, with their love of detail and through purely empirical methods, must have enjoyed unique opportunities for the cultivation of abnormal skill in the reading of character and forecasting of the future.

Young Seki graduated as a doctor in 1901, and between 1904 and 1905 served with the Japanese field hospital staff in Manchuria during the war with Russia. In 1906 he settled down at his then residence in succession to his father as an exponent of the *ninsō* art. He assured me that at the outset he found the work terribly tedious and repugnant to him, and he would have preferred to continue his medical practice had the decision rested with him. In Japan, however, parental authority is virtually all-powerful, and the idea of running counter to his father's wishes never even entered young Seki's head. Gradually too he grew to like his work and was perfectly satisfied with his lot in life.

In Japanese the term *ninsō* has a considerably broader significance than the English word "physiognomy" in that it embraces not only the purely facial characteristics of the subject but also the shape of his body, his manner of walking, sitting posture, manner of sitting down, the clothes he wears and numerous other details. Moreover when at the commencement of each seance the subject was required to write the Japanese figure 1—a horizontal stroke—with a Japanese brush, Seki derived more than one hint as to personal character from the style in which the brush was held and applied to the paper, as well as from the stroke itself which was very closely scrutinized on occasion. The study of calligraphy is also a branch of the *ninsō* art and Seki claimed to be able to learn a great deal from the handwriting of a client in conjunction with the quality of the paper used for the purpose.

Turning to the physical features of the client, it is explained that importance is attached to the contour of the face, the shape of the nose, eyes, eyebrows, cheek-bones, chin, mouth, teeth, ears, forehead, etc. The lines of the forehead, nose and mouth furnish many clues to character and fortune. The lines on either side of the mouth, Seki stated, are studied in relation to length of life, success or failure in business. Astonishingly elaborate is the *ninsō* classification of facial colours, the terminology of which is so complicated that in several instances I have failed altogether to find satisfactory English equivalents for subtle shades, though doubtless they are included in the spectrum analysis. The chief basic colours mentioned by Seki are red, dark red, yellow, green, black, white and three shades known as *anshoku*, *moshoku* and *junshoku*. In deciding the meaning of every one of these colours Seki explained that a great deal depended upon the exact spot in which they appeared in the face of the subject, the latter's age, and the season of the year. Very naturally Seki preferred not to reveal the esoteric portions of the system and therefore did not explain the precise manner in which the foregoing modifications were estimated. Thus the assignment of meanings to the respective colours, as explained below, must be accepted only in a general sense and not as an infallible guide.

As a rule red is not a colour of good omen; it commonly implies trouble or dispute of some kind, the failure of the business or enterprise in which the subject happens to be engaged. I white is shown in conjunction with red in a certain section of the face, the sign indicates severe or fatal illness of some relative of the subject.

Dark red, on the contrary, is a felicitous colour and wherever it appears it indicates good fortune and the fulfilment generally of the subject's hopes.

Yellow is also a happy colour, implying that the future will turn out in accordance with the subject's wishes.

Green in conjunction with light red is not a fortunate colour; it usually means that things are going wrong for the subject. Governed by location, green sometimes indicates that the subject is going to move or to travel. If green and red show up together in relation to moving or travelling, then the subject will move or travel in a very short time.

White has reference to death or the occurrence of misfortune; it is emphatically a bad colour. Should it appear in a certain place and when the subject has reached a certain age, it shows infallibly that the victim's hours are numbered. He is not long for this world.

Anshoku may perhaps be defined as a dark grey shade, and is not at all desirable, for it means that the object or wish of the subject will not be realized, whereas if it gradually disappears improvement will as surely set in.

Black has much the same signification but is even more emphatic. When black and green appear in conjunction with the lines of the eye, the front part of the ear, and about the nose and nostrils, they point to death by drowning or on the water. When the darker shades are noted round the eyes of the subject, the subject may safely be set down as a thief or a liar. Care, however, must be taken to discriminate between discolouration due to ill-health and a *bona fide ninsō* symptom.

Moshoku, a cloudy shade, is an unfortunate colour. Subject to location, the person in whose face it appears cannot hope to succeed in what he has in hand.

Inshoku, also a dull, cloudy shade, though different from the above, is a happy colour, and no matter what other colour it may cover the subject is sure of good fortune in relation both to his own personal affairs and those of others in whom he may be interested. Thus if some friend or relative is ill he or she will recover. In a word, *inshoku* is a shade of happy augury.

Lines, wrinkles, moles, pimples etc., have all to be carefully studied by the *ninsō* expert. As a rule no one indication can be wholly isolated from the rest; colours, lines and contours have to be scrutinized in combination and it is in his ability to do this that the skill of the *ninsō* expert lies.

Another very essential factor is the division of the face into right and left. Speaking generally, indications noted on the subject's right side affect himself, whereas those noted on the left side apply to another person whose fate is associated in some way with his own. For example, when a certain kind of pimple breaks out on the subject's right temple it means that he is worrying over some love affair; while when the same kind of pimple appears on the left temple it means that some girl or woman is in love with the subject and worrying on his account. I have had ocular demonstration that these signs will make their appearance simultaneously on the face of a man and woman, but on the right and left temples respectively, in strict accordance with the rule above cited. What is more, just as they may appear suddenly overnight they are known to disappear with equal suddenness when the exciting cause is removed.

"It must be noted," said Seki, "that when in an anatomical sense the eyes, eyebrows, ears, mouth, nose and so forth are well shaped, everything goes much better. Nevertheless, even if the shape is good but the colour emphatically bad, the result is unfavourable; while when the shape is bad but the colour decidedly good, the total indication must be pronounced favourable. The hair of the head, beard, in the nose, the eyebrows, eyelashes etc. exercise modifying tendencies. Often from the manner in which the beard or moustache grows, or from the line of demarcation between the hair and the forehead, I can foretell good or bad fortune, long or short life for the subject—whether a woman will change her husband or how many husbands she will have, whether she will enjoy prosperity or the reverse. The colours help to decide questions concerning sickness, death, pregnancy, genius, natural ability etc. When a client is writing and suddenly looks up, I instinctively gain an insight into his character. I cannot explain precisely how I do this—it is the outcome of long practice and experience."

Although such a statement may provoke a smile of derision from the sceptical, Seki and others who pursue the same calling have proved their ability to reveal the past of a client even to the extent of describing the locality in which he lived in early youth, the kind of house he lived in, the number of rooms, and various topographical features connected with the neighbourhood

It goes without saying that in Seki's business the identity of the client is a matter of secondary importance. Seki never inquired the name of the visitor and no cards were submitted. Nevertheless it was an open secret that men occupying very high positions in business, the professions, and the Government service constantly availed themselves of Seki's art with a view to determining their course of action. His advice was sought not only in person but by correspondence and photograph. He was in receipt of letters from all parts of the country in such volume that he could with difficulty keep pace with them, and it frequently happened that distant clients who had enclosed the required fee grew impatient over the delay in reply and addressed subsequent inquiries to the local police authorities. The latter, however, were all on the most friendly terms with Seki and after seeing the mountain of mail matter awaiting treatment could always reassure impatient and suspicious clients on this point. It may be added that the police themselves often submitted to Seki photographs of criminals or suspected criminals in the hope of gaining information on which to base their investigations.

In conclusion, I think it is conservative to say that an art which has stood the test of centuries, which is practised, not by vulgar charlatans but by men of education and refinement, scholars and qualified physicians, and which enjoys the patronage of Japanese of all classes, ought not to be lightly dismissed by the superior person as a ridiculous superstition.

A short time ago I was highly gratified to hear from a correspondent in Japan that Seki had survived the Tokyo Blitz and was still a hale and hearty octogenarian practising his art in the same neighbourhood, if not in the same house.

CHAPTER XVIII

THE SOCK AND BUSKIN

THE colloquial Japanese for theatre is *shibai* which also means a dramatic performance. Literally the two ideographs of which the word is composed stand respectively for "*shiba*", or "grass" and "*i*" or "abode", and the word can therefore be used to signify "sitting on a lawn or grass plot", as in the expression "*shibai wo suru*" meaning "to sit on a lawn". The derivation of the word is uncertain but there is reason to believe that in early days representations took place in the open air and the literary equivalent for theatre *rien*, means also "pear garden or orchard" and would thus point to a similar origin. Without attempting to trace in Japanese fashion the pedigree of the theatre as far back as the mythological age, I shall merely sketch as briefly as may be the known facts of the subject.

A young woman named Okuni, attached to a temple as sacred dancer (*miko*), during the sixteenth century undertook tour through the empire with the object of raising subscription for the repair of the famous Izumi Shinto temple. At Kyoto sh performed a sort of mythological play symbolizing the dance of th gods before the cave in which the Sun Goddess (Amaterasu ōmikami) had hidden herself and thereby plunged the world int darkness. Unfortunately for Okuni's reputation, scandal soo began to attach to her name, for it is recorded that she was some thing of a beauty, and so in the course of a few years we find he launched as a full-blown professional actress in Kyoto. It surmised that the plays then produced were recitations in charact of primitive poems and folk-lore. Okuni used to perform the plays or dances on the dry bed of a river, to which fact may l ascribed the subsequent fashion of speaking of actors as *kawara-z mono*, or "performers on a dry river-bed".

The *Nō* dances antedate the modern drama which the la Professor Chamberlain thought was a development of the sho *kyōgen*, or farces with which the *Nō* were and are intersperse

The *Nō* have survived until the present day and although somewhat tiresome in themselves to the uninitiated, possess a distinct antiquarian interest. The *Nō* are, in fact, a highly aristocratic distraction, entirely unintelligible to those who have not made them a special study, since the language of the chorus is the classical one of a byegone age. Besides the chorus there is an orchestra which evokes strains which to the barbarous Occidental are extremely weird. There is no scenery, but the actors are magnificently clad and wear masks of the most hideous description, some of them of great age. The late Lord Redesdale defines the *Nō* as a kind of classical opera performed on stages especially built for the purpose in the palaces of the principal nobles and, he might have added, in connexion with certain Shinto temples. In fact, it was on the occasion of the visit of one of the famous *Nō* companies to Yokohama—for even the *Nō* had become to a certain extent democratized during the Meiji era—that I sat out a performance for at least nine hours at the well-known Noge temple. The choruses are intoned in a strange recitative which sometimes rises to a squeal, not unlike the sounds which emanate from a tom-cat on the tiles, and again descends to the notes of the lower register and appears to proceed from the singer's stomach. One's natural inclination to laugh is at once repressed on looking at the solemn faces of the members of the audience to whom the *Nō* is no idle jest to while away an hour or so, but a cult to be cultivated and nurtured with the devotion of a lifetime. Every motion, every gesture of the actors is cut and dried, and one can readily believe that to memorize a series of such dances must entail an enormous amount of both physical and mental labour. I have even been told by a Japanese friend, now unfortunately no more, that in some of these dances the performer is supposed to keep himself constantly covered with his fan in such a manner that a skilful fencer would not be able to detect an opening for attack. Apropos of this theory, he narrated the story of how a certain famous *Nō* dancer was once performing in the presence of the Shogun, and how in the midst of the dance he was seen suddenly to make a slip in an unaccountable fashion, while at the same moment a voice from the ranks of the spectators was heard to exclaim gleefully, "I've got him!" The speaker was an equally famous master of fence, who had been watching the performance from the beginning with lynx-like eyes in the faint hope of discovering a weak spot in the dancer's hypothetical defence. And then the unexpected happened and, carried away by his professional feelings, the fencer, mentally delivering the fatal thrust or cut, gave vent to the ejaculation above recorded. The poor Nō dancer at the close of the performance approached the Shogunal box, prostrated himself in the accepted style, and craved permission to explain how it was that he had been guilty of what must appear to the Shogun an unpardonable piece of maladroitness. He went on to say that while in the act of bringing off a more than usually difficult *pas* he had been disconcerted to notice that part of the stage had not been properly cleaned, and it was owing to the shock caused by this discovery that he had lost his head and blundered! In any event, he hastened to assure the Shogun of his willingness to atone for his offence by there and then committing *harakiri*, if the Shogun so desired. It is pleasant to be able to add that this final proof of professional enthusiasm was not exacted of him by his august master.

The subjects of the Nō are taken from the old folklore and national legends, and their literary form is said to be of the highest excellence. Among the more notable of the pieces inflicted upon me on the occasion referred to was the famous *Sumidagawa* which tells how the child of a noble family in Kyoto was kidnapped by slave-dealers and carried off to Tokyo, but died and was buried on the banks of the Sumida river. The distracted mother sets off in search of her son, and on reaching the river overhear the passengers on the ferry speaking of the death of a kidnapped child some time before, and finally comes to a willow-tree where the villagers are weeping over a grave. She questions them and learns that the dead is none other than her son. She is distraught and during the night the ghost of the child appears and holds converse with her; but when she seeks to embrace it, it vanishes into air, and she hears but the sighing of the breeze. No doubt the recital is pathetic in the original, but for me the ghastly white and inane mask of the actor who impersonated the mother spoilt all the poetry. When in the performance the mother would fain embrace her son, the youngster who played that rôle simply slipped under her outstretched arms and ran behind the stage property which represented the grave. The story is nevertheless suppose

JAPANESE GIRL IN TRADITIONAL
OUTDOOR COSTUME

to be authentic and to belong to the tenth century, and today on the banks of the Sumida at Mukojima may be seen a small shrine erected in commemoration of the tragedy, and here a special service is held every 15th of March.

I attended the above-mentioned performance in the company of my Japanese teacher, himself an amateur *Nō* singer of some pretension. After a solid nine hours at the *Nō* theatre he must needs drag me off to his home and there condemn me to endure for another hour his own particular version of some of the unearthly strains to which I had been listening for so long. His younger brother squatted at the other side of the little Japanese table and ably seconded the vocal efforts of his senior, the while I tried to look as intelligent and appreciative as the circumstances and my powers of dissimulation would permit. I have reason to believe that I succeeded. But having thus satisfied a curiosity which has more than once involved me in difficulties, I have never since invited a second ordeal of that description.

Although the Japanese theatre may be said to have been founded by a woman, it has since become virtually a monopoly of the male sex. It is true that nowadays there are a few companies composed entirely of women, in deference to the former law which would not permit the sexes to perform together, but they enjoy no great reputation and, save in the so-called *sōshi-shibai*, more elegantly and correctly the *shin-engeki* (new drama), men and women are never seen in company on the stage. It is curious to observe that whereas the *Nō* actors have always enjoyed the highest reputation it is only within comparatively recent years that the players in the popular theatres which produce the so-called *kabuki*, or old-style classical drama, have begun to be recognized as human beings, inasmuch as in the old days they were denoted in all official documents by the auxiliary numerals used in counting animals. The insult inflicted by such a practice will scarcely be appreciated by readers unacquainted with the Japanese language. The actor was also forbidden to appear abroad without wearing a *zukin*, or hood which covered the head and face.

Things are rather better nowadays, and the great actors of Japan are among the wealthiest and most popular subjects of the Emperor. But although the theatre is generously patronized by the lower and middle classes, the more old-fashioned and refined scions of the *shizoku*, as the former samurai caste is now designated, are still loath to extend encouragement to a form of distraction which they regard as frivolous and even immoral. I myself had a Japanese friend who, despite the fact that he had travelled in Europe and America, spoke perfect English and wore foreign clothes every day, would not enter a theatre himself nor permit his children to do so. His determination to adhere to this principle was strengthened many years ago, when as the representative of a leading metropolitan daily he was once induced to attend a gala performance at the Kabukiza, the principal theatre of the metropolis, where the late Danjuro, Japan's most famous modern actor, was cast for the leading rôle—the impersonation of a former Shogun. My friend, whom I shall call Mr. S, arrived in good time and occupied his box. All went well until the entrance of the star and then, carried away by the intense realism of the production, and more especially by the majesty of Danjuro's appearance and address as he stalked towards the footlights, poor Mr. S forgot that it was all make-believe and made a profound obeisance in his box and in the direction of the great actor! His feelings when he realized what he had done may be readily imagined. That he, a samurai, should have thus demeaned himself in honour of a plebeian and a member of the despised class of Thespians at that, was none too pleasant a reflection, and the "noisy laugh and ill-bred chaff" of his many male friends did not help to mend matters. He had his revenge by never again extending to the playhouse the smallest moral or material support, albeit forced to acknowledge the consummate art of the great Danjuro. Kikugoro, Sadanji and Fukusuke were also names to conjure with on the Japanese boards in my time. Kikugoro died in 1903, almost at the same time as the late Prince Komatsu.

The leading Japanese theatre in Tokyo in my day was the Kabukiza where the "legitimate" had its habitat. The usual performance at this and other houses of the same school began and today also begin at 10 or 11 a.m. and last eight or nine hours, for some Japanese plays contain as many as sixteen acts. In fact in this as in other diversions the Japanese like to make a day of it and so they have their meals brought to them in the theatre. One reason assigned for the comparatively early closing of the Japanese theatre is that it tends to check immorality, since it is notorious that professional women in Japan, as well as others inclined to be "fast", frequently lose their heads over professional actors and pursue them quite openly in the most unblushing manner. The actors on their side confine their love of romance to the stage, and off the boards are apt to set a very practical price upon their favours, for which, sad to relate, too many infatuated women are prepared to pay.

In Europe and America one may drop into a theatre casually, at least in principle, provided that tickets are available, and pass the evening there. Not so in Japan. The mania for surrounding the simplest acts of life with useless formalities is once again exemplified, and he who does not want to be looked down upon as a mere vulgarian will find it necessary to apply beforehand to the *chaya*, or teahouse, which is connected with every theatre—a sort of parasite which absorbs a big share of the profits for discharging functions which would seem properly to belong to the theatre itself. But in Japan etiquette is a remorseless tyrant and apparently a theatrical manager would rather go "bust" according to Hoyle than refuse to let himself be robbed by these chartered bandits. So instead of going direct to the theatre and reserving a box you must go to the teahouse a few steps away and there make all arrangements three or four days ahead, if the representation is at all popular. On the day appointed you are conducted to your box by the teahouse attendant who waits upon you between the acts and expects to be liberally tipped for his services. It is usual to supply a Japanese patron with a programme, a cushion, a tobacco firebox, a pot of tea, cakes, lunch, fruit and *sushi*—the last named a sort of sandwich made of rice and fish. At the Kabukiza and some of the other larger houses foreigners are provided with chairs. The different sets of seats in a Japanese theatre are thus named: There are the *sajiki*, or gallery boxes; *uzura*, or ground tier; *takadoma*, or raised pit; *hiradoma*, or level pit; and the *oikomi*, or topmost gallery where the *hoi polloi* most do congregate. *Oikomi* means "driven in" place and well deserves its name, its patrons being commonly packed therein as tightly as sardines in a tin. They stand behind a grated pen whence the stage is barely visible.

The two most distinctive features of the inside of the Japanese theatre are the *hanamichi* ("flower-path") and the *mawaributai* (revolving stage). The former is a raised platform branching off on either side of the auditorium and serving as an alternative means of exit and entrance for the actors, in addition to the wings. The latter is what its name implies—i.e. a sort of turntable comprising a big section of the stage floor on which two different scenes can be built up, the second being exhibited with scarcely a moment's delay by simply causing the stage to revolve and carry off the actors and properties of the first scene. The curtain (*maku*) in first-class theatres is drawn sideways, but in second and third-class houses is rolled up much the same as in Europe. It is the fashion for the admirers of a celebrated actor to present him with a curtain beautifully decorated, and such gifts cost hundreds of yen. The adoption of electricity and other foreign appliances has led to remarkable improvements in stage scenery which today can challenge comparison with that of the West in not a few departments. Anything more horribly realistic than a Japanese stage killing it would be difficult to imagine. Japanese spectators demand plenty of gore for their money, and they get it.

Mr. Suteta Takashima, an authority on Japanese theatricals, states that actors are classified on the basis of the parts they act, chief among which are *Aragotoshi* (rough characters), *Jitsugotoshi* (historical characters representing loyalty or chivalry) and *Jitsuakashi* (wicked characters). "Female parts," says he, "are acted by men. It was at the beginning of the seventeenth century that women were prohibited from appearing on the stage along with men. The above remark does not mean that there are no actresses in Japan; as a matter of fact there are, but the two sexes could not in olden days and do not at present perform together on the same stage. The training and discipline undergone by actors who play the rôle of women are beyond adequate description. It is not enough that they are made the very image of women by means of facial make-up, dress and toilet, but more still their manners and action must reflect those of the fair sex. It is natural that from childhood they should be placed as much as possible in female society, and while at home they put on female dress and are disciplined until the last trace of masculine proclivities is obliterated. The *Onnagata*, or impersonators of female characters, wield no mean influence in the guild of actors, this fact being shown by the principal positions their names occupy in programmes. No green-room but theirs is locked from the inside, and no other actors can enter without first asking the permission of the occupant. Dancing is considered the first and last qualification of an actor, and it is to this end alone that his early training is directed. Of course a novice must perform a humble part in a play; he usually makes his début as *Uma-no-ashi*, or 'horse's leg'! On the stage in Japan the employment of a real horse being out of the question, a framework is used representing the head and body of the animal with the poor actors serving as its legs! Those born in theatrical families are spared such an ordeal, but to others who have no pedigree to save them, the apprenticeship to the stage is not very smooth sailing."

This humble rôle has passed into a proverb, to wit, *Bakyaku wo arawasu* ("to disclose a horse's legs", or, in other words, to reveal one's true character, betray oneself, show the cloven hoof, or one's natural form is bound sooner or later to reveal itself however much one may try to hide it).

The popular taste lends itself to heavy tragedy, the historical play based upon some authentic case of loyalty or revenge being highly esteemed. Chikamatsu's version of the story of the forty-seven *rōnin* (*Chūshingura*), who in Yedo at the end of the seventeenth century avenged their lord's judicial suicide, is a universal favourite. There is usually an orchestra and a soloist as chorus (*joruri*) which reminds one of descriptions of the ancient Greek drama as well as of the *Nō* already described. The strange falsetto which is the Japanese substitute for singing is always painful to foreign ears, though it has power to move the female portion of the audience to tears. One of the special functions of this chorus is to narrate in convulsive recitative the mental processes of the actors, thus sparing them the necessity of thinking aloud as is the case with us. The *pièce de resistance* is often preceded by a kind of curtain-raiser, or *mae-kyōgen*, commonly broad farce.

The language of the classical drama is an archaic form of Japanese unintelligible even to foreigners who are thoroughly conversant with the colloquial. To understand a Japanese play one must be familiar with the incidents, manners and customs with which it deals, in addition to the mere grammatical form and vocabulary of the piece. Without denying the great histrionic talent of actors like the late Danjuro and Sadanji I must confess that, as in the *Nō*, the manufactured stage voice and stilted gestures, whether a faithful reflection of the old-fashioned Japan or not, are to me a source of irritation. The costumes are superb and the value of the Japanese drama as a mirror of the ancient regime can scarcely be overrated.

Many of the best Japanese judges are themselves alive to the shortcomings of the old classical school which is but ill adapted to the intellectual and moral needs of the rising generation. One Koda Rohan, an eminent novelist, has said in this context:

"Judged by high standards Japanese acting today is very poor. But this is to be attributed to the fact that stage-acting, like so many other things in this country, is now in a state of transition. Progress is slow because the majority of the people who habitually frequent theatres are essentially conservative and prefer to see their old historical plays acted according to traditional rules. To obtain new dramas and new actors is no easy thing. It must be borne in mind too that to numerous actors Western methods of acting do not commend themselves at all. Now to get rid of all these actors at a stroke is impossible, as the men to replace them are not to be had. To convince them that their acting is out of date and that they must alter it is very difficult. Hence the slow progress made. But there are some things demanded by the present age which, though not impracticable by any means, are not effected by the managers of theatres. Why, for instance, are the performances stretched out over so many hours in these busy times? This practice keeps many people away from the theatre.

"Then since acting is an appeal to the eye, an appeal to the ear and an appeal to the heart, it is important that those who cater for the public today should realize that Japanese eyes Japanese ears and the Japanese mind are not what they were half a century ago and that hence what amused theatre-goers in Tokugawa times is today deemed wearisome. The want of new plays being keenly felt, the fashion occasionally followed in the West of making ordinary works of fiction serve the purpose of dramas has been adopted here; but the result has in most cases been far from satisfactory. Only a few of the many novels which have been published in recent times len:

themselves to treatment of this kind. In stage-acting the appeal
to the heart is often made very powerful by stage scenery,
music, gestures and the like. It is not the spoken word only but
the sights and sounds which precede, follow, or accompany
them that produce a strong impression on the minds of the
audience. Now in many of the attempts to adapt fiction to
reproduction on the stage this has been entirely overlooked—
with disastrous results. Some modern actors are neither well
versed in old ways of acting nor in the new style which is gradually being introduced. . . . But I am convinced of one thing,
and that is that stage-acting is progressing, though the progress
is slow. The old-style actors are gradually disappearing. As
time goes on, new dramas representing modern Japan and its
new views of life will take the place of the historical plays
which have lost much of their significance and interest to the
men and women of today."

Analogously, Dr. Inouye has compared the Japanese and
Western stages to the disadvantage of the former. In regard to
operas, operettas and ballets, he rightly asserts that Japan has
nothing worthy of comparison with the production of Wagner and
other composers.

"Our *kappore*, though possessing a few points of resemblance
to Western ballets, is lacking in dignity and refinement. The
miyako-odori and the *sansha-shigure* approach nearer to foreign
ballet but they are wanting in spirit and 'go'. Japanese dancing
consists too exclusively of mere posturing, bending to the right
and to the left, extending the limbs in this fashion or that, the
hands playing the principal part and the feet being used only
to keep time, which is done in a grotesquely noisy fashion. In
foreign ballet-dancing the adroit use of the feet is the main
feature, and it is far more exciting to watch than an attitude-
striking stage performance. We have only one ballet-dance
that may be said to be permeated with energy and that is the
sambaso, but this is quite an exceptional performance."

This testimony from a qualified Japanese is very interesting
as an offset to certain attempts on the part of former foreign

writers to prove how infinitely superior to our own dancing is the Japanese in all that pertains to true refinement, imagination, and poetry of motion.

The same expert protests against the way in which tragedy is overdone on the Japanese stage.

"Our actors are not content with mere killing; they must add every horror attached to a slow and painful death that ingenuity can invent. After being covered with blood from the wounds received, a man deliberately begins to disembowel himself and does not die until he has made the audience sick with the sights witnessed. The everlasting appeal to our pensive feelings on the Japanese stage is unwholesome and wearisome, and as for the tragical scenes which appear on our boards, their tendency is to encourage cruelty by familiarizing audiences with revolting sights. In regard to those plays whose chief design is to give pleasure to the audience, it seems to be thought in this country that it is impossible to attain the object in view otherwise than by the introduction of scenes between men and women which are quite indecent. This is an entire mistake. . . . There are many serious objections to our practice of assigning women's parts to men. There is little doubt that it has a demoralizing effect upon the audience. The class of women cleverly imitated by our actors are mostly persons of loose morals, and the effect of such acting is to elicit the admiration of young girls for heroines whose characters are unworthy of imitation. I should like to see the practice of men taking women's parts entirely abolished."

However, as previously intimated, even before I left Japan a rival to the stereotyped and "classical" school of acting had sprung up in the so-called *sōshi-shibai* or *shin-engeki* which seeks to depict life as it really is, in contradistinction to the rigid conventionalism which reigns supreme in the old-style historical drama and, as it were, dictates every movement of the limbs and features and every vocal modulation, not in accordance with Nature as Nature is known to be, but in deference to canons of art which imply that the ancient Japanese was an unqualified abnormality. Thus in the latter-style drama the hero who makes his exit along the "flower-path" does not walk like any human being in twentieth-century life but with a preposterous stride in which the feet are extended and raised to the greatest possible altitude and held there almost to the limit of human endurance, while between every stride the entire frame is shaken as though in the throes of an exaggerated ague. It is true that the old-time samurai did affect a special kind of gait on state occasions, but the classical actor's reproduction of that gait has been carried to the last degree. Now in the *shin-engeki* these stereotyped tricks have been abandoned, together with the special language in which the classical drama is couched, the "vulgar" speech of everyday existence having been adopted instead. There is, in short, a very real effort to hold the mirror up to Nature.

I myself attended a marvellously modernized version of "Othello" staged at the Meiji Theatre, Tokyo, early in 1903 by the then well-known Kawakami of the *shin-engeki* school. In partnership with his wife, whose professional name was Sada Yakko, he had earlier made a very successful tour of the European capitals in genuine Japanese drama. This Japanese adaptation of "Othello" transferred the scene of action from Florence to Tokyo and from Cyprus to Formosa, transforming the characters from Italians into Japanese. Nevertheless a playbill of huge dimensions proclaimed the following in English "as she is Japped":

" 'Othello ', to be produced here by our Mr. Kawakami and Madame Sada Yakko, is the adaptation from Shakespeare's play which they have seen the performance in Europe, where they have engaged with their troupe previous year and learned about the art of acting much differing from our conventional. No foreigner ever had such a good opportunity as this time to see Shakespeare's drama in its almost (*sic*) original form in Japan because it is the first experience to us to play the Poet's work, etc."

Othello, played by Kawakami, was General Muro, Governor of Formosa; the fair Desdemona was re-named Tonome; her father, Brabantio, appeared as Count Fura; Cassio became Major Katsu Yoshio; Iago, Lieutenant Iya Gozo; Emilia, Omiya; Bianca, a geisha called Biaka, etc. the resemblance in nomenclature being ingeniously contrived. Ignorance of Occidental history and geog-

raphy and the unpronounceable character of foreign names fo
the average Japanese served as Kawakami's justification for thi
disguised "Othello".

Instead of strangling Tonome (Desdemona), General Mur
(Othello) adhered more closely to Japanese usage in such cir
cumstances by slaying her with his sword, and in the same accom
modating spirit was allowed to commit *harakiri* instead of simpl
stabbing himself as Othello does. For the rest the acting wa
excellent and the play achieved a popular success, the theatr
being packed nightly for a protracted run. Thus again wa
demonstrated the universality of Shakespeare's appeal.

On analogous lines a Japanese company later gave a moder
Japanese version of "The Taming of the Shrew" at the Toky
Imperial Theatre. I attended the performance in initial ignoranc
of its nature and can well recall the vague stirrings of memor
excited by the familiar unfolding of the action until final realiza
tion of the truth was borne in upon me. In this case the fact tha
a Japanese woman (played by a man) would be very less likel
than an Italian to "cut up rough" with her lord and maste
apparently enhanced the piquancy of the various situations an
the house laughed till it cried.

I have little doubt that since those spacious days Japanes
entrepreneurs have "done" other Shakespearian plays into th
Tokyo colloquial and that "Hamlet" itself has not escaped.

Among the more noteworthy efforts of the new dramati
school to improve the national taste must be mentioned a
admirable performance of Gogol's inimitable Russian comed
Revizor (Inspector-General) by a company of actors at the Yur
kuza. As I was myself fairly proficient in Russian and therefor
quite familiar with the original Russian text of this great maste
piece I naturally took keen interest in this praiseworthy enterpris
With the exception of certain condensations necessitated by th
length of the original the production was a faithful Japanese tran
lation from the Russian. The Russian costumes of the day of whic
the immortal Russian satirist wrote were faithfully reproduce
and although the performance was not free from some inevitab
shortcomings the leading rôles were very cleverly represente
and the humour of the situations met with a ready response fro
a series of crowded houses. I learned subsequently that much

this success was due to the kindly co-operation of a young Russian student of the Tokyo Imperial University, a Mr. Eliseev who, thanks to his wonderful command of Japanese which he had acquired in fewer than three years, was able to coach the actors with perfect ease. This young Russian student was destined later to win a world-wide reputation as an Orientalist. He became a Professor of Japanese at the Petrograd University, then after the Russian Revolution he was attached to the Sorbonne and the Institut Oriental and also to the Japanese Embassy in Paris. My latest information relates to 1926 and I have no knowledge of his subsequent fate. The Japanese company responsible for this production appeared to have a preference for Russian plays, having just before this one staged a Japanese version of Chekhov's *Bear*, also with considerable success.

A typical Japanese and even oriental microcosm of the stage actor is the *hanashika* or *kokakushi* (story-teller) with the ability to hold his audience spell-bound for several hours on end. Personally in the heyday of my study of the language I occasionally attended these recitals and since the *hanashika* always tells his stories in the colloquial (*zokugo*), I am sure that I must have derived considerable linguistic benefit from these excursions into native life. Singularly enough, one of the most popular members of the story-tellers' guild was an Englishman named Black, born in Japan, who combined perfect command of the language with a phenomenal memory which enabled him to make use of plots culled from non-Japanese sources and to "put them over" in fluent Japanese to the evident edification and interest of his hearers. The only two concessions made to his alien origin were his European clothes and the chair on which he always sat, instead of the native cushion, or *zabuton*, when thus performing in his professional capacity.

This far from complete survey of the Japanese theatre would be guilty of a hiatus were it to omit all mention of its corollary and dangerous rival, the kinematograph (*katsudo-shashin*, in Japanese), whose introduction into Japan cannot have lagged far behind either Europe or America. It is hardly surprising that virtually all the early silent foreign films should have been imported from the United States. Concurrently, however, Japan had established a film industry of her own long before the First World War. And in this context it may be of interest to note that the early Japanese films differed from those of the West in that they were not strictly speaking silent pictures relying upon screen letter-press to record the dialogue only suggested in mime on the screen but actual stage plays in which the players were clearly engaged in living speech. And when these stage plays were being shown on the kinematograph screen several compères were always stationed in the wings where they very cleverly synchronized their own spoken words with those originally uttered by the actors while being photographed for the screen reproduction. A modified form of the same device was also adopted when imported foreign films were being shown. And in this context it should be added that the Japanese compère often permitted himself a verbal latitude calculated to prove somewhat embarrassing to any foreign lady chancing to be among the audience and familiar with the language. One such occasion I well remember when the compère signalized the exit of an actress on the screen with the facetious remark, "The lady has just gone out to the W.C.!" (*Fujin ga benjo ye heya wo dete itta tokoro da*), which naturally evoked an outburst of cacophonous cachinnation from his appreciative hearers. In matters of this kind the Japanese, despite their inborn love of etiquette, are apt to be much less reticent than the Anglo-Saxons.

Since those pioneer days the embryonic Japanese film industry has developed out of all recognition and has achieved the un-challenged status of a separate art in its own right. In its present-day producer Akira Kurosawa it possesses a genius whose work has been hailed by the best foreign critics as unique in its own particular genre. Thus when writing about one of his latest films entitled *Seven Samurai*, William Whitebait, film critic of *The New Statesman and Nation*, observes:

.   "Hitherto in his two films we have seen he has dealt with legend, with stylized drama and anecdote. This new film shows him as a master of realism that embraces more of humanity while it succeeds in sustaining the same heroic, if terrifying ideals. . . . Completely fascinating, a masterpiece of cinema. . . The samurai caste was to maintain its tradition for a couple of centuries and the leader who helped most to reunite Japan was of peasant stock. Whatever one may think of this sanctification of the fighting man, it has deep roots; and roots—in conviction in life and history—are what the general cinema lacks. Without them one may wonder how near Kurosawa could have approached his present intensity and skill. There have been strong movements elsewhere—in Russia, for example, and Italy—but am I wrong in thinking that in Japan there exists a *school* of film-making comparable to the old religious schools? We should have to see a great many more Japanese films before we could answer that question or satisfy a curiosity about their approach to contemporary themes."

A survey of Japan's splendid achievements in the fine arts of painting, carving, sculpture and architecture does not come within the purview of my book, but I am loath to close this chapter without paying my tribute to the memory of the great craftsmen of past centuries whose creations in those fields, which I have been privileged to see and to admire, may rightly claim a place among the world's masterpieces.

CHAPTER XIX

THE JAPANESE ETERNAL FEMININE

"You may call it a Japanese craze—a craze,
You may say a weak mind it betrays—betrays;
But go to Japan and see O Yu Cha San,
And you'll have it the rest of your days."

THUS warbled a United States naval officer who was badly
smitten with the charms of the fairer sex of Japan. If another
mere man may be permitted to add his "sum of more to that
which has too much" already in the way of literature on this
subject, I would say that, in my opinion, the Japanese woman is in
many respects the chief glory of the nation. Of course, like Mrs.
Solomon, there are a good many rows of her, and it would be
asking entirely too much of human nature to expect that every
Japanese girl or woman should be a Venus for beauty and a Diana
for chastity; but whether virtuous or "immoral" in the narrow
sense of a W.C.T.U. or a Christian Endeavour Society, it must be
said of her that she is essentially feminine. Whereas, on the one hand,
curses both loud and deep used to be the portion of the Japanese
male when his characteristics began to be discussed at the old daily
round-up before the club bars of Yokohama, Kobe and Nagasaki,
the merits and demerits of the Japanese female, when submitted to
a similar symposium, on the other, would most decidedly elicit a
consensus of opinion in her favour. Such a tribunal may not be
entitled to vast respect as a court of highest instance, but at least
its decisions usually reflect fairly faithfully current opinion among
foreigners in Japan. A verdict from this source on the side of the
Japanese woman is invested with some additional value from the
fact that the judges can have had very little experience of higher-
class types; and it must be frankly said that with rare exceptions
the relations between the normal foreigner and the lower-class
Japanese women are not confined to the intellectual plane. The
majority, then, of foreigners, admit the charm of the Japanese girl.

218

On the other hand, there is a minority whose members are not attracted by her, but they are commonly men of ultra-occidental type who live entirely aloof from all Japanese influences and who, at the end of many years' residence, may return to Europe or America knowing far less about the country and its people than might have been acquired by a stay-at-home from the most perusal of a guide-book on Japan, Murray's for preference.

Much of the Japanese girl's charm may be due to contrast. The newcomer, accustomed to associate with women who ride bicycles, play tennis, row, hunt, travel, and, in short, strive to compete with the man at every turn, often succumbs without delay to the fascination of their antithesis. Stern necessity has taught the Japanese woman the lesson of self-effacement, and in one sense perhaps her gentle and submissive manners which appeal so powerfully to many tourists and residents are in reality a serious indictment of Japanese chivalry. Needless perhaps to add, this appraisement has reference only to the "non-professional" woman, not to the geisha or to the representative of the *demi-monde*, although even these contrive to retain infinitely more femininity than their occidental sisters.

Physically, however, the Japanese woman leaves much to be desired. Dr. C. H. Stratz, in a work entitled *The Forms of the Human Body in Japanese Art and Life*, specifies the requirements of female beauty in Japan to be as follows: a tall and slender shape, long and narrow face, almond-shaped eyes, a long and narrow nose, slender arms, long and narrow hands, narrow chest and slender body and long, thin legs. Broad hips are considered a great defect. There is thus a radical difference between the occidental and Japanese conceptions of female beauty, and there are not wanting foreigners prepared to argue that the Japanese standard is correct! Personally, I still remain enough of a European to prefer the occidental standard, one reason being that it typifies a healthy animal. The Japanese type, on the contrary, is essentially anaemic, and while no doubt "refined", to my mind it is one which should not be encouraged in the interests of the physical well-being of the race. It is quite conceivable, indeed, that the Japanese ideal of female beauty, conjoined with unhygienic habits of life, has helped to produce the comparatively stunted Japanese physique. Things might have been much worse than they are if the evils inseparable from this false standard had not been and are not being modified by gymnastic exercises in the schools, the spread of the practice of judo, and the system of conscription. Moreover, although the classical female type has won theoretical approval, yet in practice there must have been numerous deviations, since human beauty is generally scarce. Besides, tastes differ even in Japan, and less favoured ladies in the past married and begot children, as well as those diaphanous creatures who have been immortalized by misguided artists. It is lucky for Japan that they did.

Racial partiality has really very little to do with the question. A Japanese doctor, equally with his foreign confrere, knows full well that pallid cheeks, contracted chest, narrow shoulders, narrow hips, thin arms and legs do not in either sex indicate health and strength. The man of science, therefore, and not the patriot, is the champion of the occidental type. The pretty neck and shoulders—seen from behind—for which Japanese women are noted and which are primarily due, it is said, to the national way of sitting, are purchased at too high a rate. Dr. Stratz himself includes among the physical defects of Japanese women the smallness of the hips. But it does not follow that because one finds fault with the classical Japanese type one admires its extreme antithesis, the big, raw-boned, long-striding, athletic foreign female. There is such a thing as the happy medium, and my point is that the happy medium is more likely to be developed in lands where practical allegiance is not given to the Japanese ideal of female beauty. After all, the percentage of those who can emerge unscathed from the test of nudity is painfully small. Carlyle was right when he insisted upon the debt which both men and women owe their tailors and dressmakers. In Japan the case is even more so. At the same time, in justice to the Japanese female physique, it should be said that the object of the Japanese costume would appear to be to conceal and not to accentuate those curves which are more effectively displayed in foreign dress, when they exist, so that occasionally one might justly paraphrase in favour of the Japanese girl the remark which the Princess passes on Kitty in V. A. Krylov's amusing Russian comedy "The Society for the Encouragement of Ennui", viz. "She is better built than I thought; these Japanese sometimes give us very agreeable surprises" Irrespective too of mere physique, the Japanese woman's face often possesses a distinctive allurement which is due as much to expression as to feature; and it is true that foreigners after long residence often see reason to modify previous standards. If there is one custom more than another that tends to spoil the Japanese woman's shape it is the suckling of children for three, four and even five years before weaning them. The strain upon the mother must be highly detrimental and conducive to premature old age; but it is to be feared that the practice is too deeply rooted to be easily eradicated.

I once enjoyed the privilege of a long conversation with a Japanese lady of superior education and one, too, familiar with foreign habits of life and thought. I took ample stenographic notes of this conversation at the time, thinking that a translation might prove interesting to foreign readers.

"The status of Japanese women as compared with that of the women of Europe and America," she said, "is very low indeed, scarcely better, in fact, than that of a better-class servant. Our women have gradually become almost absolutely dependent upon the male sex, and instead of possessing, like the women of Europe and America, a certain amount of personal independence, they are generally driven into marriage as a kind of profession. There are few other openings and in such as there are the salaries paid are extremely small. Even if a woman has acquired an exceptionally good education, she has few means of utilizing it and must be content to labour for a mere pittance. A faint idea of the estimation in which the scx is held by the men can be gathered from the manner in which a husband will sometimes refer to his marriage, viz. 'Rusui wo moraimashita', which literally means that he has taken something to look after the house during his absence! Now and then, even in Japan, there will be born into the world a female with strength of character and ideals approximating to those of her occidental sister; but if so she is condemned as awkward and pert, regarded askance by outsiders, and not greatly loved by her own parents because when they want her to get married she has opinions of her own on the subject which do not coincide with theirs.

"A Japanese woman is driven into marriage willy-nilly, and often with a man for whom she does not entertain a particle of affection, whereas in Europe and America, if the woman cannot find some one to her taste she is at liberty to remain single. On the other hand, when an American or a European woman finds somebody she does like, she will go to him and work for him untiringly and with constant interest in the affairs of the household, whilst a Japanese woman too often degenerates into a drudge.

"Nowadays there are many women in Japan employed in the post-offices, telephone exchanges and in other Government offices. Whether, however, it is due to some lack of the spirit of independence on the part of the women themselves I do not know, but the fact remains that the usual comment of the male sex upon all such appointments is, 'Oh, she's only a woman, after all!' and this attitude tends to keep down women's wages, though the female employees may be competent to perform the duties allotted to them. A woman myself, I must nevertheless confess that the bulk of Japanese women really are more or less dolls in their way and that they are not invariably efficient.

"In Japan if a woman remains single after twenty people begin to talk about her and to ask questions. They think there must be something seriously wrong about a girl who does not get married after seventeen. A girl enters the married state rarely with feelings of real pleasure; she goes more as an ox to the slaughter. In the husband's house she enjoys the refined society of the father-in-law, mother-in-law, and a crowd of other relatives. If the house were constructed in foreign fashion this state of affairs might not be so bad, but in a Japanese house the wife rarely has a room to herself or any place where she can spend a quiet hour or so over a book. In the morning she must rise early, together with the servants, and must participate in the cleaning, while her lord and master lies snoring in bed. The mother-in-law is the next to rise, and her first duty is to kneel down before the household shrine (*butsudan* and *kami-dama*) where she strikes the bell, claps her hands, and spends about an hour in howling out her devotions. She is then put into an appropriate frame of mind for scolding the wife for carelessness in her cleaning. Finally the father-in-law and the husband get up and begin to create a disturbance. The wife does not take breakfast with her husband; she waits upon him and subsequently eats with the servants. If the husband has business to attend to he leaves the house after breakfast, his wife following him to the door, where she kneels down upon the mats and bows as he goes out. The rest of the household follow suit and a chorus of *'Irasshai!'* ('Deign to go!') greets his lordship's departure. During his absence the wife again has to endure a tongue-lashing from the old lady, and has soon to set about preparing her husband's tiffin. His return is the signal for another stampede in the direction of the porch, where everybody flops down once more, and the jinrikishaman who brings back the master having given the hint, a shrill cry of *'O-kaeri!'* ('Honourably return!') is raised and repeated. The object of all these attentions accepts them calmly as his due and languidly allows his female kind to relieve him of his overcoat. At tiffin the wife acts as handmaiden, squatting down at a respectful distance. The husband eats his fill, and after his second exit the wife has a chance, though the mother-in-law usually secures the leavings.

"Then comes the sewing which is commonly done at home for the entire family. Preparations have then to be made for the evening meal, and the return of the master is anxiously awaited. As a rule, however, he does not come back; more usually he seeks distraction in a geisha spree or even in less reputable society. Still, the wife must wait up for him, however sleepy she may be, and when finally at some unearthly hour he does return he needs plenty of food and *sake* to revive his drooping spirits, and it is the wife's duty to supply his wants. She puts him to bed, and in many cases has to massage him for a quarter of an hour in order to compose him for slumber. The balance of the day's work must be attended to before she can seek repose, and if at the end of it all she can snatch four or five hours' sleep she has reason to esteem herself lucky.

"Care of the children when these come, is no easy task. They are reared for the most part in Chinese style, and the work falls to the wife. Of course in some better-class houses wet-nurses are employed, but these are usually women of scant intelligence and as the wife has so much to do, the home education and physical comfort of the children are more or less neglected. Foreigners often marvel at the spectacle of youngsters with their heads covered with scabs and their noses in a filthy state; such conditions are directly traceable to the care-lessness of nurses in not seeing that they are properly clad, and the seeds of consumption are often sown in this manner. A pregnant woman should be most solicitous of her health and observe regular hours of rest; but in a house regulated in the manner I have described, where the woman is constantly on the move, the development of the embryo is clearly not what it ought to be. In these circumstances, therefore, you cannot expect strong and healthy children and the prospects of the rising generation are badly affected. The women become so disgusted that it takes them a long time to settle down. Divorce is very frequent and some women marry two or three times before they finally reconcile themselves to double harness.

"It may seem a curious anomaly to a foreigner, but it is none the less a fact that the women of the middle and upper classes are really worse off in this respect than those of the lower classes. The latter enjoy a far greater measure of equality with their husbands, and it is in this stratum that one must seek for an exemplification of the principle of *danjo dōken* (literally, 'male-female same rights', i.e. women's rights). The position of the upper-class woman may also be gauged by their comparative scarcity at palace levées and other social functions, the men being in an overwhelming majority.

"Social intercourse between the sexes, as foreigners under-stand it, is virtually forbidden. The jealousy which dictates this prohibition has probably been borrowed from China, and in Japan is well summarized in the phrase, *Dannyo shichi-sai ni shite seki wo onaji sezu*, which means that the sexes should not be permitted to remain together in the same room after the age of seven. The husband is jealous; the father and mother are opposed to social intercourse between the sexes, and the wife herself, thanks to her upbringing, does not like it.

"Besides there is another point which militates against the adoption of the Western usage in this country, and that is that there are very few women who would be capable of keeping up an intelligent conversation with one of the opposite sex. Their mental horizon is bounded, for conventional purposes, by theatres, dress and novels, and even Japanese men need more stimulating mental pabulum, at times. Especially is this so when the men in question have been abroad and possess some knowledge of the world. They naturally begin to talk about politics and other matters of public interest. The average Japanese woman in such company would be helpless; she would merely sit and feebly giggle at what she could not possibly understand. So women do not commonly go into society, and especially male society."

"What, then," I asked, "is your opinion of the moral qualities of your countrywomen?"

"As a rule," she replied, "instances of domestic infidelity on the part of the wife are rare. Still, I should think that, as Japanese women are kept in such seclusion and are usually married to men with whom they are not in love, ignorant too of the world, they would be very apt indeed to yield to the solicitations of men who should lay themselves out to flatter them, to treat them courteously, and to play upon their feelings. In fact, it is owing to this fear and, I am sorry to say, to a certain amount of practical experience which supports the fear, that dances in the foreign style, at one time the rage, have become unpopular. I suppose there is such a sentiment as pure love in Japan, as in other countries, but I should say it is rare, and that the relations between the sexes are entirely physical. How indeed can they be otherwise in view of our marriage customs? How are most marriages brought about?

"Here is a young man, say, twenty-five or thirty years of age, who is at a friend's house. The idea will suddenly occur to the friend that it is quite time the young man was married. Thereupon he and his wife or a third person will begin to cast around for a suitable partner, and they will suddenly recollect that there are a couple living two or three doors away who have a daughter of marriageable age. They will then return the visit of their young friend, open negotiations, broaching the subject in an insinuating manner. The young man doesn't really mind one way or the other. He reflects that he is gradually growing older and cannot in the nature of things remain single all his life. 'However,' says he, 'let me have a look at the lady.' The go-between (*nakodo*) accordingly calls upon the parents of the girl and tells them about the projected match. If the parents are agreeable it is arranged that the prospective bridegroom shall meet the girl at some convenient spot. Thither in due course she repairs dressed in her best clothes and with her hair done up in what is called the *shimada* style. Generally she brings in tea to the young man, and if he looks at her, accepts the tea and drinks it, it is a sign that he is satisfied; whereas if he leaves it untouched the action signifies that he would rather be excused.

"Supposing the man to be agreeable, he will again see the go-between and inform him to that effect. The go-between's next duty is to go to the girl's house and sing the praises of the young man; in short he is not ashamed to lie freely in an effort to make the parents believe that their future son-in-law is a veritable paragon of all the virtues. So notorious are his powers of speech that the expression *nakodo-guchi* ('the mouth of a go-between') has become proverbial as applicable to one who can talk glibly and is very persuasive. Should the parents consent to the match it is as good as settled. They may, perhaps, institute a few inquiries about the young man on their own behalf, but these are not usually very thorough and the wishes of the girl herself are virtually ignored. She is summoned and informed that the day of her marriage is at hand.

" 'Who is the man?' she may ask.

" 'Oh, you remember the young man you met at such and such a place the other day, to whom you served tea? That's the man.'

"It is rarely that a girl has sufficient courage to avow before both parents her distaste for the contemplated arrangement, even should she feel any. She may confide in her mother, but in that event the latter pooh-poohs her objections and paints with a lively imagination the horrors of old-maidhood, should this opportunity be lost. Whether the girl likes it or not, the parents clinch the agreement. The first formality is to present the man with a pair of *hakama* (native form of loose baggy pantaloons), the signification of this observance being that as the *hakama* are broader at the bottom than at the top it is hoped that the wearer's luck will continue to unfold as he grows older. On his side the man sends the girl an *obi* (sash) which implies the binding of the girl to the contract. Other presents are also exchanged, the term for such being *yuino*."

I may here interrupt my lady friend's recital to say that one of the best and most succinct descriptions of the Japanese marriage ceremony may be found in Professor Chamberlain's *Things Japanese*. I may state briefly that the social ceremony has no legal validity whatsoever except, as Mr. Gubbins points out in his introduction to his translation of the Japanese Civil Code, in the somewhat remote contingency of its being adducible as evidence of a marriage having taken place. The legality of a marriage is determined by registration, the marriage taking effect when notice is given to the registrar. "When the registrar has satisfied himself," says Mr. Gubbins, "that the marriage is in accordance with the provisions of the law the name of the person entering the other's family is inscribed in the register of that family, and is expunged from the register of the family to which he or she previously belonged."

As a rule the bride enters the family of the bridegroom, though the reverse is sometimes the case. The marriageable age for men is seventeen, and for women fifteen—according to the foreign method of calculating age. The bride leaves her parents' home at night for her husband's home. She wears a white dress—white being the Japanese mourning colour—to indicate that she dies to her own family, and that she will never leave her husband's house but as a corpse, albeit I have shown elsewhere that this tacit pledge in not infrequently more honoured in the breach than the observance. The wedding takes the form of a feast at which the bride and bridegroom drink *sake* together, or pretend to do so, three times out of each of three cups of different sizes. This ceremony is known as *san-san ku-do*, or "three three, nine times". The white dress of the bride is also exchanged for a coloured dress brought from her own home, while the bridegroom also changes his dress in a separate room. The go-between and his wife, already mentioned, are important figures at this function, and escort the happy couple into the bridal chamber where nine more cups of *sake* are drunk.

The bride's first visit to her parents' house is called *sato-gaeri*, or "return home", and takes place the third day after the marriage. When the bride leaves her parents' home to enter that of her husband her coiffeur is altered from the *shimada* to the *marumage* style, by which most married women can be distinguished.

Divorce between the parties is easily effected. There are two kinds of divorce, viz. divorce by arrangement and judicial divorce. The former is managed in much the same way as the marriage, and when the registrar who receives the notice is satisfied as to the legality of the step he simply expunges from the register the name of the person leaving the other's family and reinscribes it in the register of the family to which he or she originally belonged.

The Civil Code specifies the several grounds on which judicial divorce is granted. These include (*vide* Gubbins) "cruelty of one of the parties to his or her lineal descendants, cruelty received by one of the parties from the lineal descendants of the other, and the dissolution or annulment of adoption in cases where the adopted person is connected with the adoptive family by both marriage and adoption."

I asked my Japanese lady friend whether those girls who today are being educated in up-to-date establishments in Tokyo and elsewhere did not enjoy greater latitude than their progenitors.

"As to that," she replied, "I find it somewhat difficult to decide. Such persons remind me of those who wear a mixture of foreign and Japanese dress. The system of education, moreover, is thoroughly hybrid. Girl students inevitably enjoy more personal freedom than other young women, and scandals occasionally arise in consequence. But Japanese parents will not allow an unfortunate liaison to force their hand in the matter of bestowing their daughters in marriage. There are secret methods of averting the consequences, and if the girl is of good family and her parents are influential an indiscretion of the kind I mean is by no means an insuperable obstacle to an advantageous match. There are scores of men who will conveniently ignore such details for the sake of their father-in-law's future assistance."

The same informant and my own observations extending over a residence of many years in the country have furnished me with an insight into the sentiment entertained towards the foreigner as a son-in-law by most Japanese. Frankly, then, it is antagonistic. The causes of this distaste are probably many and far-reaching. Different manners and customs, ideas and appearance are not the least potent factors in the problem. A Japanese woman who marries a foreigner is not infrequently spoken of as unpatriotic. My lady friend assured me that the Japanese dislike foreigners far more than we ourselves sometimes imagine, and that they themselves scarcely know why they do so. Perhaps it is because, as the Japanese believe, our hair is always red and our eyes blue or green.

"In fact," confessed my informant, "I myself at one time thought foreigners very peculiar. The foreign mode of life is so opposed to all Japanese ideas that there is not one Japanese woman in a thousand who could accommodate herself entirely to the new environment. There is the clashing between old and new ideas; ancestor worship is in the blood of our race, and with this few foreigners have any genuine sympathy. The women are often more biased than the men."

And yet, I would add, it can easily be shown that they are under no light obligation to the alien they despise. The foreign invasion has opened up new occupations for women, although, unfortunately, as elsewhere admitted, the remuneration is entirely inadequate. One of the best paid callings is that of hospital nurse. The probation is severe, since it includes a three-year course of training, in addition to a good education, as a basis. The duties too are extremely arduous and comprise much of the rough manual work which has to be undertaken in a hospital. But Japanese nurses are justly famous, more especially those attached to the Red Cross hospitals. The medical profession is also open to women, if they care to enter it, but female doctors are not popular in Japan; they do not command much confidence, and even women patients prefer a male practitioner. The calling of a midwife (*samba*) is well patronized by Japanese women and is among the most profitable. Japanese midwives, indeed, are reputed to be very skilful.

But the duties of a housewife are of paramount importance together with a proper knowledge of female etiquette, and it not infrequently happens that girls of good family are sent into service in order to learn housekeeping. The status of the maid-servant is, in fact, very different in Japan from the corresponding thing in Europe and America. The maidservant is sometimes almost the friend and companion of the mistress; the line of social demarcation between the two is by no means so sharply defined as in the West. The servant is more like a member of the family. On the other hand, a Japanese servant is worked harder and paid less than her Western sister and for her there is no such bliss as privacy. Nevertheless, foreign residents of Tokyo and the old treaty ports will bear witness to the circumstance that, with rare exceptions, even the inducements of better wages, less work, and more leisure in a foreign household are powerless to undermine the allegiance of the Japanese Abigail to her own compatriots.

The average Japanese woman is a slave to etiquette and not free from superstition. When a foreign lady calls upon a friend she tries to avoid wearing out her welcome and leaves early. But among the Japanese of both sexes there would appear to be no sense of moderation or proportion. It often seems to be equally a point of honour on the part of the visitor and the visited not to give way first. However, the hostess is fertile in resource, and when even Japanese patience finds itself on the verge of breakdown she gives a sign to the servant who procures a broom which she stands up on end in another room, and ties around the top of it a native towel as if it were a chaplet. In front of the broom are placed a pair of sandals. This charm is said to be very efficacious; the unwelcome guest soon becomes very sleepy and takes his or her departure! Many women can scarcely do anything without consulting their fortune-teller, and particular acts are restricted to particular days. They are commonly unwavering in their belief in the power of foxes to bewitch human beings and always take great pains to be on the right side of the fox goddess Inari.

In Japan, the land of contrasts, apparent inconsistencies and paradoxes, one is struck by the frequent mention of liaisons between young women and actors or other professional men, in which the former make all the advances. As a rule, no doubt, these violations of the moral code are confined to the professional or semi-professional class of women, but even "respectable" women may sometimes be guilty of similar laches and take advantage of their husband's absences to attend the theatres and the wrestling arenas.

The practice of giving presents is universal, but holds the

women more particularly in its thrall. In the West only the more intimate friends presume to exchange presents, whereas in Japan mere acquaintances are constrained by the rules of etiquette to do so on various occasions, and thus useless and pernicious habits of extravagance are fostered. And yet withal I am an avowed champion of the Japanese eternal feminine. Your Japanese girl may be dollish but in her way she is an artistic and a pleasing doll, and the cavalier manner in which the husband often treats a wife of this description invariably arouses the indignation of the foreign male. Doubtless today many of the older abuses are falling into disrepute, but it cannot be denied that the habit of keeping concubines in the same house as the wife is still practised by persons of wealth and distinction. The practice has been denounced by the native press but no very thoroughgoing reform in this direction can be expected to occur for some time yet to come.

I admire the Japanese of both sexes for the classic indifference they evince towards physical exposure which is not gratuitous. On the other hand, the low-necked dresses of our foreign ballrooms inspire in the pristine breast of a Japanese female unutterable horror.

Said my Japanese lady friend:

"The Japanese can never understand why you should object to a woman's being seen in a bath or suckling a child in public, and yet see nothing improper in one of your countrywomen displaying her neck and shoulders for no other reason than to attract the admiration of men. The air of mystery which surrounds the foreign woman's toilet strikes us as ridiculous. Why should she lock herself up in the bathroom as though she feared assault?"

In this regard the Japanese woman is fearless and unashamed, though her toilet is perhaps more complicated than that of her foreign sister. The bath is indeed almost a religion among the Japanese. Bath-houses (*yuya*), more elegantly *kokyo no furuya*, or public baths, swarm in every town, and here the sexes sometimes bathe in full view of each other, although, in deference to ideas of decency imported from abroad, in some instances they have been separated more effectually, and in others a purely nominal barrier exists which actually conceals nothing. What is more, male attendants wait upon either sex indifferently, and scrub the ladies' backs with the most complete sangfroid in the world. Among the better classes the women bathe at home, but they must wait until their lords and masters have finished their ablutions. The male head of the house then leads off, and he may even be disrobed and rubbed down by a female attendant before he actually enters the water. The rest of the household, down to the servants, follow suit in due order of precedence. The lady of the house spends fully an hour over the ceremony. Lady readers may be interested to know how she manages to be so deliberate. Here, then, are a few of the weapons in the Japanese lady's armoury of beauty. We find the *akasuri*, a piece of rough cloth used in rubbing the dirt off the body; *karuishi*, or pumice stone; *araiko*, a washing powder made of pea-beans; *nuka*, or bran, enclosed in little bags; ordinary soap (*shabon*) and a dark sort of sugar supposed to improve the texture of the skin of the face; *nori* and *oshiroi*, a face powder in liquid form; *hechima*, or snake-gourd—i.e. vegetable sponge; *beni*, or red dye for the lips, eyes and nails; *tenugui*, or Japanese towel which is first of all wetted and then wrung out before being applied to the body for drying purposes, perfectly dry towels being rarely used in the bath; and the *yōji*, or tooth-brush. There are other accessories but I think I have mentioned the chief.

The Japanese lady's dress is, after all, admirably adapted to her peculiar physique and helps to conceal its radical defects. There are few prettier sights than a group of girls in holiday costume.

"Our dress is comfortable," said my lady friend, "until you want to work and then it is very much in your way. It drags on your arms and fetters free motion. Moreover, it is very expensive and easily tears and spoils. Dress is among the chief of female luxuries among us as among your own countrywomen, and our women are fond of buying new garments whenever they can afford to do so, and of putting them away in wardrobes. A woman of the upper class will probably have stowed away as many as ten or twelve wardrobes stuffed full of valuable clothing which she can never possibly wear, but which she loves to gloat over like a miser over his secret hoard."

The prices quoted by this lady for various articles of female dress relate to many years ago so that to repeat them here would serve no useful purpose. But considering that Japan today is reputed to be about the most expensive country in the world it may be taken for granted that the corresponding retail prices are very much higher than they were then.

It is perhaps significant that the favourite booty of the Japanese burglar is female dress, the poor construction of many Japanese houses facilitating his raids upon them. It is nothing short of a dire calamity for a woman of the people to lose in this or any other manner a wardrobe which she has managed to accumulate at the cost of endless scraping and saving, for she is thus deprived of an asset which can always be converted into money in an emergency.

"What," I asked, "do Japanese women think of foreign women?"

"Well, they impress us as sharper, brighter and more energetic than ourselves. But from the native point of view they are awfully forward and pert. Their outward appearance too is strange to us. They seem tall, angular and masculine, with red hair, large blue eyes, and immense noses which stick out in front of their faces. The tight sleeves of their dresses look awkward and uncomfortable. Japanese women think foreign women rude in their manners and exceedingly 'cheeky' to the men. They are chatterboxes and in short terrible tomboys. Nevertheless, those of us who can look below the surface deeply admire the independence and self-reliance of foreign women. For instance, when the husband dies the wife is far less helpless than a Japanese would be in similar circumstances, and is capable of working for and supporting her family in a way few Japanese women would dream of."

Although intermarriage between Japanese women and foreign men and between Japanese men and foreign women is not unknown and is not always unsuccessful, I should not be inclined to advise it as a step to be taken without the most careful deliberation on the part of both sides. In the nature of things, however, a union between a Japanese woman and a foreign man has far more to recommend it than the reverse phenomenon. Speaking generally, there are few foreigners sufficiently versed in the language to make their Japanese wives anything like real companions and, worse still, when a Japanese woman and a foreign man are seen in company they promptly become objects of unpleasant curiosity and of vulgar comment. For the reasons already mentioned it is rarely possible for a foreigner to marry a woman of the better class, and those accessible to him are usually so immeasurably his intellectual inferiors that they can hardly ever aspire to any higher position than that of a confidential servant. Liaisons between foreign dwellers in the former settlements and Japanese women of the lower orders were not uncommon in my day and were the outcome of economic and social conditions which often rendered it impossible for a young man to think of saddling himself with the expensive luxury of a European or an American wife. Most Japanese look down upon the foreigner's concubine with unconcealed contempt and in speaking of her sometimes use the insulting expression *rashamen*; the more polite equivalent is *gaishō*. In too many cases, no doubt, this contempt is well deserved. The foreigner is, as a rule, exploited solely for his money, and as these women in their ignorance imagine that in Europe the female is the superior being they not infrequently grow by degrees as impertinent, obstinate and extravagant as a really good Japanese wife is the reverse. But even better-class Japanese women may sometimes mistake the superior kindness of the foreigner for an admission of weakness and presume accordingly. The foreign husband of a Japanese wife does well from the outset to make the lady understand that he is the master, otherwise he will never have any peace in his own household.

A few marriages have taken place between foreign women and Japanese, but as a rule the latter have belonged to the nobility or wealthy classes. The most familiar instances are those of Viscount Aoki, for many years Minister to Germany, and Baron Sannomiya, one of the highest Court officials, but these cases cannot safely be accepted as proper criteria of the value of such alliances. When the foreign woman has married a plausible Japanese abroad, in the belief that Japan is an earthly paradise and that conjugal relations between herself and her husband will continue the same in Japan as in Europe and America, the migration to the Land of the Rising Sun has often brought with it swift disillusionment. She has reckoned without the mother-in-law. In the Occident it is usually the bride's mother to whom the journalistic humorist owes an eternal debt of gratitude for lurid inspirations, in which the bridegroom plays the passive rôle of the crushed worm. Quite appropriately the conditions are reversed in Japan, where the groom's mother is the unhappy wife's Nemesis, and more than one foreign wife of a Japanese has found this statement to be only too true. Of course there are other contributory causes. Foreign women are rarely proof against the Japanese climate and speedily lose their good looks, when they have them, and together with their loss their influence over their Japanese husbands who all too soon obey the call of their blood and seek consolation elsewhere. Fortunately the number of these international *mésalliances*, using the term without invidiousness, is strictly limited.

It is interesting to note that historically speaking the subjection of women in Japan is comparatively recent. In ancient days the sex was prominent in politics, literature, art and social life, some of the greatest names in native literature being those of women. The introduction of Confucianism, with its doctrine of female inferiority, brought about the lamentable change which has since been witnessed. The leading tenets of Confucius regarding women are thus summed up:

1. Women are naturally inferior to men.
2. The education of women should be restricted to elementary reading and writing.
3. Woman's primal duty is obedience.
4. Men and women (above seven years of age) shall not sit together.
5. Woman shall have no voice in selecting her husband.
6. The husband shall have the absolute right to rule the wife.

Even the modern Japanese Criminal Code, which declares adultery to be a criminal offence, restricts the right of instituting an action to the husband.

While admitting the charm of contrast in the women of Dai Nippon, I have reason to suppose that beneath a demure and placid exterior they may sometimes conceal depths of feeling for which the average foreigner rarely gives them credit. Witness the numerous lovers' suicides, known as *shinju*, committed in a variety of ways. Sometimes the lover slays his mistress with a sword or dagger and afterwards stabs himself. Or he will bind himself tightly to the woman with a sash or towel and jump with her into a river or the sea, or lie down across a railway track and allow the locomotive to cut them both in twain. In most cases the actresses in these dramas are geisha or prostitutes who find it impossible to be united with the objects of their affection in a lawful manner, and thus prefer death to separation in this world. Hysteria among women, loosely styled *kanshaku*, is all too common in Japan, and assumes aspects quite as violent as anything of the kind in the West.

CHAPTER XX

"THE NIGHTLESS CITY"

ANY description of the Japanese "eternal feminine" which, through a misplaced feeling of delicacy, failed to touch upon its inevitable association with the "social evil", would be guilty of a serious hiatus. What perhaps the "Sage of Chelsea" would have called a remorseless "concatenation of sublunary things, bodeful of much", cannot logically omit this link in the chain which loosely connects the upper and the under worlds of "civilized" human life on our planet. And thereby hangs a tale which, in its relation to Japan, I shall try to unfold.

Certainly the manner in which the Japanese authorities have sought to solve one of the vexed questions of all ages is worthy of study by Western sociologists. However, since I am not posing as either a sociologist or a moralist, I shall refrain from pragmatical analysis of the merits or demerits of the Japanese system and more or less restrict my survey to what may loosely be called the "human interest" aspect of this phenomenon based too in some degree upon personal observation during my long residence in Japan. Yet in fairness to the Japanese "solution" I may be permitted to quote the conclusion reached by two such trained investigators as the late Basil Hall Chamberlain and the late W. B. Mason who, in their *Handbook to Japan* (John Murray), remark: "Their method, though running counter to Anglo-Saxon ideas, preserves Tokyo from the disorderly scenes that obtrude themselves on the passer-by in our western cities."

In the first place I must correct an initial misconception which has gained wide currency throughout the world since a United States fleet in 1853 under the command of Commodore Perry compelled the Shogunate to abandon its policy of isolation. I refer to the erroneous idea that the well-known Japanese word *Yoshi-wara* is a generic term for the so-called "Flower Districts", otherwise licensed quarters, everywhere in Japan. Actually the word applies solely to the Tokyo licensed quarter. The name dates from the early seventeenth century when the licensed quarter was fixed at a place called Fukiyacho which, on account of the quantities of rushes which grew there, was named Yoshi-Wara, or rush-moor. But another explanation is that the name is derived from the town Yoshiwara because it was said that the women of that place furnished many of the beauties of the old Yedo Yoshiwara. Even in my day the word Yoshiwara was by a process of synecdoche extended by foreigners to the Yokohama "tenderloin" and all other Japanese licensed quarters. But the correct designation for licensed quarters in general is *kuruwa* or *yukaku*. Nevertheless old custom dies hard and I have little doubt that the rank and file of present-day visitors to Japan are still under the impression that the name *Yoshiwara* means a licensed quarter.

The Tokyo Yoshiwara, with which I am chiefly concerned because it is more truly representative of Japanese metropolitan night life than the bastard and infinitely more vulgar substitutes of the old treaty ports, is situated about a mile to the north of the great Asakusa temple. Many of the houses within the district are four, five or more stories in height, of almost palatial appearance, and after nightfall brilliantly illuminated with electric light. This fact has no doubt given birth to the would-be poetical name "Nightless City" as a euphemistic synonym for the Tokyo habitat of the licensed hataerae.

I am frank enough in these pages to admit and I make no apology for so doing, that in those far-off days of my unregenerate youth I was in the habit of visiting from time to time the Tokyo Yoshiwara, not to pay tribute to a Japanese Phryne but for the more prosaic, not to say prudent and practical purpose of improving my knowledge of Japanese as spoken by the lower orders of the fairer sex and in quest of "local colour". At the same time these occasional excursions off the beaten track of the more staid elements of the foreign community afforded me an opportunity to study at first hand the distinctive etiquette and even elaborate ceremonial which invest licensed prostitution in Japan with a superficial glamour and in a measure tend to mask its fundamental coarseness and mercenary character.

When I first arrived in Japan about 1897 and for some years afterwards the unfortunate inmates of the second-class houses, decked out in gorgeous raiment, wearing a headdress of light tortoiseshell hairpins, sat in rows behind their *hibachi*, or charcoal braziers, with gold lacquered screens in the background, and shut off from the street by what may be described as immense show-windows protected from the outside by iron bars. These show-windows were colloquially known as *harimise* (*hari* meaning to stretch, to spread, to extend, etc. and *mise* a shop or store), hence the familiar expression *harimise suru* meaning to solicit guests to a house of ill-fame. Very often these girls would be seen smoking their Japanese pipes called *kiseru*, the miniature bowls of which hold only a fragment of tobacco consumed in a few puffs. Now in lieu of this direct bid for salacious suffrage the management of these vast and ornate establishments dedicated to male lust has had to substitute pretentious photographs of the various inmates exhibited in a special vestibule gallery to right and left of the main entrance. Consequently the former popular practice of standing in front of the caged windows and engaging in ribald talk with the girls within has perforce been discontinued.

My own attempts in my best high-stepping Nihongo at rather more conventional conversation with one or more of the girls standing just behind the window-bars (in summer the windows were open to the street) never failed to attract a crowd of curious, amused and quite friendly male onlookers and listeners who would speculate audibly on my nationality. As my hair in my youth was very dark and my stature not more than five feet six inches, the consensus of opinion usually was that I must be an *ainoko*, or a Eurasian. Comment upon my linguistic efforts was also generally favourable, for in these matters the Japanese are by no means exacting, which is a good thing when one recalls St. Francis Xavier's agonized appraisal of their language as long ago as the early sixteenth century, viz. "the contrivance of a conciliabule of devils to torture the faithful!"

The best time to visit the Nightless City is during the summer months. Then the pedestrian corso, if one may say so, of prurient native manhood is in full swing. The majority are clad in light coloured summer deshabille called a *yukata*, open at the neck, the sash, or *obi* being tied not round the waist but immediately above the hips, with the knot to the left and slightly in the rear. The weather being dry all favour the *zōri*, or straw sandal, rather than the high clogs yclept *geta* invariably worn in wet and muddy weather. The contact of these thousands of sandals with the soil and gravel underfoot makes a sustained, distinctive shuffling sound which once heard can never be mistaken or forgotten. The younger "bloods" take long bold strides in the fashion sometimes described in the vernacular as *kata de kūki wo kiru* (literally, "to cut the air with the shoulders"), heedless of the resultant exposure of brawny lower limbs with their often splendidly developed calves for which the Japanese are noted. Here and there raucous voices are raised in snatches of bibulous song, for albeit the ordinary streets of a Japanese city are, as already stated, commendably free from the more obtrusive and audible manifestations of night life with the lid off, in such a privileged environment as the Yoshiwara men are less reticent and give franker and more audible expression to their feelings. Amid these surroundings, at any rate, the cult of an Oriental Priapus holds undisputed sway.

Should any of my inexperienced readers fondly imagine that a would-be patron of a Japanese brothel in the Tokyo Yoshiwara may simply approach the house of his fancy, knock or ring and enter without any further parley, let me hasten to disabuse his mind of any such unbecoming notion. The procedure is much more complex. To begin with all visitors to the Yoshiwara who arrive at the entrance gate in any kind of vehicle must alight outside and proceed farther on foot. There is a police post at the entrance to enforce this rule and to maintain strict order in every other respect. Immediately beyond the main entrance to the licensed quarter itself and, as I recall, to the right-hand side, are rows of houses known as *hikite-jaya*, or "introducing tea-houses", through whose offices access to the better class brothels is effected. The candidate is politely ushered into a private room where an attendant brings him, together with a cup of tea, an album containing photographs of the inmates of the establishments for which the house is catering. If and when the guest decides upon a particular brothel on the strength of the overall appearance of its inmates, a guide with a Japanese paper lantern is assigned to him and together they wend their solemn way to their destination. Here the guide retires and the guest, after having discarded his foot-gear in the porch or vestibule called *genka* in Japanese, is politely ushered into a handsome matted reception room where he squat on a cushion behind the inevitable *hibachi* and awaits further developments.

It may be of painful interest to mention that before the wearing of swords was interdicted in 1876 four years after the abolition of the feudal system in 1871, when a samurai visited a house of ill-fame he was required to leave at the door both his long sword, or *katana*, and his dirk, or *wakizashi*, and this for two reasons recorded by the late Lord Redesdale in his *Tales of Old Japan*, first, to prevent brawling and secondly, because it was well known that some of the women inside so loathed their existence that they would have put an end to it could they have got hold of a weapon.

Harking back to modern practice: In due course a courtesan in full regalia enters the room, makes a lowly obeisance to the guest and awaits his pleasure. If his survey of her charms proves satisfactory he invites her to drink *sake* with him in accordance with the ceremony of three-times-three exchange of nuptial cups known as *sansankudo no sakazuki wo suru*, which is regarded as tantamount to his "marriage" to that particular girl with whom alone thereafter, if he again visits the same house, he is permitted to have intercourse. On the other hand, if she is not to his liking he makes no move and she withdraws to make way for another aspirant, As a rule, unless more recent usage has led to further relaxation. not more than a second choice is granted.

A high-class courtesan of a first-class house is called an *oiran* and the ambition of every *oiran* is to have as many generous patrons as possible. On the patrons' part, in their turn it is good form to bestow upon their favourites expensive bedding called *futon* of which displays are proudly made.

Until more recent years an outdoor ceremony called the *oiran-dochū*, or courtesans' parade, was a great occasion within the Yoshiwara precincts. Upon such an occasion the queen *oiran* of the quarter under an escort of male and female attendants and in full regalia, dressed up in gorgeous brocade of gold and silver, with white painted face and gilded lips, would slowly make the round of the enclosure watched by a vast concourse of admiring spectators. Mounted upon her high *geta*, or clogs, and supported by a male attendant on either side, she would sedulously banish from her face all expression in the *de rigueur* fashion technically known as *sumashita kao* (an indifferent or unconcerned face) which should not from start to finish of the procession be for a single instant relaxed. In earlier days this ceremony had retained relics of the ancient phallic worship, or *seishokki-sōhai*, and the phallic emblem (*engi*) itself was triumphantly borne aloft in the procession. Needless to add nothing of the kind would nowadays be tolerated. The foregoing details have been culled from my own interested inquiries. Now with due acknowledgment of their source I quote the following passage from Lord Redesdale's *Tales of Old Japan*:

> "A public woman or singer on entering her profession assumes a *nom de guerre* by which she is known until her engagement is at an end. Some of these names are so pretty that I will take a few specimens from the *Yoshiwara Saiken*, the guidebook upon which this notice is based: 'Little Pine', 'Little Butterfly', 'Brightness of the Flowers', 'The Jewel River', 'Gold Mountain', 'Pearl Harp', 'Sea Beach', 'The Little Dragon', 'The Stork that lives a Thousand Years', 'Village of Flowers', 'Little Purple', 'Silver', 'Chrysanthemum', 'Waterfall', 'White Brightness', 'Forest of Cherries'—these and a host of other quaint conceits are the one prettiness of a very foul place."

Old residents not of the Tartuffe tribe can hardly fail to remember the notorious "Number Nine", otherwise more symbolically dubbed "Nectarine", of the Yokohama licensed quarter. With an eye to the main chance and to meet a specific and growing demand, an enterprising Japanese business man constructed an imposing brothel more or less in European style with quite luxurious and opulent inside furnishings to conform to Western needs and tastes. This establishment was designed solely for foreign patronage and no Japanese "guests" were admitted. And understandably although the inmates were Japanese, the etiquette observed in relation to them was far more lax and latitudinarian than in the purely Japanese houses of ill-fame. It is also characteristic of the mental and moral flexibility of this founder of "Number Nine" that he was identical with the proprietor of the almost world famous European-style Fuji-ya of the celebrated mountain spa of Miyanoshita which deservedly enjoyed and doubtless still enjoys the reputation of being one of the most comfortable hotels in the Far East and one too which provides the best cuisine. This being so it is not surprising that at almost any hour of the day or night "Number Nine" could furnish its foreign patrons with a first-class meal. If report does not lie, cases have been known where in an emergency and unable to obtain accommodation at a *bona fide* European-style hotel in the Yokohama foreign settlement, a weary wayfarer has put up for the night at "Number Nine" solely for the sake of a square meal and a bed and without ulterior motive!

The inmates of the Tokyo Yoshiwara and other Japanese licensed quarters are for the most part recruited from the ranks of the needy lower classes. One of the most highly-prized of the social virtues in Japanese estimation is filial piety, or *oya-koko* in Japanese. Another social symptom is the traditional predominance of the male in virtually all family relations. This fact suffices to account for the presence of most courtesans in Japanese brothels because generally speaking a Japanese girl is not disgraced if for the sake of her parents or even a brother, e.g. to discharge a monetary debt, she sells herself to a house of ill-fame for a longer or shorter period according to the size of the indebtedness incurred.

It is significant that until almost the eve of the outbreak of the Russo-Japanese war in 1904, the inmates of the licensed quarter were little better than slaves and were not free to leave its precincts without permission of the brothel management and under escort. The police post at the entrance to the quarter would undoubtedly have detained any girl attempting unauthorized exit. Credit for fighting the cause of these unfortunate women and extorting from the authorities reluctant admission that under Japanese law their persons might not be forcibly held in bondage must be given to a resolute and altruistic Irish Roman Catholic missionary who carried the case to the highest legal instance and finally won the day. His victory coincided with a large-scale exodus of women from the licensed quarters all over the country. It was not always easy for the inmates to elude the durance vile imposed upon them by the male bullies of individual brothels, but once a girl succeeded in doing this and in reaching the gateway of the enclosure she was

244   THE FIGHTING SPIRIT OF JAPAN

safe because the police were under orders not to detain any such refugees.

Yet in the ignorant popular view this phenomenon was regarded as a strike and as such afforded the inspiration for a ditty which was for some little time thereafter all the rage among the *hoi polloi*. As I vaguely remember the refrain of this ballad ran something like this:

> "Su-tsu-rai-ki! Sari to wa!
> Dō ka kō ka
> Osshaimashita ne!"

A very free interpretation may read:

> "Strike! Cut your stick!
> By hook or by crook
> They've said, you see!"

This dramatic turning-point in the sordid history of licensed prostitution in Japan excited my special interest at the time in my dual capacity of journalist and human being because it chanced to follow closely on the heels of a personal adventure in the Yokohama licensed quarter and serves therefore as a mnemonic factor in this particular context. For reasons associated, I fear, less with a vow of continence than native caution and the representative faculty, I had generally confined my excursions into Japanese night life to the rôle of onlooker, while too my addiction at that date to the strenuous athletic life and the practice of jujutsu strengthened my resolution and enabled me to steer clear of the flesh-pots of Dai Nippon. But when some time before the "strike" a friend of mine, ignorant of Japanese, asked me to act as his cicerone and interpreter on a projected visit to one of the Japanese-style brothels of the Yokohama *kuruwa*, I was too good natured to refuse. Thus it happened that one evening we found ourselves in the reception room of the house in question. My friend's choice fell upon a girl whose *nom de guerre* was Komurasaki, meaning literally "Little Violet" and probably assumed after a famous proto-type—a beautiful *oiran* of that name who figures in the tragic story of the loves of Gompachi and Komurasaki as told in Lord

Redesdale's *Tales of Old Japan*. Even at this chronological distance I well remember that this nineteenth-century Komurasaki would, by any Western standards, have been deemed exceptionally beautiful alike in form and feature. What is even more to the point, her expression was wholly devoid of any hall-mark of her profession; it bore no vestige of coarseness and one might well have imagined that she would have felt at home in the highest Japanese society. Indeed my modest knowledge of the language sufficed to convince me that she must have been a person of gentle breeding. Soon afterwards my friend paid the house a second visit in my company and alike according to etiquette and from personal inclination he patronized the same girl. Then came the so-called "strike". A few days later my friend and I once more repaired to the same trysting place but although disappointed we were not at all surprised to be told by the female "receptionist" that the lovely Komurasaki had fled. And my friend was sufficiently sentimental to rejoice at the news and to decline with thanks the receptionist's importunate request that he should console himself with a substitute. Let us hope that the gentle Komurasaki's home-coming was such as to justify the courageous step she had taken and that her enforced term of thraldom in the unsavoury purlieus of the Yokohama *kuruwa* was never allowed in any way to mar her future happiness.

Under the former unwritten law a courtesan's engagement was never life-long. Women age early in Japan and soon after twenty, especially among this social stratum, are already in the sear and yellow leaf. Then after the age of twenty-seven she would become her own property. Among the geisha sisterhood the dancers are mostly teenagers and after twenty, if a woman is still in harness, she is usually relegated to the "orchestra" made up of players on the *koto* (Japanese equivalent for the harp) or the *samisen* (three-stringed guitar).

But no amount of official supervision and control which subject the inmates of all licensed brothels to periodical medical inspection can wholly eliminate unlicensed prostitution which persists for the most part in the old treaty ports of Yokohama, Kobe and Nagasaki. In the wake of the war and a foreign military occupation this moral malaise, which is their inescapable concomitant, has deepened and extended to other parts of the country including the capital itself and the various coastal naval stations. From all accounts Tokyo has evolved a decidedly hectic post-war night life which depends for its sustenance almost entirely upon foreign military and naval patronage. But since these excesses lack even the superficial "glamour" of the traditional indigenous practices I shall say nothing more about them.

CHAPTER XXI

POSTSCRIPT

SINCE the immeasurably more halcyon days of my turbulent youth when I penned and typed this book, a considerable volume of water has flowed under the bridges of the Sumida river on the banks of which Tokyo still stands.

I doubt not that were I to revisit that terrain today I should feel very much like some resurrected Rip Van Winkle and at a loss to orientate in the face of the countless changes wrought by the lapse of time generally and the cataclysmal impact of war more particularly, which have rendered the Japanese metropolis almost unrecognizable to an old resident so ill advised and venturesome as to return to the scenes of yore. In melancholy contemplation of the ruins of the Nishi Honganji or the Shiba temples he might be moved to imagine, with some readjustment to his environment, the feelings of Macaulay's traveller from New Zealand, perched in the midst of a vast solitude on a broken arch of London bridge "to sketch the ruins of St. Paul's". And from all accounts after American "conventional" bombs had wrought well-deserved havoc on the Japanese capital, it was not in much better shape than a future London, as visualized by Macaulay, albeit countervailing credit must be conceded to the characteristic Japanese energy and industry responsible for its incredibly swift recovery, phoenix-like, from the ashes of this almost wholesale devastation.

Thus am I only too well aware that the first fine careless rapture redolent of youth can never be recaptured, and that even the meagre residue of the subjective idealism which imparts a superficial glamour to novel exotic surroundings, viewed through its rose-tinted spectacles, would be shattered by the almost ubiquitous evidence of the moral deterioration inseparable from an alien military occupation. I should no longer be able to survey the scene from the vantage point of a mental Parnassus or to echo with fervour Ancient Pistol's ill-starred apostrophe: "Where is the

247

248 THE FIGHTING SPIRIT OF JAPAN

life that late I led?" say they. "Why here it is; welcome these pleasant days!" In short the retrospect even at this distance is pregnant with disillusionment.

I hasten to say that this remark does not apply to the basic subject-matter of this study which remains immutable, but to the dismal failure of the Japanese to live up to the lofty claims of their vaunted *bushido*, or "Way of the Warrior", publicized long ago by the late Dr. Nitobe, and to the alleged moral precepts underlying *bujutsu*, or martial arts. "O! what a fall was there, my countrymen!" Rarely has practice lagged so far behind theory as in the record of Japanese militarism during the last war. Unhappily for too many victims, the Japanese warrior's "Way" was all too often anything but a bright exemplar of chivalry.

Upon a much smaller stage and to a far less degree, no doubt, this criticism is also applicable to the case of both jujutsu and judo, with the history of which my book deals in part. As regards judo, I should be the last to question the good faith of its illustrious founder, the late Dr. Jigoro Kano, when he emphasized the ethical postulates of his brilliant eclectic creation, or the good intentions of present-day votaries of the art, both Japanese and non-Japanese throughout the world, when they volubly extol the manifold virtues of judo and its superiority over all other Western sports, insisting that it must be differentiated from the latter in that it is actuated by moral principles and is therefore capable of evolving a species of superman, wearing perhaps an outsize in haloes, or else a Sir Galahad justified in assuring us that "my strength is as the strength of ten because my heart is pure", and, of course, all on account of judo! We hear and read *ad nauseam* fulsome praise of the "WAY" (MICHI in Japanese), always spelt in capital letters, and of how its followers can and do attain this enviable superiority over the rank and file of mere mortals. Frankly, from my own observation I regard such claims as unfounded and plead for retention of the sense of proportion. Let us take Dr. Johnson's advice and clear our minds of cant. This is not to deny that for the most part in both Japanese and non-Japanese judo circles a reasonably high standard of good sportsmanship obtains, but are there incontrovertible grounds for contending that it is any higher or more widespread than in other Western branches of amateur sport? On the other hand, it would not be difficult to adduce evidence to prove that the practice, as distinct from the theory of judo, has of recent years become hardly less vulnerable to the malign influence of commercialism than any other Western sport not quite so grandiloquent and articulate as judo and *bujutsu* in its pretensions to produce the Simon Pure Admirable Crichton of the field or mat.

Thus it is difficult to resist the impression that since the war the grading panels of the Kodokan have been considerably more lavish in their bestowal of Dan grades to foreign pupils drawn more particularly from the ranks of the forces of occupation than were the grading panels of the Meiji era during which I practised at the Kodokan. Doubtless the tendency to curry favour with representatives of the victorious Allies is a natural weakness, but it must not for that reason be allowed to cloud our objective judgment of the facts. In the light of this evidence all *à priori* assumptions that modern judo is impeccable in all its manifestations are untenable and must be abandoned and in their stead substituted a wholesome respect for the eternal verities. "Tell the truth and shame the devil."

These reservations must not, however, be interpreted as in any way invalidating the esoteric element which has always been inherent in the theory and to a far smaller degree in the practice of Japanese *bujutsu*. I may here recall that I was the first non-Japanese to discover this esoteric element and to reveal its arcana to Western readers in the original edition of this book. The paramount importance which Japanese fighting men have from time immemorial attached to the development of the lower abdomen, or *saika tanden*, by means of deep abdominal breathing, or *fukushiki kokyu*, and to what may perhaps be called its vocal expression, the *kiai*, or occult "spirit-meeting" shout, supposed to emanate from that region, was also first explained in its pages. And to this source, whether knowingly or unknowingly, Western judoka owe their present-day familiarity with most of the terminology of *bujutsu* esotericism. And being only human I frankly admit that I am deeply grateful to my publishers for enabling me to remind my prospective readers of a fact which the lapse of time has tended to obscure.

Reluctant realization that under the conditions of our modern manner of life with its materialistic Leitmotiv, few if any aspirants are likely to emulate the feats of the old-time Japanese masters of the martial arts, should not deter members of the younger generation from undergoing the severe mental and physical discipline essential to any progress in their chosen branch, and it is certain that such discipline cannot fail to be salutory under both heads. Indeed I can think of no *summum bonum* more rewarding to mortal man than a sound mind in a sound body, since the former presupposes ethical and the latter physical attributes. Nor should these activities be exposed to carping criticism on the ground that they are a form of "escapism" which blinds their votaries to a situation described by Sir Winston Churchill as "measureless and laden with doom". The obvious rejoinder is that if the worst should come to the worst and should our frail humanity be eventually, in the words of the immortal Mr. Manta- lini, relegated to the "demnition bow-wows" and our "goodly frame, the earth" transformed into "a foul and pestilent con- gregation of vapours", then those of the younger generation tempered by this stern discipline may well prove better prepared to confront the inevitable Armageddon than their weaker brethren.

Finally, for myself, as a member of the older generation and therefore perhaps less likely than they are to be subjected to that valedictory test, this inadequate but nostalgic evocation of some chapters in a not wholly colourless past helps to reconcile me to a crepuscular present and moves me to end this record with old Adam's sage reflection, "At seventeen many their fortunes seek, but at four score it is too late a week".